Praise for the book:

"Spangles..." provides an insight into the glamorous world of the circus that is breathtaking in its scope. The book is heartbreaking, and yet such a positive read because of the amazing courage and spirit of its author. Above all, it is a story of a life well lived, and of the author's lifelong love affair with the circus. Three rings and three cheers for Victoria!

—Berry Lubin:
Grandma, *Big Apple Circus, NYC*

It's a pleasure to find a well written circus book from someone who understands both the joys and the frustrations of the business.

—Don Covington:
Company Manager, *Big Apple Circus, NYC*

Spangles is totally circus—the real thing. Once you start reading this book you won't be able to put it down

—Evi Kelly-Lentz:
Widow of the legendary hobo clown, Emmett Kelly

Love the descriptions of the circus, the atmosphere and the tents—draws the reader right into it, and the pictures are great.

—Kay Kipling:
Executive Editor, Sarasota Magazine

Victoria's prose is as flawless as it is beautiful. If you missed your chance to run away and join the circus as a kid, then your next best bet is a read of Victoria Cristiani Rossi's "Spangles, Elephants, Violets and Me." Page by page you will become more magically transported back to the grand old circus of yesteryear. But don't be surprised if you start visualizing circus wagons, hearing the staccato toots of a calliope, or smelling popcorn, cotton candy and the sweetly pungent aromas wafting from the menagerie tent.

—Dr. Rodney Huey:
American Press Rep. for the Federation Mondiale du Circus
(under the auspices of H.S.H. Princess Stephanie of Monaco).

You needn't be a circus fan to enjoy Vickie Cristiani Rossi's book. But you'll be a circus fan by the time you finish it! I fell in love with the circus when I was a child. I fell in love with the circus all over again, between the covers of this book. You will too! Does the author have sawdust in her veins? Tell you what....when I finished Spangles I had sawdust in mine! Oh, and about those elephants, watch where you step! That's how realistic "SPANGLES" is!

—Gary C. Payne
Circus Fans Association of America (membership, circusfans.org)

Victoria B. Cristiani Rossi promises an exciting circus train ride. Expertly and memorably, she delivers that and much more. Filled with rich detail, her memoir is an important contribution to understanding the complex world of the circus. From fascinating glimpses of Hollywood celebrities to stories of the sometimes naughty, all-too-human, but ever-inspiring nature of the big top, Spangles is a must-read. Lifting the sidewall for an insider's view of the spectacle, she also reveals something of its soul.

—Dr. Mort Gamble:
Circus Fans Association of America

A must read book for anyone interested in Americana.

—John Hart:
Circus Fans Association of America

A fascinating story about a fantastic family told in an interesting and entertaining manner.

—Jack T. Painter:
Past President, Circus Fans Association of America

What an interesting look at life and growing up in the circus! I couldn't put the book down.

—John Goodall:
Vice-Chair Circus World Museum, Baraboo, Wisconsin

Victoria Cristiani Rossi's well-written memoir takes readers back into what it was like growing up in the world's most honored circus family. Her most interesting story provides a rare inside look at this multi-talented group of artists. Compelling! I could not put it down.

—Fred D. Pfening Jr.:
Editor of Bandwagon:
The Journal of the Circus Historical Society

Spangles is about real circus elephants and real circus people. Nothing but good comments about this book!

—David P. Orr:
CFA (Circus Fans Association of America)
Representative and fundraiser for the OABA

Delightful new circus book about a lovely member of the famous Cristiani family. The fifty pages of outstanding circus photos are an absolute treasure.

—Col. Frank Robie:
Reputable circus historian
and past CFA President

SPANGLES, ELEPHANTS, VIOLETS & ME

SPANGLES, ELEPHANTS, VIOLETS & ME

THE CIRCUS INSIDE OUT

A MEMOIR

Victoria B. Cristiani Rossi

iUniverse, Inc.
New York   Bloomington

SPANGLES, ELEPHANTS, VIOLETS & ME
THE CIRCUS INSIDE OUT

iUniverse books may be ordered through booksellers or by contacting:

iUniverse
1663 Liberty Drive
Bloomington, IN 47403
www.iuniverse.com
1-800-Authors (1-800-288-4677)

Because of the dynamic nature of the Internet, any Web addresses or links contained in this book may have changed since publication and may no longer be valid. The views expressed in this work are solely those of the author and do not necessarily reflect the views of the publisher, and the publisher hereby disclaims any responsibility for them.

ISBN: 978-1-935-27810-8 (pbk)
ISBN: 978-1-935-27811-5 (ebk)

Library of Congress Control Number: 2009926457

Printed in the United States of America

iUniverse rev. date: 4/29/09

C ONTENTS

Author's Note xi

Credits xiii

Acknowledgments xvii

Introduction xxi

Chapter 1   SAILING TO THE NEW WORLD 3

Chapter 2   AMERICA 8

Chapter 3   ENTER THE EQUESTRIANS 13

Chapter 4   RUDE AWAKENING 19

Chapter 5   CARDOME ACADEMY 24

Chapter 6   PACKIN' SAWDUST 37

Chapter 7   ON WITH THE SHOW 43

Chapter 8   BETWEEN SHOWS 52

Chapter 9   THE CIRCUS TRAIN 58

Chapter 10 CIRCUS MAGIC IN MOTION 62

Chapter 11 FAMILY FEUDS 66

Chapter 12 WINDING DOWN 118

Chapter 13 THE MACON YEARS 124

Chapter 14 MOUNT DE SALES ACADEMY 130

Chapter 15 CHRISTMAS AT THE OLD PLACE 141

Chapter 16 RELATIVE OBSERVATIONS 149

Chapter 17 A NEW VENTURE 157

Chapter 18 THE GREAT ALASKA TOUR 162

Chapter 19 IN THE CLOVER 175

Chapter 20 CHICAGO 183

Chapter 21 ROLL OUT THE SKY 188

Chapter 22 WEST COAST HOPE 195

Chapter 23 THE ELEVENTH HOUR 216

Epilogue...229

AUTHOR'S NOTE

Let it be known that any statements in this book about persons living or dead represent my views alone. Readers should also keep in mind that, even if the emotional truth is there as I saw it, certain events are somewhat filtered because they were revealed purely by memory.

To recall every experience in one's life at a very young age would be next to impossible. Hence, all the names at Cardome Academy have been changed— except one. Much has been written about the Cardome experience over time. To my knowledge, the stories vary from bad to worse. Know, too, that although I made every effort to remain true to my childhood recollections at that point in time, I took liberty where details were unclear; however, in sum, I'm satisfied that my rendering is not all that far from reality. Be that as it may, readers may form their own opinions, if they so choose.

According to the Cardome Center Web site, the school closed in 1969 due to a variety of circumstances that led to declining enrollment. The visitation community disbanded in 1987, and the property was sold. The site is now owned by the city of Georgetown, Kentucky.

Victoria B. Cristiani Rossi
spanglesvi@hotmail.com
Visit the author at www. spanglesvb.com

CREDITS

Front Cover: Cristiani Bareback Riding Graphic Design—Jack Haunty
Interior Photo Layout—Ben Rossi:
BenRos Worldwide Entertainment
Back Cover Copy—Dr. Mort Gamble
Back Cover Caption—Peggy J. Russell

Cardome Academy ink sketch—H. B. Goyert
(Permission Cardome Support Staff)

Cristiani photographs and personal snapshots posing with stars (1937):
Edward G. Robinson, Wallace Berry, Barton MacLane, George Raft, Jack
Okie, and Joseph Cotton
—Cristiani family personal album

Joe E. Brown photo with Cristiani family (1937)—Frank Fernekes,
Hollywood, CA
Photo of Clark Gable and Carol Lombard watching the Cristianis perform
(1937)—Hyman Fink

Autographed MGM Studios head shot of Franchot Tone (1937)—Hurrell
Autographed Metro-Goldwyn Mayer Studio head shot of Jean Harlow
(1937)—Ted Allan

Rare circus posters and photographs courtesy of
Fred Pfening Jr., Editor of Bandwagon—Journal of the Circus Historical
Society

Alaska newspaper clips 1954—*Anchorage Daily News*
Courtesy of prominent circus fans
—Hank Fraser and Jack T. Painter

NBC-TV's 1959 Kaleidoscope documentary, *Roll Out the Sky*, publicity
photographs with Gene Rayburn,
Corky Cristiani, and host, Charles Van Doren, in Sarasota, FL—news
photographer unknown

Roll Out the Sky wrap party photo with Cristiani family members dining
with NBC-TV cast and crew at the Colony Club—Longboat Key, FL
—local photographer unknown

Roy Rogers snapshot with Rex and Jimmy Rossi—Rex Rossi Collection

Publicity photographs taken under the big top in LA, 1959
Bob Cummings and family with Mama Cristiani
Jeanne Crain with her child and Caesar Romero with his family watching
the Cristiani Bros. Circus performance
—Joe Friezer, news photographer, Los Angeles, CA

Publicity photo showing Shecky Greene posing
with Jane, Victoria, and Corky Cristiani on opening day in LA
and
James Garner photo with Hadassah sponsors under the Cristiani big top
—Cliff Kalick Photography, Hollywood, CA: 1959

In memory my of beloved parents, guardians of my soul,
Oscar and Marion Cristiani

Oscar Cristiani   Marion Cristiani

and
in honor of my extraordinary grandparents for sacrificing
all they had to produce the greatest equestrian family
the circus world has ever known,
Ernesto and Emma Victoria Cristiani

Ernesto "Papa" Cristiani   Emma Victoria "Mama" Cristiani

ACKNOWLEDGMENTS

First and foremost, I would like to thank professional writer Peggy J. Russell—coauthor of *Sing Me Back Home*, the acclaimed 1980 autobiography of country-music legend Merle Haggard—for sharing her innate talent and giving me the tools to transform stacks of scribbled notes into a legible manuscript.

For his significant contribution and untold hours of hard work, I wish to thank my husband, Benny. All the photograph composites in the book are the result of his creativity and imagination. In addition, I offer my never-ending gratitude to our dear sons, Ben Jr. and Ryan, for showering me with their unconditional love and staunch support—and for offering a multitude of marvelous suggestions that worked like magic. Further afield, I have been greatly encouraged by my sisters, Bonnie and Carin; my nephew Brian; my niece Sa Sa, and my great-niece Felicia—along with my cousins, Tony, Eva, Desi, April, and Antoinette.

This project has been long in the making. Hopefully, it was worth the wait, for now outsiders will be privy to the true Cristiani story—no holds barred. Of course, I must convey my heartfelt gratitude to the entire Cristiani family (including those who have since passed) for purging their souls—and, more importantly, for giving me free rein to record their actions, however damning.

Beyond question, Spangles would not have been possible without my family's full cooperation. Deep appreciation goes to my uncles, Pete and Belmonte, and my aunties, Norma and Corky, for their support and assistance along the way. To Fred Pfening Jr., who knew the Cristiani family better than anyone else, I offer my humble gratitude for his time and generous effort on my behalf—and for kindly providing a rare treasure of vintage photos from his personal album. Shalom, Fred—you are the best of the best. Also, my thanks go to Hank Fraser for all he has done; he of all people should know what a ride it has been. To Jack Painter, thank you for believing in my project and sharing my dream. In addition, I would like to commend lifelong family friend, showman, and decorated Vietnam War hero Allan C. Hill (Allan C. Hill Productions, Inc.) and passionate circus fans, Jim Cole, Denny Gilli and Harry Kingston, for their combined effort in getting the word out to the right people at the right time.

I would like to name a few articulate residents of Sarasota, Florida, who agreed to read one of my earlier drafts—and, for whatever reason, had enough faith in me (and the work) to believe that I would eventually pull off the miracle of getting it right: (friend and committed circus benefactor) Rita Adler, (former NYC editor) Ellen Hawes, Nicholas Tsacrios, and Annie Solomon. My thanks always to Kay Kipling—executive editor of the award-winning Sarasota Magazine—for her confidence inspiring advice and uplifting support in the final stages.

With great pleasure, I would like to express my gratitude to each and every member of the Circus Fans Association of America (CFA) for recognizing the Cristiani family for their accomplishments throughout their years of hardship and joy—and for continuing to keep the circus spirit alive in the hearts and minds of children of all ages. You know who you are.

At this point, I would like to express my indebtedness to the much admired CFA member and OABA circus representative, David P. Orr, and his lovely wife Sharon. Lucky for me, Mr. Orr (who seems most content when at work juggling countless projects on any given day) is recognized throughout the circus industry as a masterful and inexhaustible marketing powerhouse. I've been further blessed to have received additional help from *White Tops* magazine editors, John and Mardi Wells and revered showman, Buckles Woodcock (distinguished creator of Buckles Blog). And where would I be without the wise counsel of Dr. Mort Gamble (veteran in the field of higher education and admired member of the *White Tops* advisory committee), and the invaluable backing of Dr. Rodney Huey (George Mason University Professor/*ShowTime Magazine* contributor and American *Press Rep. for Monaco's Federation Mondiale du Circus*.)

I mustn't forget to mention a bandwagon full of zealous circus fans and industry experts who have gone out of their way to publicize the work. In a very real way, Spangles is their book as well: Don Covington (Company Manager, Big Apple Circus NYC); Globetrotting, world-class clown, Barry Lubin (Grandma, Big Apple Circus NYC); John Goodall (Vice Chair, Circus World Museum); Buckles and Barbara Woodcock (Buckles Blog); Jerry Cash; Henry Edger; Ben Trumble; Bill and Trudy Strong (Bill Strong's Blog); Joanne Wilson; Penny Wilson Rodriguez; Kristin Byrd Parra; Colonel Frank Robie; Mike Piccolo; Paul Ingrassia; Bob Snow; Don Curtis; Charles Hanson; Bill Biggerstaf (Circus Report) Bob Connor; John and Mary Ruth Herriott; Catherine Bliss; Richard Georgia Jr.; Gary Payne; Vern Mendonca (CircusVern); Ed and Lynn Limbach; John &

Bari Hart; Dick Dykes; Clark and Cathy Beurlen; OABA (*Outdoor Amusement Business Association*) President, Bob Johnson; Evi Kelly-Lentz—widow of circus icon, Emmett Kelly; and most recently, Laura van der Meer (Executive Director of the Federation Mondiale du Circus—under the patronage of H. S. H. Princess Stephanie of Monaco).

Special thanks to my faithful band of cheerleaders on the WDW Boulevard: Sal and Paula Perillo, Wayne Hall, Harriet Jeffrey, Beatriz Perez, Rosa Mejia, Irene Blackman, Susie Dixon, Rosie Bueschel, Gloria Arango, Betty Lopez, Sara Lo, Sonia Constanza, Joe Ferguson, Ruth Adams, Sharie Russi, Flor Solivan, Maqsood Ahmed, Maribel Diaz, Margaret Spittel, Pearl Lark, Marenilda Font, Antonia Arocho, Diane Fitzpatrick, Kathleen McCarthy, Rebecca Chappell, Marianela Nogue, Maggie Molinaro, Angela Casino, Barbara Taylor, Alan Orris, Stephen Saroka, Shanni Moy, Karla and Tammy Jenkins, Keith Billy, Jerry Connors, Norma Haili, Louisa Torres, Gail Dempsey, Diane Morris, Lois Kohan, Christine Johnson and the boulevard's dependable magazine distributor, Pete Harrigan.

Lastly, a world of thanks to the entire iUniverse staff for making my experience pleasurable from beginning to end—namely, Shelley Rodgers (iUniverse Publishing Program Manager), Schyler Simpson (iUniverse Marketing Consultant) and my wonderful PSA, Rosalie White. Their prompt assistance throughout the project put my mind at ease. Unquestionably, the professional services provided by iUniverse exceeded my expectations. No doubt, the editors' insightful suggestions inspired me to grow as a writer and ultimately helped me reach a goal I would have otherwise been unable to achieve.

Introduction

There was a method to my madness when I set out to write Spangles. The idea of writing a memoir came about rather suddenly, without my ever planning it. There were many questions I had never before confronted—not only questions about my family's eventful history and dysfunctional lifestyle, but haunting questions regarding my own personal struggle to pull away, almost forcibly, from the fanatical Catholic teachings that had emotionally enslaved me since childhood. Faced by these questions, I could not dismiss the lasting impact of my first convent experience at the tender age of six.

In the beginning, piecing together the shadows of my past was an exceedingly difficult and lonely voyage. However, I soon found myself in the company of a throng of ghosts from circus past who kept me focused on my self-appointed mission. Slowly, I rediscovered my unique heritage and realized its important place in history. Through the years, I had somehow separated myself from a world I no longer recognized as the enchanting playground of my youth. Vowing mentally to never give up, I navigated my way through a maze of perplexing issues that plague many first-time writers on the verge of making every mistake in the book—casting aside reams of discarded drafts in the process.

Eventually, I inched ahead, determined to gift future generations with an up-close and intimate inside look at the circus—the amazing way it entertained us, the magical way it took us away from the ordinary, and the unfortunate way it has almost disappeared. Not surprisingly, I became increasingly intrigued with the vibrant big-top era I was privileged to have experienced firsthand—a spectacular era no one should wish to forget. As an insider, I felt empowered to present a refreshing panoramic view of a half-forgotten time, recounted with the grit and passion of one who has lived it—thereby rectifying a swell of misinformation provided by those with limited insight.

No doubt, I've spent a good part of my life grappling with the embarrassing stigma resulting from most outsiders' perceptions of circus people as a group. Whereas certain negative assumptions are justified, others are baseless, heartless, and cruel. Everyone is aware of the changing mores; I don't mean to be presumptuous, but no one knows better than this lifelong animal lover that some things should be changed. For example, all animal handlers, in my view, regardless of experience, should undergo thorough background checks because certain crimes can signal sadistic tendencies. Logically, anyone working with animals should be monitored regularly—without exception. Certainly, being born to parents reared in opposing worlds has helped me tackle the subject fairly. I suppose that if, in some small way, Spangles serves to provide a better understanding of my heritage, my efforts will not have been in vain.

Most fittingly, Spangles begins at a time when the circus was in its heyday and my equestrian family, "The Internationally Famous Cristiani Troupe," was enthroned as circus royalty. Using each chapter to represent a layer of time, I sought to cover every aspect of the old-fashioned circus and its cast of characters, while intuitively melding the good, the bad, and the magic. Hopefully, I've charted a journey that will take my audience on a thought-provoking train ride through a landscape of fairy tales, nightmares, and miracles. If that is the case, I've succeeded in baring the inner core of the operation—the part I knew and loved, the part encased in the phantasmagorical pageantry of arc lights, glittering spangles, and hullabaloo.

The popular phrase "children of all ages" is synonymous with the circus. Therefore, now, at our moment of departure, I offer the young at heart a free pass to shed the constraining trappings of maturity so they can escape, unapologetically, into the tangles of their imagination. None can deny that, through the ages, an awesome mystique has surrounded those muscle-toned artistes who flew through the air with the greatest of ease. Even so, it is only when reminded of the pungent odor of dampened sawdust that we find ourselves wishing we could revisit that fabulous Cracker Jack and cotton-candy era of yore. And because my mind has embraced the flight of imagination from birth, my fervent desire is that Spangles will ignite that marvelous fantasy by offering readers from every stratum of society a unique opportunity to experience the weird and wonderful world of circus performers, clowns, and freaks from the inside out.

∗   ∗   ∗   ∗

It was my good fortune to have been born in Sarasota, Florida, in 1940, when my equestrian family performed with the Ringling Bros. and Barnum & Bailey Circus. My family's illustrious history is memorialized in the archives of the Circus World Museum in Baraboo, Wisconsin, and at the headquarters of the Circus Historical Society as well as the highly regarded circus magazine, *Bandwagon*—edited by Fred Pfening Jr., a distinguished gentleman (and longtime Circus Historical Society trustee) who has spent a lifetime gathering the final relics of a bygone day.

Notably, the absorbing documentary (first shown on A&E) that celebrated the one-hundred-year anniversary of the American circus aired many rare film clips of my handsome family—renowned for peerless routines and choreography within the sawdust furrows of the center ring. While performing, the Cristianis were the epitome of perfection—however, their private lives were riddled with scandals. By their own admission, they were not a perfect family, nor did they pretend to be. Rebels at heart, my family members didn't hide behind the mask of normalcy. Instead, they lived life according to their own ideology, pandering to no one—not even for the sake of acceptance by the closed circus society to which they were born.

Hollywood beckoned during their whirlwind California tour with the great Al G. Barnes Circus in 1937—a momentous year indeed. The entertaining Pete Smith special (The Great Picture) that features the Cristiani riding act was filmed by MGM and has been shown repeatedly on TCM (Turner Classic Movies). Here, the Cristianis won the admiration of award-winning directors like Josh Logan and the sensational *On the Waterfront* writer/director Bud Shulberg. Various prominent actors sought the Cristianis out backstage to pay tribute and schmooze after their performance. The list is staggering: Clark Gable, Carol Lombard, Joseph Cotton, Harold Lloyd, Fredric March, Ethel Barrymore, Charley Chaplin, Edward G. Robinson, Wallace Berry, Burgess Meredith, Joan Crawford, Jean Harlow, Gilbert Roland, and Cesar Romero, to name a few.

∗   ∗   ∗   ∗

John Ringling North referred to the Cristiani family as a "circus miracle." Although the Cristianis' final attempt to preserve a fifth-generation heritage was a welcomed effort, their struggle to do so was compounded by their refusal to accept life beyond the orbits of their own existence. Little did they know that time would soon cast dark shadows on the golden era of colorful circus trains, gigantic big tops, exotic menageries, and titillating side shows. By the look of it, the Cristianis were fighting to maintain their place in a drastically changing world that threatened the only way of life they knew—a world whose oblivion contributed enormously to the downfall of a very important part of Americana. As a result of that struggle, this amazing equestrian troupe procured an indelible mark upon—and ultimately wrote a most remarkable chapter in—the pages of the American circus story.

Over a period of time, the great mystic poet and humanitarian Bob Lax became a dear friend of the Cristiani family. He was especially close to my uncle Mogador, openly praising the flowing elegance of Mogador's performance. Mr. Lax—a modest, soft-spoken saint of a man whom I was privileged to know— actually traveled with my family through western Canada in the summer of 1950, expressly to gather material for his incredibly moving book of poems, *Circus of the Sun*—and his later work, *Circus Days & Nights*. Mr. Lax had in fact followed the Cristiani family since 1943, and from that point on he was never out of touch. At the age of twenty-seven, the young poet was so inspired by their performances that he actually visualized the Cristiani riding act as an unexampled work of art.

James Hartford, emeritus executive director of the American Institute of Aeronautics and Astronautics, paid final tribute to Bob Lax, his friend of forty-eight years, in National Catholic Reporter—October 20, 2000: One of Bob Lax's most acclaimed works was *Circus of the Sun*, a book of poems metaphorically comparing the circus to Creation. Called by a critic in The New York Times Book Review perhaps the greatest English language poem of this century, an excerpt was handed out to those attending Lax's funeral at St. Bonaventure University September 29.

$$* \quad * \quad * \quad *$$

Among the Cristianis' historic achievements are Alaska's first circus and a pet project videotaped by NBC.

A sense of history pervades the fascinating chapter that explains exactly why the Cristianis decided to roll the dice and take their novel outdoor circus, including a herd of elephants, on an extremely risky odyssey to the wilds of Alaska. The perilous 1954 voyage, via the treacherous Alcan Highway, took place four years prior to Alaska's statehood.

Interestingly, the 1959 account of NBC-TV's Kaleidoscope special, *Roll Out the Sky*, was the show's first videotaped project shot entirely on location. The successful documentary, sponsored by the trendy Polaroid Land Camera, was narrated by the infamous game-show contestant Charles Van Doren shortly before his fall from grace. Sharp-witted celebrity host Gene Rayburn represented Polaroid.

✳   ✳   ✳   ✳

The Cristiani family had many dealings with the late Walt Disney over several years. In 1955, Mr. Disney consulted with the family regarding his tentative plan to add a Disneyland circus to Disneyland in Anaheim, California (this was well before the inception of Walt Disney World in Orlando, Florida). The story was covered in detail in the August 1955 issue of *Cosmopolitan* magazine. What's more, the Cristianis gladly responded to Mr. Disney's personal request to collaborate with the Sarasota Chamber of Commerce in a combined effort to prepare for the premiere of the 1960 production *Toby Tyler* at the Florida Theater. Putting all else aside, the Cristianis provided the colorful circus atmosphere for the occasion—along with a parade of clowns, wagons, costumed performers, and the line of Cristiani Bros. Circus elephants.

In future years, the Cristiani elephants were featured in Epcot's unprecedented *Daredevil Circus* (1987–88). Trivia buffs may be interested in knowing that the Cristiani pachyderms were the first live elephants actually housed within the vast expanse of Disney property (right behind Epcot's quaint English Village)—before Disney's Animal Kingdom park was even on the map.

The Epcot management team treated the Cristiani elephants like royalty and provided the most comfortable elephant quarters on the planet. Later, when WDW needed an attractive, well-disciplined Dumbo look-alike to lead the *Aladdin* premiere parade at MGM Studios, they hired Shirley, a beautifully rounded, dimple-faced Cristiani elephant. However, because Johnny Carson's brilliant sidekick, the one and only Ed McMahon, had a very difficult time straddling her neck (ouch), he ended up walking rather sorely at her side, dressed in an Aladdin costume and turban. Soon after, the Cristiani elephants were signed to work on Disney's nonanimated classic *Jungle Book*—partly filmed on location in the backwoods of South Carolina and Tennessee.

*   *   *   *

As I've looked back, the sparkle of tender eyes has unleashed memories of a glorious heritage I would like to share. So all aboard, don't be late … the circus train is scheduled to leave on time. May my heart touch yours—and may my story inspire you to rekindle the rich tapestry of olden times … which, I pray, will include either personal or passed down recollections of family outings to the grand big-top circuses of yesteryear.

PROLOGUE

▼

Christmas 1951, spent at my paternal grandparents' home in Sarasota, Florida, proved particularly memorable. I was eleven at the time, and life was good—very good. Lost in the glorious rhythm of holiday cheer, I could not have foreseen the parallel between the evocative painting of *Custer's Last Stand* (fixed on the foyer wall) and a future battle—one vicious enough to trigger bitter estrangement from my relatives for over thirty-five years of my adult life. Given the reality of our prosperity back then, how could anyone have predicted that my seemingly invincible family would end up torn apart by obsession and failed dreams?

The child I was back then might have asked, "What failed dreams?" The tide had flowed in the right direction for as long as I could remember. My internationally famous circus family appeared virtually unscathed after suffering through decades of punishing blows in order to reach the pinnacle of the circus world.

Collectively, the Cristianis had accumulated a vast fortune as owners of one of the largest and most successful circuses in the business. Beyond that, they still benefited from singular talent, looks, drive, entrepreneurial spirit, and business sense. So what could possibly go wrong in their almost-perfect world? And what soothsayer could have prophesized the virtual demise of the enormous big top circuses that had entertained generations of youngsters through two world wars—or the life-altering injury I was destined to suffer in Los Angeles, at the promising age of nineteen?

That Christmas in 1951, I had every reason to be positive, for I had been blessed with wonderful parents and had been loved and nurtured by a flock of caring blood relatives, all of whom I loved doubly in return. As far as I was concerned, my family's virtues and kindly deeds cancelled out their vices—so why should they be skinned, I reasoned, as the majority of their detractors supposed they should?

Growing up, I mostly overlooked my family's ongoing war of words and personality clashes; beneath it all was a comfortable balance that made me feel safe. But nature works in strange ways, and flawed human beings are not always adaptable to crushing changes. The truth is, as life speeds by, nothing appears reasonable—or fair. In time, we're presented with a number of surprises that will either shuffle the deck in our favor or deal us a losing hand—the latter of which can transform decent people into cold, hard-hearted beasts, trapped in denial.

Writing this book forced me to reassess the ugly rivalries and hostile attacks that destroyed my family's bond. Somewhere along the way, I came to analyze their bitter feuds—together with a multitude of joys, regrets, setbacks, triumphs and accomplishments—from a whole new perspective. Thankfully, the process made me all the wiser. In due course, a change of heart caused me to rethink everything about my family I had previously condemned. Ultimately, in an unexpected twist, the miracle of forgiveness relieved my conscience from the agonizing pain of detachment from the family I so cherished—before it was too late.

CHAPTER 1

▼

SAILING TO THE NEW WORLD

Not a hawthorn blooms but is felt by the stars,—
not a pebble drops but sends pulsations to the sun.
—Victor Hugo

The American circus—a magnificent spectacle beyond compare in the field of family entertainment—celebrated its heyday from 1880 to 1920. John Ringling's circus empire collapsed in 1929. Unfortunately, while his shocking 1.7 million dollar purchase of the American Circus Corporation put six major competitors in his pocket, the move proved to be a disastrous mistake: Not long thereafter, the country suffered the paralyzing effects of the Great Depression. Accordingly, the Ringling family board of directors appointed show business prodigy, Sam W. Gumpertz, executive manager. Fierce competition forced Mr. Gumpertz to search the far reaches of the earth to sign the highest caliber acts for Ringling's grand show of shows. By the time the Ringling Bros. and Barnum & Bailey scouts initiated talks with the Cristiani troupe in early 1933, my family had already headlined every major European circus and had given a number of command performances before kings, queens, and other royals.

Though past offers had been refused, Mr. Gumpertz wouldn't give up—and with good reason. After Ringling's insightful razor-sharp agent, Clifford Fisher, witnessed the equestrians' triumphant stand at Medrano's in Paris, France, he was once again astounded by the troupe's original choreography of movement, which the Cristianis so beautifully brought to an apex of achievement.

After one command performance at Cirque Royal in Brussels, Belgium, Ringling scouts approached my grandfather, Nono, with a reworked contract that gave him cause to reexamine his goals. Their generous offer presented a lofty range of brow-raising possibilities for this superconfident family—perceived as a human cluster of sheer talent—exhibiting all the signs and sounds of ambition. The fusion of expert horsemanship, flashy staging, and imposing Hollywood looks was, by any measure, a winning combination—and enough to ignite Mr. Gumpertz's passion for acquiring the Cristiani troupe. Still, his past offers were made to no avail and this would meet the same fate.

My shrewd grandfather Nono (respectfully called Papa Cristiani) hadn't nurtured his family to such acclaim for anything less than the perfect deal. As would be expected, the perfection he demanded in the circus arena also ruled his business mind. Nono studied Ringling's new contract carefully, with pardonable distrust and the usual pinch of genius, insisting that every minute detail be addressed. According to Nono, his equestrians were entitled to certain hard-earned privileges. Even the American three-ring circus concept was alien to Nono, so the prospect of signing on with Ringling's five-ring spectacle hoisted a red flag. Nono felt the Cristiani riding act merited undivided attention according to the European tradition, in which all eyes were trained on *the* featured act in a single ring. This was a huge issue for him—and a totally unsolvable one at that. Besides that dominant concern, Nono was bothered by the arguable matter of security. In those days, tabloid warnings created images of an unsafe America, populated by notorious gangsters such as Al Capone, John Dillinger, and other machine gun-slinging criminals who terrorized the streets. Newsreels of blood-soaked, motionless bodies stacked along bullet-riddled gangland automobiles reinforced his fears. Transportation was another factor, not only for Nono's large family, but also for five horses; the horses' irreplaceable master caretaker, Fachini; and the family's wonderful adopted dwarf clown, Bogonghi. Both men were considered part of the family, and any substitution was unthinkable—not that Mr. Gumpertz ever posed such a suggestion.

Talks remained at a stalemate. Some issues of disagreement remained, so the current Ringling contract went unsigned. With no lack of confidence, the Cristianis decided to accept a new contract at Great Yarmath, in England, before filling in seasonal gaps in their itinerary.

My Nono was headstrong and proud; he was small in stature, but he remained in control, even from that limited vantage. For him, success was not a dream; it was a duty. Nono, known for his shameless womanizing, was an inflexible disciplinarian in constant pursuit of perfection. Regardless, he was not deaf to good advice or impervious to reason. All these qualities contributed to his strong character, which led to the inspirational role he played in his family's ascent to fame.

Nona, my grandmother (called Mama by almost everyone), was of generous build, with a heart even larger than her size. Moreover, she was blessed with wonderful Italian genes that gave her fair, unblemished skin and a thick crown of wavy, black hair that never turned completely gray. She was also a deeply religious woman who prayed night and day (first for family harmony, and then for all else) and who wouldn't be caught without her Vatican-blessed scapular and gold Madonna medals hanging from her neck. Nona preferred to stay behind the scenes of public scrutiny; she never concerned herself with Nono's business, although she surely understood that her children were drunk with vision. She remained backstage, but openly applauded their tenacity. For these reasons and many, many more, Nona remained the Cristiani family's steadfast pillar of strength. She was honored as an adoring wife and mother who had enormous faith in her family's grandiose ambitions.

By mid-1933, political turmoil in Europe increased as the free world watched with dread. The prospect of unimaginable opportunities seemed to lift the young jocks like a magic carpet. And since timing had always been important to Nono, he recognized that America was his family's only salvation from Europe's hotbed of political unrest. (At the time, non-Nazi parties were forbidden in Germany.) Meanwhile, the Cristianis, known throughout the circus world to be passionate antifascists, were foolishly incapable of concealing their ever-increasing disdain for that faction. Because their childhood had been lost to practice, the ornery jokesters had a ravenous appetite for fun. In fact, stirring up excitement and controversy became such a liberating outlet that they seized any opportunity—damaging or not—to employ their bold and risky brand of rascality.

One impetuous prank backfired and placed the entire troupe in jeopardy during their employ with Circus Krone in Germany. Overconfident with youthful boldness, the brothers had the gall to costume Bogonghi as the mustached likeness of Adolph Hitler. Next, they coerced the roly-poly dwarf into posing as a stable groom during the riding act, so he could clown out his lowly duties with a gargantuan manure shovel.

Nono, having been left out of the scheme entirely, had his eyes riveted on a small committee of officers in the front row. The brainless stunt that could've ruined the equestrian's career sent him fuming out of the ring. As anticipated, the officers abandoned their seats and corralled the four oldest brothers as they exited the tent—demanding an immediate apology. Instead, the cocky foursome shouted back in the most insulting German terminology they knew. Then Uncle Daviso further infuriated the humorless officers by offering to provide each with

a shovel of their own. With that provocative comment, my father, being the closest mark, was bludgeoned over the head, and a bloody free-for-all ensued. Immediately, Bogonghi landed some punishing swipes with his foul-smelling shovel
while Nono reacted, sensibly, by helping Fachini load animals and gear for their
escape. But just as the stupefied officers slouched to the ground, the far-off sound
of sirens and screeching motorcars conveyed a critical message: *Get out of Dodge!*
With the gestapo in pursuit and the advantage of angels' breath at their backs, the
Cristiani troupe barely made it past the nearby German border with their heads
intact—showing no sign of remorse or apology.

$$*\quad*\quad*\quad*$$

Finally, over a span of several months in late 1933, Pat Valdo, Ringling's gen-
tlemanly acquisitions director, made the deal in Brussels after appeasing Nono
with yet another revised contract. Compromises on both sides left each party
feeling victorious; it was the classic win-win situation. Nono was skeptical but
not bereft of ideas as he explored his newly sprung atlas of dreams. While complicated travel arrangements got under way, the self-made marvels marched onward
full throttle with heightened resolve, honoring previously signed contracts.

The Cristianis were overwhelmed. They could never get their fill of Hollywood's glamorous motion pictures and fell in love with the thrilling sport of
American boxing. The brothers knew the history of the champions and could
name every major contender in the boxing profession to date.

In March 1934, during the economic downturn of the Great Depression,
when breadlines were a common sight, the famed equestrian troupe set sail from
the coast of England in what would prove to be a fortuitous move to America—
and to *"The Greatest Show On Earth."* Destiny had played its hand; the ball was
in their court, and a new era had begun.

Consider some of the major events the Cristiani family witnessed in 1934:
President Franklin D. Roosevelt was offering social and economic reform with
the New Deal; Adolph Hitler came into power and assumed the title of Der
Führer; notorious bank robbers Bonnie Parker and Clyde Barrow were ambushed
and shot to death by police in Louisiana; feared gangster (Public Enemy No. 1)
John Dillinger was gunned down by the FBI steps from the *Biograph Theater* in
Chicago; Clark Gable and Claudette Colbert received their only Oscars for Frank
Capra's *It Happened One Night*; methodical boxer James Braddock, dubbed "The
Cinderella Man," made the comeback of his life at age twenty-nine; a select num-
ber of Ringling's most promising corporate-owned shows entertained circusgoers

from coast to coast; business was on the rise, slowly showing signs of recovery—and the Cristiani family was sitting on top of the world.

Interestingly, the Cristiani family tree, which dates way back to biblical times, names an impressive list of authors, lawyers, philosophers, and scholars. Records indicate that the Cristianis are direct descendants of the first nobility of Italy, so their coat of arms was established way back in the twelfth century. Nono made a point of keeping the striking gold and blue crest on display as a proud symbol of the Cristianis' aristocratic lineage.

The entourage en route to the United States included Ernesto (Papa—my Nono); Emma Victoria (Mama—my Nona); Oscar (Daddy); Daviso; Lucio; Belmonte; Mogador; Pete (Parieto); Chita; Cosetta; Ortans; Corky (Corcaita); Fachini; Bogonghi; and five prize riding-act horses.

CHAPTER 2

▼

AMERICA

There are two worlds: the world that we can measure in line and rule
and the world that we feel with our hearts and imagination.
—Leigh Hunt

From 1934 to 1943, the Cristianis performed with Ringling and other Ringling
corporation-owned shows, including the Al G. Barnes and Hagenbeck-Wallace
circuses. Meanwhile, as young American men were swept into uniform, the
troupe found themselves filled with patriotism. Without hesitation, the Cristianis volunteered for countless benefit performances across the country. They
received star billing in the tenth annual police show, *Koppers Capers*, following
such luminaries as Bing Cosby, Bob Hope, Jack Benny, and a list of popular
entertainers of the day—such as famous funnyman Charlie Kemper, and George
and Helene Riley (from the hot radio show *Furlough Fun*). On one rare big-top
hiatus, the family performed in San Francisco's magnificent 1944 presentation
Frisco's Follies Bergere—a jubilant and most rewarding experience, I was told. In
1945, the Cristianis coproduced the beautiful and much-discussed Russell Bros.
Circus. This dicey enterprise was, to some extent, an artistic success, but it also
represented a financial letdown—an unsettling yet minor blow.

Those early Ringling years encompassed both smooth and rocky periods. My
family battled with management and refused to compromise until John Ringling
North (who had taken the reins, in 1938) intervened on their behalf, which infuriated rivaling performers. Many times, the unpredictable equestrians refused to
perform if the surrounding area was irresponsibly contaminated with props or
other paraphernalia that wrecked their concentration. The troupe would literally
walk out of the arena immediately before or during the riding act, evoking fits of

anger. It was a time of adjustment, of learning a new language and culture. The Cristianis had sailed to America with one goal in mind: to make their mark in the New World.

As arbiters of style and precision, the troupe made progress with astonishing speed; their vision was unfolding before their very eyes. But despite their focus, the Cristianis were never devoid of humor. Their attitude was, in fact, daring, unique, and liberating. In 1938, the family briefly returned to England for special engagements. Once again savoring the accolades of European fans, they entertained the Duke of Windsor in pantomime from the ring. They even charmed the incomparable Ethel Barrymore into riding their prize rosin-back, Baby, around the packed amphitheater of the Palladium—much to the delight of the cheering crowd. On opening night (at the Olympia Circus, in London) the Cristiani women were brought to tears when they were singled out to receive a lovely bouquet from the Lord Mayor himself. In years past, the Cristianis had been honored when King Albert of Belgium requested a private tumbling display after the show. So it was not out of character when, after settling in America, the troupe happened to tease good sport Mayor LaGuardia in New York City's Madison Square Garden about his trademark black hat.

The charm and wit of the Cristianis lured many stars of stage and screen to their performances during the memorable 1937 California tour with Al G. Barnes. The ever-returning luminaries sought the troupe members out backstage—openly praising their unique routine, signature strut, and trademark sizzle. Apart from being passionate followers of professional boxing, the Cristianis were, by their own admission, motion-picture fanatics, so such celebrity praise was accepted most humbly. Because of the many photo opportunities that came about naturally, the Cristianis accumulated a number of signed autographs from the greatest names in Hollywood.

The stars thoroughly enjoyed their visits between shows, after the matinee. Amazingly, they had a hard time leaving the big-top scene—often taking in the night performance as well. The very tall and exceedingly friendly actor, Barton MacLane, returned several times, always forgetting to bring in a promised head shot. When he did finally remember, he signed it on the spot: "To the Cristianis—a great troupe. Best wishes—better late than never—and don't forget to look out for the tomatoes [meaning babes]." Mr. MacLane, a regular man's man sort of guy, was a favorite.

Eventually, my family befriended icons Wallace Berry, George Raft, Edward G. Robinson, Joe E. Brown, Joan Crawford, Fredric March, Jane Withers, Harold Lloyd, Frank Buck, Jean Harlow, and Franchot Tone, as well as Clark Gable and Carol Lombard.

The year of 1937 was full of milestones. MGM signed the family to star in *MGM's The Great Picture*—meant to be one of *Pete Smith Specialties,* known as "shorts" because they were only ten or eleven minutes long. The popular black-and-white short, narrated by Pete Smith himself, was filmed in Hollywood at the ranch of Leo Carrillo—the actor who played Pancho, the Cisco Kid's sidekick. The filming took six weeks, affording the Cristianis the pleasure of meeting a litany of stars who frequented the set, including Charlie Chaplin, Fred Astaire, and Joseph Cotton, just to name a few. Coincidently, Charlie Chaplin, being a family friend since his circus career days back in Europe, graciously invited my grandparents to stay at the guest cottage behind his Hollywood home for the entire shoot. The project introduced my aristocratic circus family to theater audiences from coast to coast, bringing in stacks of letters from awestruck fans. Shortly thereafter, the Cristianis, itching to reap good fortune in their newly adopted land, proudly became American citizens; Nona and Nono's fondness for America left little room for regret. Though pierced by the sorrow that had befallen friends and relatives abroad, their loyalty was bequeathed to their new home.

America was free and beautiful, and the Cristiani family was under her spell.

✳   ✳   ✳   ✳

My father, born June 24, 1905, became a man quick to learn. Moreover, he was innately honest, and spoke in five languages. His comprehension of world history amazed me. In the formative stages of the Cristiani riding act, Daddy created a winning jockey act with my uncles, Lucio and Daviso. Together they performed a cycle of unique stunts on a speeding, halterless horse. The stunts gained the troupe recognition around Europe and attracted crowds to Nono's *Fratelli Cristiani Circus.* As the firstborn, Daddy grew up assured and self-reliant—and settled for nothing less than perfection after Nono awarded him the task of training his younger siblings. Those who knew Daddy best viewed him as a man who never relaxed his standards.

My mother, Marion Bendixen, was born in Derby, New York, on May 25, 1916, to full-blooded Norwegian parents. My maternal grandfather, George Bendixen, was a gifted landscape artist—mostly known for his trademark feathery strokes in watercolor and oil. Initially, my grandfather made meager sign-painting wages in and around Buffalo—a paycheck that didn't quite meet the needs of his large family. To his credit, he earned extra grocery money by writing articles for journals and local newspapers, so he managed to support his family without ever borrowing. My maternal grandmother, Martha, behaved like a protective mother hen, ever feuding in defense of her children. She had an irrefutable green thumb and verbally chased trespassers out of her showcase rose garden, in which she took utmost pride.

In due time, the Bendixens moved to Portland, Oregon, where Mommy grew up. Fortunately, my grandfather invested well (mostly in land), so Mommy spent her teen years living in a lovely white two-story home the family named Wood-haven. Their traditional wood-frame home, with private boathouse, ruled proud on an isolated stretch that extended along the banks of the Willamette River. But my seven-year-old mother's lighthearted world came to a halt in 1924, when she fell ill with diphtheria and scarlet fever, which left her with a damaged heart valve and total deafness in one ear. Almost immediately upon word of her daughter's fatal prognosis, my defiant grandmother singlehandedly carried her sickly daughter out of the hospital and nursed her back to health at the family home.

Countless times, Mommy told me that she had never once questioned her survival, because one particular nurse (a clairvoyant nun, to be exact) had appeared at her bedside midway through her ordeal and uttered the following words in her good ear: "My dear little Marion," she said with a compelling gleam in her eye, "you will live to marry and have two beautiful daughters." Mommy smiled, and the nurse was gone.

After a difficult convalescence, Mommy insisted on resuming her ballet lessons while she still had it this side of heaven. Her parents, feeling blessed by their daughter's energy after such a serious illness, allowed her to dance through grade school and high school, only to keep her happy. In fact, Mommy's once-professional ballet teacher, an avid follower of the stylistic school of Martha Graham, recognized her ability and offered to arrange specialized ballet training in New York City. My mother's frustration over persistent parental rants, along with the gravity of her nagging heart murmur, wrecked that grand idea—but just barely. Having lost her passionate dream, Mommy became an observer, a seer breathlessly in search of all that contributed to her creativity and spiritual needs. Ultimately, she interlaced the exterior duties of life with that inner search, which eventually led to the circus, where she found proper balance. Mommy considered time a valuable commodity, so wasting it was not her style—due to her precarious health, I'm sure. She was driven by her persistent memory of the strange circumstances of her blessed recovery; rain or shine, she woke up hungry for the day. I'll never forget her words of wisdom—which, unbeknownst to me, carried a prophetic message. "There's beauty in time," she said, looking off reflectively.

"This won't mean much to you now, but one day, you'll discover the true meaning for yourself."

My parents met under the most unusual circumstances. From what I've learned, an advertisement stating that the Al G. Barnes Circus was seeking production dancers for the 1937 season caught my mother's eye. After Mommy's successful audition, my grandfather found himself in a hopeless battle to keep his twenty-year-old daughter from joining the Al G. Barnes Circus ... which happened to feature the Cristiani family. Only months into the season, my parents married at the courthouse in San Francisco. Because Mommy had been raised in a family of three boys and four girls, Daddy's large, cohesive family didn't intimidate her in the least.

Although my maternal grandfather had always preached fair-minded liberalism, condoning his dearly loved daughter's marriage into what my grandmother called "a totally ridiculous, wandering rat-pack family," no matter how distinguished, was a real stretch.

"Marion," he said with outright conviction, "Mom is incensed. You'll be living the life of a gypsy. It's unthinkable!"

Daddy, being eleven years older than Mommy, took her condition seriously and promised his in-laws that, under his protective rule, circus work would be made simple to avoid jeopardizing his wife's health. Even so, my grandparents' acquiescence came later—three years later, in fact, after my birth. I came along in 1940, after the troupe signed another Ringling contract—"a good time to be born," said Daddy. Thereafter, Mommy's grace and sense of style carried her through all her endeavors. The circus issued a valuable passport that enabled her to nourish an insatiable appetite for investigating all cultures. She befriended all sorts of people; she condemned no one for their beliefs, however bizarre. Before my handsome father swept her off her feet, Mommy's life had been as far removed from the circus as anyone could possible be. Consequently, I was raised with a healthy mix of both worlds.

As foretold, my little sister, Carin, came along eleven years after me. In addition, I had the solid love of my older half-sister, Bombita (Bonnie), born to my young father back in Italy, several years before the Cristianis sailed to America. Although Bonnie had been my caring protector when I was very young, she was ten years my senior, so we mostly went to different schools. I am certain that God had a hand in Bonnie's birth and all that followed. Like my mother, I've always believed in kismet; to this very day, in every instance, it just seems right to deduce that certain things in life are predesigned.

▼

ENTER THE EQUESTRIANS

The Cristianis are a circus miracle.
—John Ringling North

The Cristiani family revolutionized the American circus.
The renowned equestrians performed feats that will never be repeated
in this country or anywhere else.
—Charles Philip Fox (circus historian and noted author)

Even at my callow age, I was aware that I had been born to a unique family. Understandably, I was proud of my celebrated surname, and I preened at all the notoriety that came with it. I'd clutch my hands and wait patiently in proximity of the Ringling circus back door, anticipating the arrival of the Cristiani horses. I hardly missed the occasion, ever eager to offer valuable tips to an excited score of amateur photographers. I was struck by my family's need for absolute focus, so I dared not distract either horses or family at this frenetic cycle. Of course, no one had reason to order me aside, because I knew enough to play by the rules: I simply lapsed back into the periphery with pursed lips, duly impressed with my own perceptiveness.

That memory is significant to me.

At the appropriate time, Fachini would aim his manicured horses toward the backyard of the big top (which was always frantic when a show was in progress). Clickity-clack! I was affixed to every clattering hoofbeat, fully aware of a communion between Fachini and his bridled flock. He would express his support by cheering them in the only language they knew: "*Miei bellissimi cavalli, tu mi fai un uomo riccho* [My beautiful horses, you make me a rich man]."

To call Fachini a mere groom would be ludicrous. He was, in fact, a well-schooled and talented musician as well; Fachini was no mercenary servant. Nono made sure trusted Fachini had all the authority he needed to properly care for his valuable animals, never shunning his persuasive advice. In any event, with Nono's full consent, Fachini regularly utilized his own proven remedies, which usually worked better than veterinarian-prescribed medications anyhow. As a precautionary measure, Fachini insisted on keeping a goat around the Cristiani horse tent at all times. According to Fachini—and, to this day, many professionals in the racehorse industry—goats are more susceptible to certain diseases. Reasonably, if the goat was infected first, he'd have advance warning to save his priceless team.

This principled man was of medium height and, though age slowed his pace, he stood strong and erect. Fachini's soulful eyes were deep-set with a subjective stare, projecting integrity. Santa Claus-like spectacles found a home in the center of his structured nose, and a soiled fedora roofed his silver hair, which still had the thick form of its earlier brown vitality. What's more, Fachini had healthy teeth, and his olive skin was flecked with age spots—but absent of wrinkles, except for solid lines that added depth to his chiseled face.

The promenade of ostentatious equines formed the foundation of the Cristiani riding act. It was imperative that these bareback riding horses all share one characteristic: suitability. It took years for animal and rider to prejudge everyone's subtle signal. The horses learned to adapt to each rider's habits—allowing for a regularity of form, style, and balance that resulted in explicit confidence. The riding act was the highlight of the program, and rightly so. Cognizant of their leading role, the horses marched in euphoric splendor, empowered by an unquenchable thirst for the spotlight.

Baby, Kansas, and Alba were the horses I remember best. Fachini spoke to all the horses in the same Italian dialect. However, he mastered a slight variance in tone that made the horses acutely aware of his penchant for pleasing them individually. The team reacted immediately by nudging him forcefully on the stomach or shoulder while snorting and digging their hooves into the dirt. The affection mutually expressed between Fachini and the horses was nothing less than inspiring. I was of the impression that Fachini could read their minds. It was as if the horses knew his gentleness—it summarized what existed between them. Whenever the opportunity presented itself, I'd ask Fachini if I could assist with the grooming, with the understanding that I had to follow his instructions to the letter so as not to get stepped on. And before I began my chores, he made certain to repeat his favorite Italian proverb: *"Cara* [dear] *Victoria,"* he said fondly, *"chi ama il suo lavoro lo fa bene* [he who loves his work does it well]." In truth, Fachini deemed that job the noble feature of his life.

Baby was a glorious masterpiece of a horse—a real prize. This Trojan straw-berry-roan Percheron had an immense, muscled neck and topped the scale at well over two thousand pounds. He drew onlookers like a magnet as he trotted by the bandstand with pomposity and flair. His ears always slanted toward the bandle-ader, who cued the familiar musical score that preceded Baby's advancement into the ring. Mighty-chested Baby used his dark, melting eyes most effectively—usu-ally to invoke a tight neck hug or sustained fingernail scratches under his thick, manicured forelock.

Baby allowed my uncles to show off their steamy libidos during the act, be-cause he controlled the beat of his canter to every gyrating transfer and pirouette. He hardly wavered an inch as he withstood the weight of five Cristiani brothers, who managed to land on his muscled back in standing position—without the aid of a springboard. Baby's stabilized pace also permitted Mogador to hold a perfect handstand on his rump for almost two revolutions around the ring, which served to illuminate the beauty of my uncle's manly physique. Mogador's style was dis-tinctively different from the rest of the family. His solo routine, though elegantly polished, appeared totally natural and seemingly off the cuff. I understand ex-actly why Bob Lax was so inspired by Mogador's performance. At his best, he came very close to resembling a Herculean figure performing for the Gods in the mythical age of Ulysses. After Mogador completed his pattern of imposing ballet movements, Kansas joined Baby in the ring. Baby and Kansas gave Lucio and Belmonte an opportunity to engage fans in a series of difficult maneuvers—which then segued into a succession of synchronized horse-to-horse, full-twisting somersaults that jostled the crowd to their feet.

Kansas was a crafty white gelding with a sizable, gray-dappled rump. Though not as large as Baby, he possessed a certain kind of elegance—and what I found most amazing was that he responded to a woman's touch as if given the vanity of a human mind. His proud stance and willingness to hold a pose made him circus-poster perfect. (The few existing circus posters, inspired by the image of my bru-nette aunt Chita—positioned next to his white-speckled head—have long since been snatched by ardent collectors.) Kansas willingly flirted with all the ladies who petitioned for a portrait by his side; he was a most handsome creature, and he knew it. This sparked a touch of arrogance that suited his Valentino image. Belmonte's athletic legs had remarkable spring, and his phenomenal jump onto Kansas—while shouldering a bulky harness-racing sulky—was not only superbly crafted, but drew intellectual praise from the most cynical New York critics when the Cristiani troupe was featured with Ringling at Madison Square Garden.

Then there was Alba—the "finish horse" brought in for the entertaining, nonstop finale. Like his legendary predecessor, Polo, Alba galloped with a fervent desire to win at the game he played so well. With Alba, the Cristianis performed various audience-teasing maneuvers that had spectators either gasping for breath or bending over with laughter. With crinkled nose and slicked-back ears, Alba persisted in his quest for victory while shaking off the intrepid jocks one by one. Snow-white Alba delighted in challenging each rider to withstand more than a few seconds on his back—except during the incomparable six-person fork jump, when Lucio, the last rider in line, positioned himself backward, facedown on the stinky crease of Alba's tail. It was uncanny, but the horse was inclined to download a steamy cascade of manure bricklets—timed precisely at the moment of Lucio's hilarious gag. At that instant, Lucio brought the house down by cleaving to Alba's rear end, fanning away the horse's rank output with his beat-up fedora hat.

In the next sequence, Lucio would make several staged attempts to stay on Alba's back. After pleading in pantomime to the crowd for the favor of one last attempt, Lucio would press upward with split-second timing—purposely landing off-balance on Alba's rump. Lucio then teased the crowd with uproarious mime-type gestures while trying wildly to gain control with one leg flung high in the air. (These choreographed maneuvers lasted for three or four laps). Then, dramatically, as if riveted to Alba's back, Lucio stiffened with his arms pressed down to his sides, like a zombie. A hush would fall over the tent as he held his position with both hands at his side for several rounds, without tipping one way or the other. At the appropriate time, Lucio completed an about-face, leaving the audience benumbed with fear—and wondering what to expect next. His body swayed with every movement in perfect balance.

Appearing mean and annoyed, the unbridled Alba would race on, ever failing to shake Lucio off. Finally, the bareback-riding comedian silenced the crowd once again by performing a double pirouette before nonchalantly high-stepping off Alba's posterior onto the safe terra firma—laughing with both hands tucked in his pockets. Upon realizing they had been duped, the crowd would shower Lucio with an electrifying ovation. Straightaway, Lucio removed his hat and jacket before hitting the springboard and diving over Alba in swanlike form—properly landing on the outer ringcurb mat. Lucio would then change the mood by strutting about in an obviously feigned stupor outside the ring, while Mogador strategically placed his coat and hat on the floor of the center ring. But as soon as the pelting horse made his second pass, Lucio took what appeared to be a suicidal tumble under Alba's belly—barely clearing his thunderous hooves. With little pause, he completed yet another tumble over his jacket and hat, then took a well-deserved bow—covered in sawdust, but perfectly intact.

Lucio's cycle of comedic stunts led the audience to new heights of enthusiasm. I kid you not: circus fans became junkies on Lucio's daredevil comedy routines. He was a born entertainer, somehow able to combine his natural athletic genius and zany jocularity with seamless realism.

Many Lucio-wannabes have performed over time, but none have made the grade; even the best have fallen way short in their copycat attempts. Many old-time fans and performers concur that there will never be another paragon like him in his field of expertise. In those glory days of yore, the equestrians were mobbed even before they reached the back door by throngs of seat-fleeing fans seeking autographs and close personal contact. Starstruck fans actually draped over the aisles in fun-loving hysteria, athirst for more … but what could top the ooh and ahhh of that finale? At the end of their performance, the riding marvels backed out of the center ring to the roar of a standing ovation, arms uplifted in humble gratitude.

Nona and Nono usually stayed somewhere in the background during the family act, radiating a swell of pride. Comfortable folding chairs were placed in front of the bandstand prior to their appearance. They would watch their children's rudimentary moves as they prepared to execute a phenomenal routine of equestrian feats without a grimace of worry—satisfied that they had always trained with the punishing control of a Russian dance troupe.

Back then, Nono kept his ultrafine, grayish hair trimmed in slick crew cut style, so he rarely wore a hat. My grandparents dressed for every occasion—and no event was quite as important as watching their children perform. Nono normally dressed in a fashionable tweed suit, adorned with an engraved gold pocket watch and chain from the old country. Despite his stern demeanor, he softened considerably when it came to his beloved grandkids; they never went unnoticed, not a single one. Moreover, Nono's grandchildren visibly removed the burden of his dogmatic character, which most outsiders considered set in stone. In other words, this overpowering figure of a man was simply my grandfather, Nono: tender and loving and witty. Moreover, like Daddy, he was by turns playful and focused—with the mark of a born storyteller.

When socializing outside her kitchen, Nona favored light, silky dresses with matching shoulder scarves and her favorite brooch—pinned off to one shoulder. Immediately after the riding act, workers assisted Nona and Nono through the back door and seated them in the shade to relax in the company of visiting circus fans and elderly show friends. Given the opportunity, I'd disappear in the cushy fold of Nona's lap, seeking her embrace. There was no other like her. Attributes of maternal wisdom and courage impregnated her heart—and the beauty that had been hers in her youth was no match for the beauty I saw in her as my grandmother. She adored all her children and strove to keep the peace. Heaven knows she wasn't always successful, but that was her masterful talent.

CHAPTER 4

▼

RUDE AWAKENING

There exists no cure for a heart wounded with the sword of separation.
—Hitopadesa

It wasn't until 1946 (the year I turned six and thus became old enough for school) that my family broke away from Ringling and joined the Cole Bros. Circus. For them, it was simply a matter of choice and refreshing change of pace. The Kentucky-based Cole Bros. Circus was the second-largest railroad show in America during the 1940s. In its heyday, this great-looking, tightly run operation—which boasted a huge big top, menagerie, and sideshow—hired an impressive list of headline acts, so avid fans and sponsors alike regarded the main performance as second to none. That's why Ringling considered the Cole show such a fierce competitor—which, of course, was great for circus business overall. The banner years of my youth, when the Cristiani acts were still at their peak, were experienced on that show.

The Cole show winter quarters was spread over several acres and many performers who could afford the purchase settled in travel trailers until the winter date season began in November. The security of our cozy, thirty-foot house trailer, palatial in comparison to our cramped stateroom on the circus train, sustained me. We were proud to own this particular winter home, be it ever so humble. Naturally, my recollections from that more advanced part of my childhood spent on the Cole Bros. Circus are quite vivid, and therefore, much easier to recall than my experiences on Ringling.

The winter dates were special engagements, produced with ceremonial hoopla and tied together with the best talent a generous budget could buy. Performers competed vigorously for these prestigious dates, because the benefits were threefold: they were longstanding Shrine-sponsored events, they paid top dollar, and—because the dates were held annually—performers could benefit from a return contract. Nabbing any one of these lucrative contracts could see circus performers through the lean winter period. And it was not to be overlooked that because the winter dates took place in major cities like Detroit, St. Louis, Chicago, and the Texas cities of Fort Worth, Dallas, and San Antonio (booked as a trophy package deal known as the Texas dates), flashy audience-pleasing acts could be showcased before a rolodex of aggressive booking agents.

Performers really looked forward to the opening-night shindigs, which gave them a unique opportunity to cozy up to influential Shriners—which couldn't hurt, given the stiff competition. When it came to spectacular entrances, circus performers took the cake. Undoubtedly, the advantage of working inside the comfort of secure, heated buildings equipped with colorized lighting effects and spotlights galore, rather than element-exposed big tops, motivated everybody to dress to the hilt. Ignorant of how tacky they really looked, most performers proved themselves incapable of separating costume regalia from street clothes. As far as the high and mighty male "cat act" trainers were concerned, the jungle look was in vogue year round: unkempt shoulder length hair, skin-tight pants, heavy gold chains—and half-buttoned shirts that exposed their hairy chest to the world. How dare any sane gal resist their advances! With few exceptions, women performers showed up in a hodgepodge of zany animal print garments and sparkly beehive hairdos—excluding feathers—thank heaven, but not always.

The banquet, however, was the main event. In order to beat the sounding bell, the cranky oldsters would toss their canes in a push-and-shove run for the free food. After the buffet tables were picked clean, everybody engaged in animated gossip sessions, sparing no one. The aforementioned amusement was fodder for the underbelly throng; it refreshed their gullets like an after-dinner mint.

While the secure buildings provided a haven from the ravages of winter's cold sting, the dense concrete flooring was a constant reminder to stay focused. This foreseeable hazard caused interminable restlessness among family members who stood vigilant as their loved ones stoically entered the spotlight. Blood relatives would posture themselves beneath the rigging, squinting upward toward the high scaffolding, scrutinizing every link for defects.

In that age, aerial stars weren't required to be secured by mechanic belts or protective wires during the performance, which certainly gives the new crop of aerialists a great advantage. Back in the old days, these devices were only used for practice sessions—never in the performance itself. Old-time aerialists were reluctant to lessen the element of danger, even for safety's sake. Of course, safety nets were compulsory for flying acts, and the Zacchini cannon jump as well. Unfortunately, other circus stars, including German-born high-wire daredevil Karl Wallenda, shunned lifesaving devices of any sort. Such risky tightrope walking offered the crowd spine-tingling drama, but wreaked havoc with ground-based kinfolk. Karl's faithful wife and adviser, Helen, was taunted with premonitions— all bad. She often lashed out at Karl about giving up his risk-taking behavior before it was too late.

*   *   *   *

Being self-taught, Daddy never failed to remind me about the importance of education. He couldn't have made it clearer that he expected me to find an interest outside the circus. He and Mommy expected such a quest to begin at Cardome Academy—my first boarding school experience, where the mighty seeds of church doctrine took root. Considering that Cardome was conveniently located in nearby Georgetown, Daddy thought the academy would be the ideal school. Reasonably, my parents figured they'd have the opportunity to rescue me for regular weekend excursions to Louisville in between the winter dates. However, the thought of leaving my parents' nest to start school in a very strange environment was quite traumatic. My parents' frantic performance schedule didn't leave me much time to talk my way out of it—not that I had a prayer of doing so. Besides, Mommy had spent a full week packing items on the provided list and sewing personalized name tags onto every article of clothing, including my socks. And a telegram had just confirmed that the required set of sterling silverware, engraved with my initials, VBC, had already been rushed directly to the school. My goodness, I could hardly believe the preparation involved.

At every chance, I studied the big top with near-mystical reverence. Altogether, I was spooked by my understanding that very soon, Cardome would snatch my circus independence like some powerful magnet. The academy was costly, that much I understood—so outwardly, for my folks' sake, I promised to tolerate the agony of isolation and conformity. *I am, after all*, I thought, *strong enough to get through the school year, and I'll prove it.* But bless the day when summer vacation would release me back into the bosom of my home on the Cole Bros. Circus. Before Daddy tucked me in for the night, I studied the sketch of Cardome Academy on the brochure—far more carefully this time. Then, lo and behold, my heart started thumping harder and harder. In the deep recesses of my mind, I was overcome with a creepy, lingering feeling. There was something ominous about that school. Of this I felt sure.

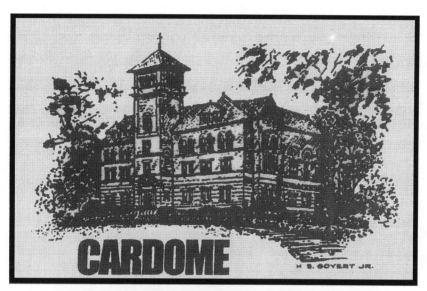

CARDOME

H. B. GOVERT JR.

Victoria Cristiani At Age 6

CHAPTER 5

▼

CARDOME ACADEMY

Fall 1946

There comes a time in every human life when the past comes back afresh.
It seeps in slowly like the morning fog.
Suddenly, you are surrounded by its presence and there is no escape.
It cannot be leaped over, ducked under or dodged.
There it is, engulfing and embracing you with neither mercy nor compassion.
One must then pass through and endure the vaporous mist until it lifts,
disappearing finally the way it came, without invitation or encouragement.
—Victoria B. Cristiani Rossi and Peggy J. Russell

Upon my arrival at Cardome, the bright wall of the sky was jewel-like blue and feathered with thin, wispy clouds. I carefully guided my feet past the traffic jam on the automobile-blocked driveway, where parents and students alike plucked out their suitcases and other belongings in an unashamed display of heartache.

In a way, I felt exiled, starting first grade in a setting that kept me shadow-boxed from the glorious environment of circus performers, exotic animals, dancing horses, and bicycle-riding bears. Without warning, I began hyperventilating. Indeed, I recognized the familiar thumpity-thump palpitations that made me disoriented—the same suffocating condition that always threw me into panic. Drawing from the powers within, I reached a compromise of sorts and fumbled through the day's orientation, which included a tour of school and grounds, without incident. And while optimism still rattled loudly in my mind, I piggybacked my gear upstairs and sprinted directly to the dorm, citing squatter's rights after

- 24 -

staking out a cheery window alcove. Following that, I fabricated a slight offering of sprightliness, sensing the cool draft of a certain nun who appeared out of nowhere like the illusionary will-o'-the-wisp.

"What are you doing, pray tell? And why did you break away from your classmates?" she asked, with a hand restraining her puffed-out chest. "I'm Sister Mary Agnes, and you're Victoria … the *circus child*, I gather? No, no, no, child! We don't race up stairs like a pack of wild animals. We move about in an orderly fashion at Cardome. We're disciplined and civilized. Do you understand?"

Impulsively, I backed away and looked up at her in surprise, answering, "Yes, Sister Agnes, I understand," with a lump in my throat. At that, Sister ordered me to relocate to a dark, windowless alcove without a word of explanation.

The girls I'd met so far weren't very talkative, and I had little to say myself—especially after being scolded. By the end of that long day, I was suffering from severe loneliness and my inability to fit in or unearth even one colorful element of circus life. I withdrew into the bondage of my achromatic surroundings, feeling that my recovery was as hopeless as that of a javelin-pierced heart. But little did I know the worst was yet to come … in the mortal form of a demented nun, hidden from view.

Darkness cast a spell of mystery that turned my blood to ice. Lights-out meant an instant hush. No one dared to utter a word. For a long while, I couldn't hear even the faintest whisper. Then it happened, like a stab in the night: unnatural cries, sounding like possessed calls from a bride of Satan, arced to the corner dormitory. They sliced through my ears like a knife. Although I was in agony, I couldn't move my limbs, so I balled my fist and—for the first time ever—wet the bed. Hail Mary, it was difficult to process the horror of that first night on the weekend before school. Understandably, I had never expected such a bizarre introduction to one of the most prestigious schools in the state of Kentucky.

The next morning, as if spirit-guided, I was drawn to a wooded hollow just beyond the play yard, where I listened to nature's gleeful chorus as it rhapsodized in perfect harmony with the sacred bells that rang from the tower. Wild violets captured my soul and landscaped a treasure trove of memories that would never fade. Their purplish blue petals studded the backwoods like gems, waving in vivid contrast to the bedded swirl of Irish green.

For the time being, my world was a convent tucked away in the foothills of Kentucky. The Catholic boarding school was run by the Sisters of the Visitation, a cloistered order of nuns whose only contact with outside life was through enrolled students. The towering building, made of dun-colored brick, had a gothic presence that seemed to wrap around me.

Nuns traveled the halls like birds of a feather, wearing immaculate black-and-white habits that cast reflections on the glowing linoleum corridors. Being a typical March Pisces, I had an affinity for anything that sparkled. I'd stoop down in complete disbelief and marvel at the perpetual shine. Bells beckoned, guiding the events of a season marked by foliage at the peak of its colorful glory. Saintly statues with dead-white faces guarded the dormitory entryway. Those giant marble sculptures appeared to come alive in the eeriness of nightfall, when their scary shadows escaped onto the floor like discontented ghosts. The monastic quiet had me dodging a whirlpool of untamed spirits, awaiting rescue by the blessed sandman.

Using the bathroom after hours presented the risk of sighting a nun gliding by in her bed habit, her shaved head exposed. Vociferous cries resonated from afar. For all I knew, they could've traveled to our school from some distant graveyard. However, the disquieting wails were rumored to echo from a crazed nun subdued within the confines of her padded cell. Every so often, a small clique of older students would secretly huddle in the dark corners of the social hall, hinting in whispers that this nun had undergone a lobotomy. I was gratified not to understand the significance of a word I could barely pronounce—a word that sounded much too scary to be good.

The hour of reckoning came one evening after nightly prayer, when I figured things out for myself. Tilting my head to listen, I overheard disgruntled utterances at the foot of the stairs. "She's the nun who went crazy!" whispered one concerned senior. "Evelyn says she was so uncontrollable that the bishop had to approve a gruesome operation that removed bits and pieces of her brain."

Oh, sweet Jesus! I broke away, swift, silent, and mute, blinking painfully into the gray hall. I sank deeply into meditation, desperate to find answers to a zillion questions—most of which I was too scared to ask. This mortifying revelation caused me to lie awake every night, bedewed with cold sweat and stretched tight in virtual paralysis, listening for the "aaaaahhhhhs" of the deranged nun who, for all I knew, had had part of her brain cut out.

As October approached, the inundation of cryptic theories ignited a number of interrelated personal problems that made me wish I were dead: sudden tearful outbursts, shameful bed wetting, and nail biting right down to the bloody quick. Regardless of how humiliating those emotional annoyances seemed at the time, they were unconquerable under the circumstances.

At dawn, the reveille bells rang from the tower. The enchanting tones bellowed while I slumbered in grim semiconsciousness, hoping to steal a few more winks before rolling out of bed. Shortly thereafter, the sister in charge stormed the halls, waving a large, silver bell. The harsh rings made it painfully clear that we had little time to shower, dress, and make our beds before inspection. Demerits were given for any type of misconduct, followed by a more archaic form of punishment for grave offenses, God forbid. Orientation on this thorny issue made me fretfully nauseated. The very subject of rule-breaking prompted a paranoiac scurry to the nearest holy water font where—for my sins—I crossed myself and genuflected in a prayerful salute to my winged guardian. "Listen carefully," Sister Clare commanded, rapping her desk with what we took to be a whipping stick. "These are the rules … If broken, there will be consequences."

Our uniforms consisted of skirts, sweaters, and ties—all in a shade of liver brown that might as well have been known as "ugh"—coordinated with tan blouses and brown oxfords. Matching brown beanies covered our heads for the daily obligation of attending Latin mass inside the holy chapel. As a matter of routine, we learned to organize all apparel on our alcove chairs for nightly inspection. Within days, the habit of preparedness was ingrained. Above all else, modesty, cleanliness, and other virtues were constantly impressed upon our malleable minds—followed by droning lectures relating to self-sacrifice, eternal damnation, and—my second-worst dread, meant for "saved sinners" only: the long, drawn-out stew in purgatory. Surely St. Joan of Arc, who had been torched at the stake back in the Middle Ages, was making progress fighting for sinners' rights. Things didn't add up, I reasoned. Once, I burned my finger on a match, and the blister hurt for days on end … so the nuns must've lied. God wouldn't do that. *Or would He?*

Every waking hour was regimented, except for recess and prolonged weekend play periods. We marched in formation as a group, with our arms folded, ushered by phantom-like silhouettes and the faintest of sounds. Before breakfast, we attended mass, which was especially difficult for me; I fainted more than a few times while kneeling on those insufferably hard wooden benches, earning black-and-blue kneecaps that didn't want to heal. During the benediction, wand-like strokes of incense emitted plumes of smoke that traversed the chapel. Its intake generated an emotional paradox—one of pious spirituality and sheer reluctance to succumb to the unbending religious views that shaped our moral conduct. Regardless, on such days, when troubled in the very heart of darkness, I was also blessed—and, by the grace of God, seized by an unfailing sense of wonder.

I'd journey time and again to my radiant cluster of trees, only to relax among the violets and daydream of what I would become in my life: singer or stage actress came to mind, but never circus performer. If I could remain still enough, a majestic flock of sentry butterflies would encircle me, at times settling on my braids or sweetly kissing my nose. I'd watch in awe as they danced merrily in delicate swirls of balletlike mimicry, while families of tiny blossoms swayed in the breeze, nodding approval. My fascination for animals must have been firmly inborn at birth. I quite naturally anthropomorphized not only animals, but also objects I loved. This might explain why my adopted hideaway became an effectual comforter—a place of unrivaled intimacy, and plausibly the one place where I could incorporate my thoughts while listening to the soothing, rhythmic chimes of nature. Normally, I'd slip away on weekends or during weekday recess—while my classmates skipped rope, played hopscotch, or bounced balls on the tennis court. It wasn't as if I had far to go.

Breakfast was my favorite meal, so I blissfully cleaned my plate. As for the other meals, my culinary recollections suggest a menu that was less than gourmet. Proper etiquette was dictated by Sister Margaret, a no-nonsense nun who prowled our pre-assigned dining tables at random. Unburdened by guilt, I frequently risked my neck by stuffing vomit-inducing vegetables up my sweater sleeve. One unlucky day, as I exited our dining hall, Sister Margaret, in normal hectoring mode, caught sight of spinach dripping from under my wrist. I expected the worst as her musing gaze surveyed the icky green puddle directly below my feet. Sister's faintly mocking smile made me shrink. "Step out of line, scalawag!" I didn't know the word, but I recognized the tone … it wasn't nice. Anyway, I surrendered in a hairbreadth, without even giving her the satisfaction of hearing my impassioned excuse. Panic-stricken and more than a little cowed, I felt her scrutinizing stare penetrate with laserlike accuracy as Sister pointed her prominent nose.

"Victoria," she said, curling her ugly purple lips, "rinse out that sloppy mess!" Shoot, my plans were thwarted. I had planned to bury the smelly strings—best suited for worms and snails.

That night, I was subjected to snickering mockery and the cruel code of boarding-school censure: one hour kneeling on a hard floor with my wet face masked from view. After enduring pangs of humiliation, however, I was only slightly repentant. Still, I promised (with gritted teeth) to refrain from future fooleries, submit to the school's exacting standards, and *never* repeat my misdeeds—for a while, anyway. Truth be known, physical punishment was a rare occurrence, but the nuns not-so-subtly implied the contrary. So inwardly, the queasy combination of ripping fear, ugly night cries, and isolation festered, causing more panic attacks: What if I were moved into throwing a fit? Might *I* be next in line for a lobotomy?

*   *   *   *

Phone calls from my parents were always met with jubilation, but I couldn't wait to elaborate on every injustice. Every Sunday, they made a point of reminding me that it was *not* the end of the world. They were right; it wasn't, and I told them so.

But nothing beat Mommy's newsy letters. Occasionally, she'd glue a spangle at the top; if tilted toward the light, it magnified splendidly and served as a looking glass that previewed my next holiday. Of course, I saved all her letters inside my tidy rose-print box, along with my three-inch elephant tusk, a couple of family photos, one silver dollar, and a tube of Mommy's lipstick.

In all fairness, I vividly recall contracting the mumps in late fall and being nursed with gentle sympathy by nuns who were kinder in spirit—and not clad in fanaticism. Any infected students needing to be quarantined were relocated to the convent's bright and cheerful infirmary—fondly nicknamed "Peanut Heaven," though I don't recall anyone ever mentioning the history of it. This safe, secluded section was conveniently situated on the top floor, overlooking the tennis courtyard. Sister Mary Angelica, a cherubic Irish nun with broad hips and rosy cheeks, served light meals on a flowery tray three times a day. She'd whisk around, delivering frisky winks, as if holding the most sumptuous, irresistible dish on earth. "S'pose you're a starvin' little imp! Lookee what I have here ... smells good!" Then she would push for a heartier chuckle. "Child of the Lord, ye feel like dancin'?"

"Maybe tomorrow, Sister Angelica," I answered. "I'm so achy, it hurts to grin."

Obviously begging for needed sympathy, I focused my eyes on hers and gingerly cupped both hands on my cheeks to ease the pain. In response, Sister pinched her habit and moved her tiny feet in a lively Irish step—and then answered in fine limerick fashion: "Remember, dearie, always offer your pain up for the poor souls; that way it's never wasted," she sang. "Have faith in the Lord's providence, child, and be comforted. For an angel like you, there's always tomorrow and tomorrow ... and tomorrow."

One moonless night, a windy storm almost bent trees double. After a crash of lightning split their topmost branches, I hid deep under the covers, listening with stiffened spine as autumn bid farewell to the airborne peels swirling in disarray. Sister Angelica was carrying an armload of towels to the linen closet when something hit nearby. Just as the lights flickered a warning, she stumbled inside, panting, to a halt. "You mustn't fret in Peanut Heaven, dearie," she said. Her words were followed by a moment of breathless expectancy. "Sleep well; it's only God's sainted helpers movin' the furniture."

Come to think of it, all the pampering spoiled me so silly that I momentarily forgot my place. Even as the stormy chill drew me deeper into the gloaming, I felt snug, much like a princess in her towered castle. Thereby, I idly rested, cooling my fever in coiled-up comfort—sucking in fragrant trails of warm sweetbread, homemade jams, and brewed tea. Occasionally, Mommy would send packages filled with various nonperishable snacks for my breadbox, and sometimes she'd sneak in a surprise fix of chewy black licorice to appease my addiction.

Once, near Easter, an express parcel came in the mail. Yearningly, I rushed to uncover the clear wrap that protected a delectable milk-chocolate bunny, roughly ten inches tall. To my dismay, I found that one ear had braved a clean break. My impromptu judgment, made while carefully holding the torn ear, was that I would not—could not—feast on this dear splintered bunny, which in my mind had suffered much pain. On second thought, it struck me that it mightn't be a bad idea to concentrate on the divine taste of milk chocolate. After I pondered for a spell longer, my resistance weakened considerably. Then and there, I made a secret resolve to let my burning *sweet* desire take full charge. *Well, what the heck, go ahead … smear your silly face and enjoy.*

Even though I was not great at socializing, I did manage to gather a handful of playmates. But Jenny Harrigan, an only child, was special. Everybody needs at least one bosom buddy. In time, we became inseparable. Jenny was an elfin child, full of singsong, tricks, and rhyme—the ideal little leprechaun friend who mischievously appeared and disappeared around corridors and stairwells in the bat of an eye. Frizzy, golden red hair outlined the quizzical expression on her freckled face as she toiled to make trouble. She started each day triggered and vainly confident, and since she never wanted suggestions, I mostly followed her lead—a truth that in large measure, I supposed, made her happy.

Pretty Jenny had the kind of unbridled curiosity that annoyed our sweatbeaded, menopausal teacher, who reacted sharply in catechism class by puffing with sour breadth and glaring at her freethinking little head with bongo-drum eyeballs. No matter, for I found my pal's girlish, uncompromising honesty terribly funny, without a whiff of contrition … though our catechism teacher, Sister Gertrude, never saw the humor in it. As punishment for disrupting the class, she had me write a line of apology until my fingers cramped up, but it was worth it.

For one thing, Jenny happened to be, by her own description, a born actress. She entertained nicely during recess by fabricating stories and interjecting laughable versions of her nanny's witticisms, like, "Wake-up call at sparrow's fart!" We giggled ourselves sick, and that particular phrase became our last whispered sack-time quote. But despite sharing many fertile-minded fantasies, as children often do, I never discussed my sanctuary with anyone, even Jenny. No—I simply wouldn't chance it. Excuses count for nothing when it comes to letting the cat out of the bag. Every kid knows full well that secrets, once told, aren't secrets anymore; it's a lesson learned early on. Besides, my fairy contract called for discretion; otherwise, I'd be blacklisted and would lose my privileges forever.

Although I arrived at the academy with no preconceived notion of acceptability, I had hoped that my classmates would be tolerant of my background, however dissimilar from their own. The majority came from well-to-do stock, most of whom I found politely civil. But a select few, caught up in an idyllic concept of superiority, looked at me uncomprehendingly. Whatever the cause, I was spurned as an outcast. The remarks behind my back were degrading and demoralizing.

"Do you suppose her parents are freaks?" Rosemary asked, raising her brow.

"Maybe so," said blond, blue-eyed Ellen. "How on earth are they paying her tuition? My brother, Humphrey, knows all about circus people. They're homeless, spooky-weird, and live in a tent. Boo!"

Rosemary laughed at the thought and added, "I wonder if she can stand on her head."

Looking back, the slurs hit me hard. But instead of dwelling on the negative, I'd stomp about, arguing with my hurt ego, insisting I didn't care. Eventually, I mastered one-upmanship and accepted their upturned noses without a tinge of remorse.

Jenny and I used to track the affairs of Olivia and Sara Jane Moffet, a pair of willowy, pink-cheeked twins whose grandmother elected to visit on certain weekends. We'd pretend the grandmother was either a wrinkly, has-been movie star from the silent era or some eccentric millionaire. At every stopover, her black stretch limousine would swerve up the driveway and park under the same shady tree. Before long, the skinny, tight-lipped chauffeur circled to the rear door in a smooth lilt as the prissy sisters ran to meet the shadowy figure—in hiding for reasons that kept us guessing. Jenny was brilliant anytime we could steal a moment to cut up in private; her laudable impersonations had me holding my belly from howling.

"Madame," she sighed, standing at soldierlike attention with her back swayed, "the brats have arrived."

Without fail, I'd lean over the warm, ever-ticking dormitory radiator with my nose boldly pressed against the windowpane and wonder where I had seen this very tall, wiry man with a long pointed nose. Time and again, the vision of his tableau lingered in my mind and left me puzzled. For weeks, I had tried to convince cynical Jenny that I knew the chauffeur from some far-off, scary place, but she never once entertained the notion, so I gave up the struggle. "That's nutty!" she would snap, blinking suspiciously. "How could you possibly?"

Although my inner voice told me differently, I agreed. It did seem preposterous. Strangely, we never saw the aristocratic recluse leave her limousine; she managed to stay hidden behind the darkly tinted glass for the entire span. Madame must've been on a precise schedule, because the interludes never lasted very long, but the spoiled-rotten twins always left with a generous payload. And, as they made their way past the light-footed chauffeur, he never failed to tip his hat in a most respectful manner. Oh my, oh me! The very idea of such formality—at all the exact and proper moments—left me dumbfounded. I reacted by mouthing an audible "wow" every time. Yet Jenny, who scrutinized everyone and everything, was unimpressed. Whether consciously or not, the twins were barely friendly, and by all indications carried an inherent air of importance that was particularly noticeable in their peppered conversations. *But never mind that,* I said to myself, *I'll concentrate solely on the puzzling figure dressed in black. He's the one to watch— not them!* Up until then, I had mostly held my thoughts, fearing the beast in him might grab me in the night.

One dark, drizzly day, at ease with Jenny in the chilly library, I thumbed through my favorite Halloween story, Washington Irving's, *The Legend of Sleepy Hollow.* He jumped off the pages in etched-out living color. After I shoved the book in my friend's face, Jenny stood mute with chin in hand, as if seriously bothered by the perfect likeness. Of course, being the person she was, she paused to study the picture even closer in order to remove any trace of skepticism.

"I'll be. It's him, all right," she agreed moments later, sitting rigid with her neck out, like a turtle. Without having to say one word, she made it abundantly clear: I was vindicated. No question about it: I'd just identified the stuffy chauffeur, Ichabod Crane!

*   *   *   *

Initially, I just wasn't capable of doing anything right at Cardome. But by applying myself after Christmas, I managed to settle in. In the following days, I picked up a head of steam and hopscotched into spring, eager to make the most of it. Interestingly, the cursed nun's night cries subsided over the course, only returning now and then in full form. Also, the valuable lesson in benevolence I'd learned from dear Sister Angelica at Peanut Heaven helped me contain my fear somewhat. Thereafter, whenever disturbed by those haunting mournful sounds, I'd stick my fingers in my ears and offer her pain (and mine) up for the intentions of the poor souls, and, if at all possible, turn my attention to something far more pleasant. While I doubt I ever fully accepted the strict regimentation at Cardome, the passage of time inspired a fresh interest—specifically, the advent of summer vacation.

Rightfully, I felt blessed to belong to another world—the world of the celebrated Cristiani circus family. So, yes, my classmates were right in one sense: I *was* different. I didn't lead the elite lifestyle of the moneyed crowd, accustomed to the privileged society of grand, lavishly appointed mansions equipped with a stilted line of uniformed butlers and sharp-nosed chauffeurs. But no question, those prim girls—especially the twins—couldn't begin to imagine the full extent of my joy when, at long last, I left the dull orb of the convent. Indubitably, I'd be the envy of every child who saw me waving from the red and gold scrolled circus train—decelerating to a crawl for the benefit of isolated rural community fans. Yes, I would appear out of nowhere, just like a happy accident, preceded by the toot-tooting blast of the whistle. Fittingly, awareness of that glorious timetable sugared my thoughts with immeasurable bliss.

The last month of school was full of anticipation for the summer ahead. School would soon be out, and, knowing things were bound to get better, I emerged from my cocoon as an agenda-driven, globe-trotting monarch butterfly, anxious to absorb the aroma of the circus. The countdown was on: Three weeks. Two weeks. Finally, news of exactly where I'd join my folks came in the mail; Dallas, Texas, was underlined on a lively circus route card. I couldn't wait to tell Jenny, though she seemed detached as of late. Things were not great at home, I was to learn. The thought of not seeing her again made me tear up. My good news seemed to pick her up.

"I wish I could go with you," she said, giving me a congratulatory hug. "I'd give anything to be part of the circus, even for one day."

"Oh, Jenny, maybe you will someday. I'd like nothing better," I replied tearfully. "I'll never forget you—never, never!"

Lovingly, I held the route card to my breast and cheek, then edged it into a corner of my bureau mirror. "Cheer up," I told my image. "You'll soon be home again." My alcove had a prophetic makeover; instantly, the drab walls transformed into Technicolor visions of spangles, elephants, and me. I could almost hear the rustle of costumes as I danced in the shower, letting the water tickle my toes. I then tapped my healthy lungs and sang, just loud enough, with a pleasing voice quite worthy of carrying a tune, "Sister Angelica, you are right … there's tomorrow and tomorrow and …"

I felt privileged when listening to the boring details of some of my classmates' summer schedules. Furthermore, I was thoroughly convinced that my weird and wonderful background was so foreign to those snobbish girls that they had to be clueless, and therefore couldn't possibly know what they were missing. The nuns took on a special glow; they became less surly and somewhat jovial, for they, too, looked forward to a slack in their regimented routine. Unimaginably, broad smiles adorned their porcelain faces as they quietly slippered down the convent halls, lost in thought—dusting, polishing, and mopping with shared determination.

"I'll bet ya a nickel they *all* feel like dancin'," I told Jenny during one of my hilarious moods.

The little stinker rolled back her eyes and devilishly stuck her tongue out. "No!" she giggled. "You'd win."

Spring was in the air. Trees were giving birth to their new wardrobes; they stood remarkably proud, eagerly awaiting the array of guests who would visit their extended boughs for the summer. The grounds were seemingly enchanted as I sported to and fro like a hummingbird, extracting syrupy nectar from the hollow of nature's leafy hand. I twirled with animated gaiety, prancing through the differing woodsy shades, exercising the mind's eye of a child while riding the gentle breeze of May. Wildflowers, energized by the warming sun, peered up, gleeful as ever, gesturing sweetly with their stems rakishly atilt. Unafraid and deliriously happy, I frolicked around my favorite trees, gazing down at their intertwining substructures, simply marveling at their solid grasp. My beloved violets showed such brilliance as each happy, petaled face bristled at the flowery gossip channeling through the air. This friendly force pulled me through each and every hour, leaving me limp as I imagined what was in store: bidding farewell to the dull convent atmosphere, reuniting with my parents, seeing the excited crowd collecting on the circus midway, laughing at stubborn animals in the menagerie, inhaling the smell of fresh sawdust, and once again watching the Cristiani riding act in all its glory.

Ultimately, I no longer had to count the days—or even the minutes. Since I'd scarcely slept a wink on the eve of departure, I was, need I say, up at sparrow's fart, dressing myself neatly to the tune of half-awakened birds and quickly ready for my nonstop ride to the airport.

By daybreak, I found myself soaring above the clouds in a silver airplane, shading myself from the orange sun—conceivably anointing yet another circus day. My window seat gave me clear views of a land of squares and rectangles—a land I'd soon be exploring on the circus train. When we taxied up the runway, I saw my parents, dressed in familiar clothing, waving fiercely from afar. My handsome, lovingly protective dad, a worrier by nature, looked rather dapper in his dark-rimmed sunglasses, ascot, and favorite hat—superbly decorated by my stylish mom, who made a habit of wearing the perfect splash of color that encouraged flattery. Both had a fine sense of sartorial elegance for which they were admired. Mommy, coded for geniality, was openly approachable—ever smiling, inviting a friendly chat. Without question, my quiet, business-wise father knew who he was, and so did I. To me, he was solid gold—a genie who softened my blows and lit my way.

My survival of the school year was my foundation for pride. I'd no longer have to cope with harsh wake-up bells, Rosemary and the gang's constant ridicule, or Sister Margaret, the spinach monster—even Sister Gertrude's tirades in catechism class were a thing of the past. Cardome was behind me now—for the entire summer. Therefore, the inequities I had endured were but dashing trivialities, escaping my thoughts in leaps and bounds. Regaining control felt good. Naturally, this tacit knowledge encouraged my warm circus blood to pump audacity into my veins, renewing my free spirit. Decidedly, I looked back with no more forethought than a rosebush devotes to blooming in the spring. The pleasantries of the summer were before me—which meant certain relief from that unforgettable little voice calling for help with long, plaintive wails.

I grimaced through the vapor of intense Texas heat that rose from the tarmac until my glowing eyes rested on the unmistakable sight of my parents. My features brightened when I saw their worried expressions soften, wonderfully, at the very sight of me. Weighted down with baggage, I crashed into the softness of outstretched arms while shamelessly wiping away a cloudburst of happy tears. I bounced up and down like a Mexican jumping bean—in absolute contrast to the stampede of adult passengers bumping into each other, stony with indifference. After we kissed and hugged, again and again, I backed away and blotted my face dry. Tears, even joyful ones, seemed totally inappropriate. This was the perfect time to laugh, not to cry. Daddy, whose eyes still smarted with tears that never fell, left to retrieve the rest of my luggage while I prattled on with Mommy, gasping for every breath.

Clarity had returned to my life, etching out a proper frame for the big top and all I held dear. The anxiety had me in such a tailspin that I actually felt a slight catch in my heart when my twinkle-eyed father whistled for a taxicab. Once inside the car, I smiled at the beauty of his words: "Take us to the lot of the Cole

Brothers Circus!" With that, I loosened my pigtails, tousled my hair, chinned up to my dad—as I gave his mustache a playful tug—and struck a glamorous pose.

CHAPTER 6

▼

PACKIN' SAWDUST

Its interior is not illuminated from without by the sun …
the radiance comes into being within it.
—Procopius

My first day home on the circus lot was enlivening. As soon as I changed into my T-shirt and dungarees, I set off to explore the neighborhood—amply armed with that certain brand of inexhaustible energy only youth is blessed to know. Actually, I could think of nothing but the joys of my summer vacation as I watched the big top rising majestically, like a grand old friend. Familiar trumpeting calls resonated throughout the lot as the elephants worked to unroll gigantic bundles of damp canvas. Dewdrops twinkled like tiny stars on the tent's surface, welcoming each horse-drawn wagon. Shirtless workers circled the wondrous city of tents, pounding truckloads of wooden stakes and jerking miles of solidly twined hemp rope with a rhythmic chant: "Hit it! … Hit it again. Hit it! …"

What a world this was!

These loyal men were part of the circus landscape—an uncommon breed, with faces carved out of poverty, guilt, and booze. Many were old hands at the trade, having long ago decided that this transient lifestyle made them feel good about themselves. Circus work was a pleasant departure from lowly jobs that paid in cash and gave them the same image of rootless drifters living hand-to-mouth. On balance, veterans were slow to accept greenhorns until they proved reliable; however, it was virtually impossible to investigate every suspect recruit.

Apologizing for nothing, our grizzled old-timers felt they were a cut above most carnival help—a breed of their own in my estimation. Justifiably so, circus workers despised the name "roustabout": "We ain't happy 'bout some folks con-fusin' us with them ne'er-do-well carnies. Noways! Downright offensive!"

Whenever we played next to some ragtag carnival, lurking malcontents and the echo of fighting words would invariably provoke a wave of ferocious melees. It wasn't unusual to learn that one of our workers had gotten his face slashed with a jackknife. Iron stakes and brass knuckles were also popular weapons. Most fights were hard to break up without police involvement … and until such inter-vention came, it was every man for himself.

As the circus city was taking shape, I skipped around the lot, visiting my rela-tives and reacquainting myself with friends—including a mob of so-and-sos, such as propmen, concessionaires, general office help, animal handlers, or anybody else I wanted to impress. Understand that circus folks watched out for each other's kids, so I didn't want to be mistaken for a "town monkey" (pesky townsperson). After completing that task, I gained confidence by introducing myself to any unfamiliar performers in the program (comprising a blend of races), so there'd be no mistaking that I was a proud member of the Cristiani family.

All at once, voices around me were saying, "Hi, Miss Vickie. How was school?"

School! Gee whiz, why did they have to mention that awful word right off? To prevent being questioned further, I answered, "Fine, just fine," while gallivant-ing in prima-donna fashion.

Instinctively, I inspected every detail with visceral insight: camera-toting fans bewitched by the spectacle, which roused a natural propensity to lend a helping hand; performers stomping behind the wardrobe wagon, impatient to claim the trunks, buckets, and folding canvas chairs that were stacked inside. The hyped-up activity was part of the daily ritual: costumes were hung, concessions set up, candy apples dipped and spun.

Typically, the cookhouse tent was pitched first. The smell of freshly brewed coffee and salty bacon motivated foot-draggers. The fairly large cookhouse was filled with rows and rows of picnic tables covered with liquid-proof red and white checked tablecloths. Seating arrangements were assigned according to status: all workingmen sat toward the rear of one end, and colored workers (as they were known then) were segregated at the other end. The workingmen never went hun-gry, their plates were loaded with generous portions but if they wanted more food all they had to do was ask. Condiments such as salt and pepper, peanut butter and jelly, ketchup, and mustard, napkins, and metal utensils were dispensed on the tables before each meal. The same piping hot food was served by neatly uni-formed waiters who would be tipped well at the end of the season, which gave them incentive to stay for the long haul. Flag up signaled chow time—flag down meant the kitchen was closed.

If we played next to a cornfield, guess what was on the menu … for days?

For us circus children, there were off-limit zones—areas where we were not allowed to freely roam. Every seedy activity one might conjure surfaced some-where, to be sure, but clearly to a lesser degree than in the carnival set. Moreover, those dark components were encapsulated elsewhere, contained within the circus back alley—the sinister zone where *bad things* happened. As a child, I was much protected—hardly exposed to that side. Despite that lack of exposure, I didn't walk around blindfolded. Certainly the circus had a naughty side; I wouldn't want to suggest anything different. Presumably, as an overimaginative innocent, I had gained enough wisdom to know that the world wasn't all fairy tales and happy endings. I wasn't stupid.

On tour, the constant motion of managers, performers, crew, and animals created an amazing relationship. The very instant barrels and troughs were filled to capacity, the circus waterman prepared to receive an array of thirsty beasts, all of which knew the daily routine by heart.

The elephants couldn't wait to plunge their trunks into the fresh water, inhal-ing long and deep, then playfully spraying their rutted, inch-thick hides with the cool liquid. These majestic, vegetarian creatures, far more intelligent than we will ever know, held everyone captive, demanding acknowledgment of their importance. Anything could set the bulls off: runaway animals, small dogs, or a screeching cat—even a critter as small as a mouse. Think of it: the very thought of some small rodent finding a getaway path up their long trunks was enough to make any elephant go on a rampage! It isn't difficult to receive a serious injury from a panicked elephant. I'd always approach my hefty friends with caution, some fear, and great respect as their tangled trunks reached for whatever I had managed to bag for them at cookhouse. But elephants are comically suspicious by nature; they'd examine each offering with their snouts before consuming it whole. However, certain treats, such as watermelon, would pass inspection immediately. Elephants view any type of melon as a delicacy; the very smell would throw them into a begging frenzy. They'd rush at you holding out their feeler trunks, at times touching your face and body while pulling at their chains—practically mowing you down in the process—without really meaning to. It could get scary if you got sandwiched in or lost your footing. There were always one or two elephants in the herd that couldn't be trusted. I recognized them by sight so I made a point to stay out of range.

The native voice of the circus was almost poetic. The entertaining mix of roaring lions, shrieking baboons, snorting horses, and lovable belching seals was music to my ears. The muzzled bears looked cuddly enough to hug; however, one peculiarity I noticed about bear trainers was the number of their fingers. They had very few … seldom all ten. After applying simple logic to decipher this similarity, I wisely kept my distance. And yet, every once in a while (usually in the course of grooming), I'd risk sitting down close enough to observe the baby bears being counseled by their mothers about the secrets of circus life—much in the same way as our parents did with us human children.

It was my fixed belief that circus animals were different too; I could relate. Animal stars exhibited a certain uppity quality, even when at ease in the menagerie. But they were especially sophisticated at showtime, when clothed in sequined regalia and anxiously milking the crowd for all the applause they could muster. I speak from experience when I say that the spotlight brings out the ham in everyone, even animals.

Meanwhile, inside the men's dressing tent, the fastidious clowns, most of whom I surmised to be peculiar and nothing more, began powdering their lily-white faces yet again in preparation for the painstaking art of tracing original greasepaint designs that reflected their personal trademarks. A group of three or four clowns entertained directly after "doors" (the traditional term for opening the ticket gates). Immediately after doors, the up-tempo fifteen-piece band helped droves of circusgoers adjust to the spellbinding vibes of the big top. Candy butchers were a crass bunch, all exceeding the bounds of good taste to make an extra buck. They'd hit every rubbernecked customer in attendance, hustling fresh (and not so fresh) popcorn, cotton candy, Cracker Jacks, peanuts, blackened hot dogs … and live lizards. The lizards came with feeding instructions and a thread leash and pin attached to a tiny collar. They sold out fast and were advertised as harmless, trouble-free pets that had been captured somewhere in Florida.

"Last chance, people! Souvenirs! Programs! Hurry, get your …"

Clearly, the obvious forces made the circle of magic complete as I traipsed the grounds, familiarizing myself with faces, animals, and circus objects. Perhaps the mite of wisdom seeded within my girlish head enabled me to perceive the circus in both its oneness and its madness. However, it was its madness that consumed me.

Troupers had to follow a fixed schedule on the road; otherwise, the circus couldn't function properly. The main show announcer was the designated clock-watcher and therefore compelled to be a stickler for punctuality. This prominent position called for a meticulous, sober individual with deep, commanding voice and a reputation as a responsible and articulate spokesperson—worthy of representing the circus both on and off stage. Veteran announcers were in such demand that show managers, fearing the appropriate ringmaster was nowhere to be found, auditioned eager "first of Mays"—hoping the pick of the crop would work out most of the kinks in a week or two. Even so, if otherwise suitable candidates appeared hippo-fat or plain wart-faced ugly, they got the same old "Don't call us— we'll call you," regardless of the fast-approaching deadline.

The burdens of this particular job could drive a man to drink—especially dealing with the vacillating moods of star entertainers, a zoo of wild animals, and fussy trainers when show-time came. Separate from that, whenever serious debacles forced last-minute changes in the advertised schedule, the announcer had to hold body and soul together. His angry mutterings had the entire work-force jumping through hoops (sometimes literally!), for all understood the scope of his authority—and the penalty of ignoring his professional call. When the take-charge announcer blew the warning whistle, both man and beast snapped to attention. "Showtime," if I'm able to correctly quote an age-old showman's line, "should *never* be in the realm of guesswork."

Not long thereafter, the backyard filled with animals listening for musical cues. Aerialists sequestered themselves on the sidelines; they posed erect, within an assumed masquerade of expressions, even as shutter-clicking fans captured the moment. Clowns, a strange lot (and not always the stuff that saints are made of) flaunted their broad-lapelled, hallucinogenic attire while pranking out mini-skits of concocted foolishness. Those conned by the spotlight overworked the crowd— fast reaching the saturation point as they gormandized the contagious laughter that, by all accounts, rated their clownish worth. My favorite clowns were Emmett Kelly, Otto Griebling, and Lou Jacobs—in that order. As masters of the art, they will be remembered in the hearts of circusgoers for generations to come.

Unless spooked for good reason, the elephants remained calm—mainly when lowering their heads for tardy bally girls (another name for a line of chorus girls) busy laddering up their creviced trunks. Maybe, to some extent, the elephants considered the foibles of humankind and forgave them. Either way, they were obliging, even during the overture. Suddenly, the cymbals would crash, triggering the select program of festivities. In response, an explosion of resplendent harmony entered through the red velvet backdoor. This procession included clowns; aerialists; bareback riders; somersaulting jugglers; flirty, hat-tipping cowboys; and caged lions and tigers—plus a train of fancy wagons and floats. When the ponderous pachyderms tailed up, the dazzling showgirls extended their arms and fish-net-clad legs in a graceful pose and, in spite of cumbersome headpieces, maintained perfect balance.

Inside, "children of all ages" satisfied their cravings by crunching down on sticky, ruby-red candy apples or other circus delights. The crowd seemed almost as eager for titillation as the toga-dressed citizens of ancient Rome, who had anticipated bloodthirsty confrontations between muscled gladiators and starved lions in the coliseum. All buckled down for an experience that would thereafter be a part of their lives. But because I was limited to mere spectating until I wormed a place for myself in spec (circus slang for the opening parade, derived from "spectacle"), I couldn't help but gasp at the splendor of the passing traffic along with everybody else. And, oh dearie me, when the magnificent white team of Cristiani bareback riding horses appeared on the scene, I felt important and proud and teary—and every bit as privileged as those snooty rich kids at Cardome. All the same, I shrank small in my seat and impulsively smacked both hands over my mouth to silence the wheeze. Presumably, I was much too stunned to stand up and brag out loud in the midst of all the commotion: *Look everybody ... those are my family's horses! Aren't they bee-yoo-tiful?*

Spotlights swung back and forth like pendulums, stroking the decadent splash of amethyst and turquoise rhinestones. Spangles glinted off the ceiling-high chrome apparatus in neon blurs. The indisputable sensory powers of purple, fuchsia, and chartreuse hit like fired sparklers. The electricity wowed me! It lifted my hair with static and accelerated my heart with excitement. Next came the blasé llamas, the bossy zebras, the blood-sweating hippopotamuses, the lofty giraffes, and the smug camels—promenading at a moseying pace, festooned with garlands of plumage and swaying furbelows. Finally, I was carried away on the wings of wonder, firmly convinced it was time for the circus—and my seventh summer—to begin.

Well, there I was, back in the swing of things, holding a half-chewed pear and once again feeling ten feet tall while experiencing the thrill of my other life—a dimension filled with elements of danger and total chaos, all of which I experienced firsthand: demanding one-night stands; exhausting rain-drenched tear-downs; drunken workingmen brawls; comical husband-stealing catfights; pasta-throwing family dinners ... the whole nine yards. One couldn't help being jarred by the contrast between this life and the rigid, dull academy I had left behind.

Regardless, I lived for it, I daresay ... and personally, I could not altogether enjoy the company of anyone who didn't.

CHAPTER 7

▼

ON WITH THE SHOW

It is well for a man to respect his own vocation whatever it is,
and to think himself bound to uphold it,
and to claim for it the respect it deserves.
—Charles Dickens

By week's end, I had undergone a complete metamorphosis. It just so happened to be an embraced change: from dispirited convent child to girlishly vivacious showgirl. Being an exemplary observer, I started my vacation by gathering many tricks of the trade from inside the nosebleed headquarters of the women's dressing tent. Though the unattractive few didn't say exactly how they turned themselves into such beautiful dolls, I wouldn't be outsmarted. It's amazing, all the useful tactics kids can learn from adults just by appearing uninterested. My eyes were peeled to each and every aspect of theatrical technique: black-waxed eyelashes, fire-red rouge, lip gloss, waist pinchers—and tweezed Bette Davis brows, arched high like the back of a threatened cat. *Glamour ... I purrr in it!*

Funny, I can remember, as if it were only yesterday, how much I profited by not being a bother at showtime—when performers' tempers flared at even the slightest sign of interference. I'd simply vanish into thin air, for experience had taught me to respect their harsh expressions as they began the dedicated ritual of limbering their disciplined, toned bodies. A flashback brings to mind a frigid opening on a particular winter date in Chicago, when my parents bought me a white bunny-fur coat, complete with hat and muff. Not unlike any other kid showing off a brand-new outfit, I had been stricken with acute self-awareness.

Although I had racked up a number of insecurities as a youngster, I could be an attention grabber if it fit me. I was definitely my father's daughter in my leanings toward melodrama. From the time I could reason, I thrived on the stimulating production of the circus. Drama was my brain food—like water and air, I needed it to survive. Needless to say, I became quite adept at creating situations in the theater of my mind. Anyhow, I was undoubtedly overcome by that inherited gene the whole while as I claimed top billing upon my self-appointed stage—starring in *The Epitome of Sophistication*. Clad in my new coat, I vamped round and about the damp building for days, acting prissy and gallingly bossy—imagining that the title of queen prefaced my first name, Victoria. The pretense was rather cute the first go-around, but my constant pivoting became infuriating. At the very edgy moment of showtime, I accidentally bumped an overmedicated juggler, and he dropped his clubs.

He was a basket case. (Jesus, aren't they all?)

"I toll your mudder … enough wis za gooofyyy bunny outfit! EEENOUGH!"

Instead of fetching the coveted Academy Award, I received a rather embarrassing booby prize, despite Daddy's crush for time. My vivid memory reminds me that he lifted all the fur padding and gave me two controlled slaps on my tender buttocks, right along with the apropos accompaniment of the opening drumbeat—which must've muted my not-so-quiet screams. Just the same, my patient father's reaction positively proved that my blue-blooded charade had lingered far longer than he could endure. Whoopsy daisy—my imperial tiara crashed down to the floor. By golly, it had been fun while it lasted … but that royal spanking had ended my reign.

Because I had to contend with other show kids, most of whom weren't sent off to school like poor ole me, I had to crusade like crazy for a prize position in spec, the opening parade. And because "The Old Lady in the Shoe" was my preferred float, I wouldn't settle for a lesser post—unless, with momentary apprehension, my happy summery attitude had me switching places for *one* performance only. It was difficult to decide whether to stow inside the donkey-pulled covered wagon or hitchhike on my second favorite float—suitably stationed on the carved-out lap of Mother Goose. Whatever the case, I would make eye contact with as many kids as I could, noting a combination of joyous anticipation, astonishment, and perhaps a little envy in their rounded doe eyes.

Zack Terrell, the imperious owner of the Cole Bros. Circus, had large Bing Crosby ears and a habit of pressing fat cigars betwixt his gapped buckteeth. He had the sadistic composition of a defrauding banker who showed no shame when sniffing for land-rich clients in dire straits. Mr. Terrell dressed to the nines in a vested suit, tipped straw hat, and cane while inspecting the lot with a cold regard for excuses. He regularly wielded his cane in tirades with the working crew, and he seemed especially intolerant of rambunctious circus children. To be spiteful, the older gang of smart-aleck kids would taunt us small fries.

"You yellow bellies, Zack Terrell will catchya, cookya, and eatya!"

Between shows, Mommy would bag me a lunch if I scoffed at the cookhouse menu. Ordinarily, I'd sunbathe on a bale of hay next to the horse wagon and snack in friendly tandem with my animal pals. But often enough, especially on rainy days, I'd climb my way up "The Old Lady in the Shoe," pull back the tarp, and drop my legs down the hollowed-out vertical shaft that stretched to the very tip. After spreading my napkin, I dined in flashlight ecstasy while marveling at my luck and poring over an important index of daily errands in the selected company of me, myself, and I. Except, one dull afternoon, just as I climbed aboard, I heard shuffling footsteps at close range. Shortly, a loud voice told me I was on the griddle. Aha—it was Zack Terrell!

"What in tarnation? Get down from that float, young lady," he fumed, pointing his cane at me, "before you take a buster, and I get sued!" He ranted on without pause: "For cripes' sake, what are ya doing climbing on my show floats? Don't you know you're not allowed in the backyard, little girl? Run home, or trouble will find you."

I fidgeted in my pinafore and sandals, absolutely tongue-tied, displaying the pallor of a corpse. But sheer urgency forced me to respond (in between a sequence of fretful sobs). "I'm a *Cristiani*, sir, (sniff) and my father is *Oscar*, sir, (sniff) and I'm sorry, and I promise I won't eat my lunch in your shoe ever again—sir!" (Sniff, sniff!) My head spun as I contemplated the agony of actually being boiled alive inside the crackling-hot copper cauldron of candy-apple syrup behind the concession tent as Mr. Terrell nervously passed his hand across his brow. Who'd find me if he cooked my flesh down to teeth and bones?

"Oscar's daughter? Do tell." His demeanor changed drastically, as if taking this unexpected revelation seriously. "So, you fancy this float?" he said, in a reasonably kind voice.

"Yes, Mr. Terrell, it's my favorite, and I love riding it in spec (sniff), but now I won't even go near it," I avowed, distrusting his softer, nicer tone. "Not ever again!"

Visibly stupefied, he pinched his nose and closed in at a scary pace. "Well, now, since you indeed know my name, carry on ... but don't leave leftovers for the vermin!" Phew! I shook my head like a rag mop, glaring with downcast eyes (misted with painful tears). As Mr. Terrell crossed by, he stopped dead in his tracks—and because my eyes were fixated on his cumbersome footsteps, so did I. At a standstill, he pushed back his hat, reached deep into his pocket, and wiped his perspiring forehead with an enormous white handkerchief. Then he reverted back to his former gruff self. Looking mad as a cockeyed rooster, he dashed toward me, waving his tobacco-stained finger in such an alarming manner. In fact, he came so close that I could count the wooly hairs in his nose.

"You'd better listen up, *Miss Cristiani*," he insisted with a corrupt smile, "the Ole Lady expects to see *you* in spec. Don't be late!" Then he laughed. I laughed too. I'd say the dynamics of that exchange restored my color—and equilibrium. Satisfied that I'd escaped the gallows, I buffed my perfect pear, bagged the mess, and scooted away with hands on hips, sporting the obnoxious Chiclets smile of a Cheshire cat.

Apart from my cozy picnics inside the splendid shoe, I couldn't wait to explore the grounds or hang in the backyard after spec, hugging family members as they prepared to enter the densely packed big top. The instant the cookhouse flag was raised after the matinee, the bustle calmed down, and all those pensive faces loosened like creamy vanilla. There was a definite change in the general mood as everyone became interested in the day's menu. Bacon time!

Immediately after the show, our four-legged troupers stepped to a concerto of hungry cries, while threading the meandering path toward shady tents and canopies for the removal of constraining gear and lavish trappings.

No two days were alike—that was the fun of it. Gutter language sounded in the backyard if performers missed any of the announced tricks that gave them star billing and top salaries. Every person in sight would duck out of harm's way if the blame game got hot and heavy, but that didn't faze me one bit ... being a Cristiani, I was used to it.

Regardless, I opted to close my ears to any cusswords God would surely strike me dead for repeating. If nothing else, Cardome had provided a kind of shielding separateness that I relied on. Even when not in fine spirit, I viewed the circus as more romantic than rugged. I felt privy to its secrets and, in keeping with my well-seeded heritage, I stayed wedded to my surroundings. While small-minded hecklers focused primarily on the negative aspects of our dysfunctional gypsy lifestyle, I remained positive as can be by painting my own picture—as seen through the pure eyes of a child born in the womb of Ringling's canvas sky. Improbable as it may seem, I was able to perceive a beauty from that to which others chose to be willfully blind. For me, everything had a language: the animals, the big top, the circus lot, and the train. It was as if all were living, breathing entities, with no distinction between animate or inanimate.

The Cristianis merited a private cookhouse table, roomy enough to accommodate the entire clan. None were inclined to miss those fabulous late-night suppers. In order to stay light on their feet, the equestrians ate a hearty breakfast and then mostly fasted until boarding the train, where Nona, my grandmother, cooked the customary feast that lured her famished brood back to her nest. Sitting down to *mangia* [eat] together was the best part of the day.

*   *   *   *

Interestingly, circus people never lost sight of their water buckets (mostly used for bathing). These utilitarian gems were vital to circus folks during their travels. Although rough handling eventually chipped at the paint, performers never left the winter quarters until their buckets were freshly painted on both sides—either in canary yellow or blood red. Considering the sought-after galvanized metal pails were practically impossible to locate outside rural agricultural areas, they were guarded with the fury of a mommy alligator. Consequently, bucket catfights, though they constituted a small fraction of daily gossip, were nonetheless a hot topic. Performers looked forward to the almost daily occurrence of calm spring showers, particularly if they were perfectly timed after the matinee. Women would stop whatever they were doing in order to collect what Mommy called "Circus holy water"—the heavenly, soft liquid gold, ideal for washing finery and shampooing hair. The theft of such a divine treasure was regarded as a capital crime. The act itself ranked way up there next to husband stealing. If taken to the extreme, the sting of fighting words, especially among female performers, could incite guerrilla warfare—leaving either plaintiff or defendant minus a fistful of hair.

"You lousy bitch, if you swipe my water again, I'll punch your ears 'til they bleeeed!"

Sponge baths were usually taken behind a strip of sectioned-off sidewall that ran across one end of the dressing tent. Since everyone had a favorite time to indulge, preferably in complete privacy, conflicting schedules could provoke another blast of testy spats. Bucket baths weren't just invigorating; they offered the only possible route of bodily refreshment when stranded on the lot.

Moments after I entered the ladies' dressing tent, I became lost in the process of discovery. Wardrobe trunks were positively *neat*. Some stood upright, with a costume rack on one side and drawers on the other. I especially loved my mother's trunk, because it opened from the top, and its lid supported a tray containing a slew of cubbies for a potpourri of items.

When safely alone, I began padding my chest with wadded tights or whatever worked to pump up the size of my seven year old board-flat bosom, just for the fun of it. Looking the part on Mommy's canvas folding chair, I enjoyed the girly pastime of playing grown-up, with finger on cheek, musing aloud about this and that and mugging before the magnifying mirror like some ham actress starring on the Broadway stage.

Beneath the trunk tray, there was sufficient storage space for extra garments, such as sweaters, raincoats, and galoshes—or whatever was needed for an "on lot" emergency. Performers utilized their trunks in a number of ways: they cooked on them, wrote letters on them, and even ate on them, as if they were picnic tables. And since most performers vowed to carry them past retirement, they made a ritual of pasting a colorful collage of favorite snapshots, doohickeys, and small keepsakes on the inside lid. However, the clowns were the most creative when it came to that.

Slop shoes were indispensable. Performers couldn't do without at least one pair of these indestructible clodhoppers, because the terrain of circus lots varied from town to town: rock, mud, sand, gravel, or clay. Parkland fields were a rarity, so these necessary platform mules (mostly fashioned from wood and customized to individual taste) were also held sacred. All were equipped with loose-fitting straps to protect the artists' rosin-powdered work pumps from getting slippery wet or mud-coated when entering and exiting the big top. It was necessary to keep at least one extra pair on hand in case a pair of slop shoes was lost, stolen, or in dire need of repair.

In order to prepare for the typical preperformance time crunch, a rack was placed in both the women's and men's dressing tents for easy access to spec wardrobe, general production costumes, and cartoonish papier-mâché hoods—mostly used for the clown walk-around number. Like it or not, arrogant star performers knew it was in their best interest to be subservient to the lady warden of wardrobe. No sense butting heads, I suppose, for they depended on her nimble fingers to restore their glimmering threads. All the same, if costumes were ill-treated, she'd deliver a stinging retort or scathing lecture. The finicky seamstress seldom left her domain, where she seemed to find life most tolerable. Normally, the place was equipped with an icebox, coffeepot, and emergency potty.

For my part, I'd never met any wardrobe mistress crazier than pantyless Leona, the long-retired hoochie-coochie dancer who, according to eyewitnesses, actually peed standing up. Gross! Incidentally, Leona believed in reincarnation big-time and wished, more than anything, to come back as a bug.

*   *   *   *

As one would expect, circus people are a superstitious breed. The large majority were taught from early childhood to believe that accidents happen in threes; camelback trunks and cracked mirrors are unlucky; and playing a harmonica on the showground portends trouble. No matter what, I contend show folks will never shake the notion that certain tragedies are solely caused by such dark juju.

It's never been a trade secret that the social fabric of the old-fashioned circus was extremely compartmentalized. (Nothing's changed in that regard.) Even so, I'd like to emphasize that, although artists, workers, sideshow personnel, candy butchers, office and cookhouse staff, and the band mostly socialized with people who worked within their respective department, the groups maintained a passive respect for one another. Furthermore, all circus employees—regardless of rank—pulled together as one whenever dark forces were in play.

Considering the vulnerability of gigantic big tops pitched in the open air, stormy weather was as threatening to circus people as to fishermen out at sea. Survival was imperative. Back in the 1940s, forecasts weren't nearly as accurate as they are today. Hence, the unforeseen evolution of spring weather could quickly undo a perfectly calm Midwestern day—ripping weakened canvas into shreds with the inordinate power of its viselike jaws. Given that scenario, workingmen had to scurry like ants in a disturbed anthill, while the darkened firmament swept up loose debris like a cosmic vacuum.

There was a sense, I recall, on a late-summer day in 1942, (a few months after my two-year-old birthday) of evil forces testing their powers. An unsettling creepiness prevailed as the soundtrack of whooshing wind gained volume. The storm appeared to chew its way through the Ringling Bros. and Barnum & Bailey Circus lot like a fiendish piranha. Without exception, circus performers tended family first; next, they saw to other business in order of importance. Instinctively, they'd band together to guy out the tents (meaning, take up the slack to withstand the storm) or drop the peaks. Whatever the call, that first decisive move represented the first of many steps that enabled them to save the circus from the disastrous aftereffects of a fearsome blowdown, which could cripple any traveling show for the rest of the season.

As soon as the night performance was officially canceled, workers engaged in the dangerous operation of loading a multitude of drenched animals and slippery props onto the wagons. While some performers coiled ropes and wires, others loaded reserved seats, blue section planks and side railings, or whatever else. The big top hummed with a vibe of urgency and reeked with elephant dung and the human smell of sweat and dirt. Elephants—or bulls, as trainers called them regardless of gender—seemed psychically attuned to the pending storm. The herd moved heroically with forceful eloquence, utilizing their mighty strength to lift poles, roll canvas, and pull stakes. At times, the beasts would release their aggression by drawing back and raising their trunks upward to the ominous sky in direct response to the crisis at hand. They'd trumpet and cry in indecipherable elephant speech, as if begging to the heavens for more strength, before soldiering ahead, freeing wagons and equipment from the sinking mire. Women and children were advised to head for the train to hunker down. Even stubborn locals knew they'd better skedaddle home.

Ordinarily, I played somewhere in the vicinity of the backyard, but on that particular day, I took a naughty turn of my own accord and strayed with pals up to the midway … until the sudden burst of thick, splattering raindrops forced me inside the big top, where I locked horns with my angry daddy. Ignoring his boundary rule was *not* a habit of mine, and he was fuming at my deviance from the norm. Soon thereafter, Mommy's hysterical call sounded close by. "Vickie, get home! Bad storm! We're going to the train at once!" I'll say *that* sent me dashing to her side as quickly as a cheetah.

As if controlled by the hand of a powerful sorceress, electrifying fingers cracked down on the metal-covered Ringling Bros. Circus "Gilley" wagon at the very moment we jumped aboard. Undoubtedly, my two-year-old mind was crammed with all sorts of hideous possibilities. Somehow, I was convinced that the evil one in the sky (that baneful witch who I had blamed for the all the bad weather) had targeted our chaotic circus village, just so she could view the drama from the best seat in the house.

When our dripping-wet Gilley driver dropped us near the tracks, I stupidly ran across the narrow and bumpy access road without looking and was struck down by a slow-moving jalopy. The poor fellow behind the wheel, no doubt blinded by the blustery downpour, came out hollering, probably thinking I was either dead or twisted like a pretzel. I wasn't. Petrified nonetheless, my mother collapsed to the ground in disbelief immediately after I wormed free from underneath the hot motor—unmarred except for my hurt pride and gravel-bruised fanny. Stunned that I was still a breathing mortal, I tugged back and forth at Mommy's sweater, checking every sign of life until she looked up, smiling. "Wake up, my mommy," I bawled. "Talk to me! Say what's wrong. Pleeeeeese say what's wrong!"

One ghostly pale showgirl—Mommy's good friend, Maggie Wise—dusted me off and wrapped me in her raincoat, tight as a drum. "Thank God, Vickie!" she exclaimed with a chastising stare. "To think you might have been … Anyway, that'll be it for now, little one—next time you may not be nearly so lucky. You had a real close call … too close. Mommy's going to be fine, but you sure managed to scare the daylights out of her!"

"Don't worry, Mommy," I whimpered. "I'm OK, but my pretty dress is all broken."

CHAPTER 8

▼

BETWEEN SHOWS

Artists can color the sky red because they know it's blue.
Those of us who are not artists must color things the way they are
or people might think we're stupid.
—Jules Feiffer

Any number of activities, apart from the performance itself, were scheduled "between shows," a phrase deeply rooted in circus vocabulary. Craps games, for instance, were held daily in the center ring, after the matinee. Propmen voluntarily lowered the contraption of overhead lights so gamblers could keep a sharp eye on their cash-only bets. Gambling, in those days, was viewed as strictly a man's game, when men of various departments intermingled with anybody willing to throw their hard cash on the mat. Cash was cash and whoever had it was in the game; simple as that.

Busybody women and children were shooed away. Trash-talking chain-smokers used pushy, broad gestures and deep, raspy cigarette voices as the dice rolled. Some phobic players, harboring scalding contempt after crapping out, foolishly hung around looking for a human punching bag to release their anger. But unless they went totally bonkers, even the worst of the lot would resist copping a Sunday punch on fellow players, for fear of retribution from the redneck crew of brass-knuckled bouncers. Usually the games ended amicably … usually!

Between shows could also be a time for flirtatious rendezvous under the big top, the idyllic setting for romance. In addition, the afternoon break gave male aerialists and ground performers time to examine the bones of their rigging while their wives shopped for sundry supplies. Between shows also offered an opportune time for all sorts of celebrations. Kids' birthday parties were full of fun, presents, and games; circus kids couldn't wish for more on their special day. Admittedly, I was somewhat envious of my playmates who benefited from the outpouring of generosity, because my March 2 birthday was celebrated back at boarding school—normally, an uneventful bore.

Animals were visibly grateful for this break in particular, for their conscious gaze had the look of rapture. Neck-to-bucket, the pop-eyed brood chomped away, constantly shifting their hindquarters just to forewarn any chow thieves sneaking up for the take. After satisfying their voracious appetites, the animals would either snore while standing up or stretch out in makeshift stalls until show-time. But by midafternoon roast, the brackish tang of animal sweat; fresh, steaming manure; and urine permeated the menagerie. The likely combination released a scent akin to ammonia that hung like sea fog; it was tough as a Texas boot and moved with the breeze, swooping underneath the canvas sidewall.

Unlike ordinary horses, the wild performing zebras—no matter how well trained—were, for the most part, troublesome creatures—perfectly capable of driving a kick to the throat without the slightest warning. They'd hardly bother nipping at their trainer's arm or leg—heavens, no. Sly zebras preferred getting right down to the nitty-gritty business of actually separating his nose from his face—Hannibal Lecter style! Even at ease, these striped renegades could change from compliant to ornery in a heartbeat. First, they'd kick the spunk out of their neighbor and then follow up with a chain of sobering, flesh-breaking bites that often sent less aggressive victims directly to the vet. But, when hurt themselves, they were such crybabies—hee-hawing and screeching with the worst-sounding voices in the menagerie. Astoundingly, though, most circus animals adapted to their unusual living conditions fairly well, considering their placement side-by-side in same crowded quarters.

Caged lions and tigers took the guise of harmless felines while grabbing a snooze. Several rested on their backsides in various catlike positions—mostly piled in a heap, with twisting bodies overlapping. But when supping, the snarling carnivores were savagely cutthroat as they hooked their curled talons into blood-dripping chunks of raw meat in deadly play. Immediately after licking their paws clean, they'd return to their usual prey-stalking mode. In order to avoid being targeted with their pungent (and well timed) spray, I never came within reach of tooth or claw.

Of all the creatures in the menagerie, the elephants were the funniest to watch. The more restless elephants in the herd pulled at their chains, bobbing and swaying their heads with powerful energy. Others were inclined to relax standing up, curving to the roll and heft of the canvas wall. Some bloated sleepyheads of course lay on the ground, seemingly in a drugged state. Their rounded bellies would inflate and deflate, keeping to a marching rhythm as their disproportionate tails played havoc with pesky flies and gnats. Long lashes protected their comparatively small amber eyes as they dreamed elephant dreams without a care in the world.

It's important to know that elephant brains are almost three times larger than human brains. Research has confirmed that these humongous creatures can warn other herds from miles away through infrasonic vibrations (vibrations of a frequency too low for the human ear to detect). Studies also suggest that elephants can recognize themselves in a mirror, indicating that they may actually have a sense of self, like dolphins and apes—which only proves we have much to learn about these marvelous, family-oriented mammals. Daddy always taught me to be cautious when approaching any wild animal, reminding me that they don't appreciate sudden moves. So whenever elephants voiced anger in their usual transcendent language—deep, vibrating rumbles well beyond our knowing—I used my head and backed away. If I've learned one lesson, it's this: a cranky expression, even on an elephant, is not to be dismissed.

After the bake, in the cooler part of day, Daddy would take a half hour or so to practice basic acrobatics with me in a corner of the big top: handstands, cartwheels, backbends, flip-flops, or other limbering moves. I can still visualize his dubious smile at my feeble attempts. I was never a natural gymnast, so my flip-flops were precisely that: a flip and a flop! On certain days, I became so disoriented that I had difficulty finding my own legs. Oh, the joy!

Eventually, all those painful athletic turns were eliminated from our practice sessions altogether. Who knows—maybe Daddy feared my continual botchery could result in possible brain damage. Nonetheless, we did carry on with a basic exercise routine, just to resurrect my slender form from the damage done by Cardome's starchy diet. Naturally, Daddy knew firsthand that performing spelled hardship even for the crème de la crème, so my deficient talent in the genera of circus artistry was something we examined daily—as we read each other's minds in amusement.

"Spino," he playfully quipped, "I'm afraid you were born bodily unequipped." Daddy mostly called me Spino, unless I was being reprimanded for some kind of mischief. I absolutely cooed whenever he called me by that particular nickname, which meant absolutely nothing to anybody else but me.

The two-show-a-day schedule (the story of our lives on the circus) was exhausting. Aside from meals and practice, my quality time with Daddy was limited to evenings on the train. We would laugh ourselves dopey—swapping a daily catalog of sidesplitting nonsense involving animals, workingmen, and performers … or the very painful subject of flip-flops.

We were on the same wavelength, he and I, in that we both had a special rapport with animals—expressly elephants. We understood their primal speech, which allowed us to converse without the noise of words. Daddy likened them to amicable giants from another age, and they certainly were. But like me, Daddy was also enthralled with all species of birds. Normally, if time permitted, Daddy would spin a medley of bedtime stories based on his boyhood experiences in Europe. The best tales centered on his adventures with a frail, young falcon, either forsaken or orphaned. My teenage father had stumbled upon the exquisite predator outside his toppled nest by accident and proudly doctored him along to a full recovery.

Of course, I was totally mesmerized with Daddy's dramatic storytelling, which never failed to transport the fanciful incarnations of his adventuresome youth smack into the realm of my nightly dreams. If I dozed off beforehand, I'd awake at the break of daylight and, with measured caution, proceed to wiggle his nose, ears, and mustache, requesting only one giant favor: "Daddy, can you pretty please, *please* say that nice bird story again?"

$$* \qquad * \qquad * \qquad *$$

Both Daddy and I were crazy about the movies—good or bad, it didn't matter, as long as it was a western. Looking ahead, I decided I would wed the Lone Ranger when of age … that is, if he would have me. While daydreaming, I took our considerable age difference into account, but love ruled. In all truth, I acted out the ceremony at least twice a week, rewriting the script in my head until it worked in my favor. Ever the good wife, I'd place my hand over my heart and promise to be true through the hardest times, whatever the costs. I even pledged to spare the silver bullet and nurse the Lone Ranger's wizened body to his wheelchair end—with Tonto's help, of course. That way, my spoon-fed movie-star husband would never suffer his most feared indignity: growing old disgracefully. (Anyhow, if things didn't pan out, I planned to dump him for Lash LaRue.)

I can't recall a time when my western-minded father didn't own at least two pairs of pricey cowboy boots, custom-made in Fort Worth, Texas. Daddy was frugal by nature, except when purchasing items of importance. He took care of things and kept them in good repair, so they would last. Furthermore, he was meticulously organized, unlike my blithely spirited mother, who had a habit of leaving stuff around, although—just as she predicted—most irreplaceable items reappeared, eventually, in some uncanny way. Mommy considered worry a waste of time, and Daddy worried about everything from noodles to nuts. Any domestic flare-ups were directed by his vocal Italian temper, while she remained a silent Norwegian cool. Mommy did have her say—she just had it later, at her elected moment, and then it was Daddy who wisely chose to remain silent.

Mommy was a rather bookish person, residing in another world when glued to a good read. She desired books that touched her soul and expanded her mind. In between shows, she'd sneak away to the local bohemian art community, where she lost all sense of time while browsing secondhand bookstores—generally located in less-than-desirable districts. Now and then, she even missed spec. The playful wink-and-nod attitude Mommy exhibited while explaining away her spur-of-the-moment excursions drove my punctual father wild. Authors such as Thomas Merton (the controversial Trappist monk) and his very close friend, poet of distinction Bob Lax (who wrote about the performing Cristiani family in *Circus of the Sun*); Charles Kingsley; and John Steinbeck (*Of Mice and Men*) wrote some of the books Mommy preferred. *The Prophet* and other prized works by the uncanny Khalil Gibram shaped her philosophy. And since Mommy painted and sculpted for relaxation, art books were stacked in every corner. On rainy days, she'd hand me a bag of licorice and snuggle up close before reading selections from the classics. "What now, Vickie Belle?" she'd inquire. "What will it be … *Ann of Green Gables*, scary *Jane Eyre*,or *Little Women?*" Certain picture pages of *Stuart Little* and *The Trumpet of the Swans*, by E. B. White, were worn onion-peel thin.

On my sixth birthday, my chosen present was a beautifully bound copy of *Andersen's Fairy Tales*; it stands preserved, along with a full body of endearing memories of Mommy reading aloud on the circus train. Although "The Red Shoes" certainly reminded me of Mommy's lifelong infatuation, I especially loved the tearful tale of "The Little Match Girl." Obviously, I had a great deal of sympathy for the little fawn-eyed child's plight. It struck a familiar cord—too familiar, I'm afraid. Whenever severe reprimands at Cardome broke my spirit, I felt as though I were living out her very sad story. I would place myself in that very scene by visualizing myself as nothing more than a shoeless little urchin girl, brittle with cold—peering through the Victorian window, peeking around curtains of red velvet. All of a sudden, I found myself waiting in suspense under the gaslit street lamp just for the vicarious pleasure of ogling a clan of rich kids collecting around the fireplace, shamelessly indulging in their fortunate legacy of ancestral wealth. Moreover, I'd feel sorry for myself as they picked, ever so daintily, at the display of hors d'oeuvres on silver trays, ignoring platefuls of glazed treats for which I hungered. Thankfully, that dark theater of thoughts never lasted very long. "I'm not all that gullible," I informed my poised shadow. "The little match girl, that's who *they* wish me to be. Definitely, they're all wrong—it's not so."

*　　*　　*　　*

I maintain the circus world has always been multivocal; it speaks out to people in different ways. Some people are driven to disregard its value, poking fun at it, while others embrace the wonder of it all. Prejudice takes many forms; intolerance can be as subtle as a look or backhanded comment, followed by a series of innocently posed questions with obvious answers. My mother was smartly aware. She made my father's life fuller by teaching him to understand the significance of an open mind. So how could I go awry, with Daddy taking me to double-feature westerns starring Roy Rogers, Hopalong Cassidy, and Gene Autry—and Mommy influencing me with classic books, crouching pliés, grands jetés, and posing arabesques?

Although Mommy faced each day with enthusiasm and defined purpose, she lived out every single day thoroughly—just as life presented it—with the cool calm of a grazing Guernsey. Daddy had always had deep faith … but gradually, through her, he learned to accept what he could not change.

By the same token, my folks were also cognizant that they both had a long list of unshared interests. My father radiated pure energy. He stayed rooted in reality, concerned exclusively with the perils he was dealt, both present and future. Predictably, my confident mother permitted her second sight to guide her along as she danced inside a pulsating ring of spiritual and earthly forces—which, in sum, helped her facilitate a partnership within the luminous expanse of both kingdoms.

All I know is, their marriage worked. Whatever good I have in me comes from them.

CHAPTER 9

▼

THE CIRCUS TRAIN

To love what you do and feel that it matters
—how could anything be more fun.
—Katharine Graham

The living accommodations my family enjoyed on the Cole Bros. Circus were almost identical to Ringling. The Cristianis occupied an entire car that was sectioned off into individual staterooms for family members—with an extended stateroom at one end for Nona and Nono. Their master suite was equipped with a full custom kitchen to suit Nona's needs—including a dining area large enough to accommodate a sturdy protracting table, so her family could relax comfortably while consuming the best Italian food around.

My Nona was an amazingly gifted cook, and—as large as she was—she moved about her kitchen with the grace of a gazelle. Nona spent most of her mornings grocery shopping and the rest of the day creating a menu of mouthwatering recipes that rivaled anything prepared by the world's finest chefs. Circus fans spread the word that the aroma of Mama Cristiani's freshly ground espresso could draw enough people to fill the big top. Probably due to his European upbringing and disciplined work ethics, my lean Nono was a light eater. He mostly dined on salad and crusty Italian bread dipped into a large bowl of Nona's homemade chicken broth—loaded with a generous pour of *vino rosso*. Actually, I thought Nono ate more like a sacrificial monk than a circus performer—mainly because he pushed his plate away before he was full. "Only eat what is good for my stomach," he insisted. Foraging for wild mushrooms, watercress, and various greenery on the grassy knolls near the circus lot was his favorite pastime on the road. For the most part, our late onboard meals were relaxing meltdowns with an entertaining backlog of good and bad jokes, juicy gossip, and witty critiques. An invitation to dine at the Cristiani table was an honor many savored.

Single showgirls resided in a separate car, called the virgin car, and most married couples were housed in yet another car with suitable quarters, assigned according to wants and status. My parent's personal stateroom in the Cristiani car was small, but adequate. Unfastened items could be hazardous, so every item had to be fastened into place. Since the lack of storage space was the most common complaint, shoppers wedged smaller, sturdier items inside berth pockets or trunks and made time to ship delicate items back home.

On the other hand, life on the train had one advantage circus people never overlooked: the swaying locomotion. The train's hypnotically soothing rolls helped the exhausted band of travelers restore enough energy to carry them through the next day. That was one consoling plus to consider, especially after slopping through nasty, rain-drenched lots, where all hands were needed to aid fatigued workers in loading tons of wet, muddy equipment onto the wagons just so the show could make the next jump on schedule.

One particular night, without ado, Daddy surprised me with a mother lode of shiny silver dollars imprisoned inside a wooly kneesock saved from his boyhood for this sentimental reason: the heel had been beautifully darned by Nona. He even promised to add at least one coin to my nest egg weekly, and so he did. On every occasion, I'd smile up at his eyes like a pampered tightwad—before sneaking away to tally my mounting cash in private. Naturally, I insisted on squirreling the lumpy heirloom under my berth pillow for safekeeping. "Who but a fool would steal it?" I boasted, making a fist. That silver reserve made me feel richer than King Midas.

The pie car (ofttimes referred to as the onboard den of iniquity) was a café-type bar and supply store. It was mostly a male-dominated hangout wherein the hairy-chested males swapped smutty stories or picked fights—just for the satisfaction of honing their gorillaship. Now and again, they'd collapse in the smelly mess of their own puke after slugging it out in fistfights (the reason for which they'd never remember). In the bargain, one and all had liberty to swear and spit, mentally frisk pinups, and pee out onto the tracks. Poker and craps games took over the entire smoke-filled car, blaring with sweeps of guttural coughs. Angry-fisted losers would shove the cheaters into tight corners, kicking their shins bloody and often holding a switchblade to their throats, declaring there'd be no next time. After the workout, the cheaters were left thrashing about in the hall like whacked polecats until they managed to disentangle their sore limbs and, if chance would have it, escape into the sanctum of their bunks—hurt and dizzy, but feeling darn lucky they hadn't been bagged and jettisoned off the zooming train.

Although the transit wagon stopped its back-and-forth shuttling to the train tracks once the lot was bare, sex-starved workers often risked a trip into town after the tear-down, either to connect with ladies of the night or to buy a caseload of beer and cheap booze. Even if none were limp-wristed wimps, most believed they were a better catch than they really were—although, once in a blue moon, they'd get lucky. Just the same, when the last whistle sounded, stragglers would clamor to get onboard. If unsuccessful, they'd go from the frying pan into the fire, for their chancy outing had dire consequences. For example, no-shows were docked five bucks on payday and received advance warning: "Three strikes, and you're out."

The tiny cracker-box lavatories were situated at each end of the sleeping cars—although we always counted on our sanctioned standby, the honey bucket. Fortunately, the shared facilities were kept clean by a smiling porter; the more he was tipped, the more he smiled. Fittingly, my grandparents' half-car cabin had its own lavatory and shower. (Knowing my grandfather, that perk was probably an addendum to his contract.)

On the showgrounds, however, the restroom quality took a severe plunge. The circus restroom was in those days an unsightly establishment—beyond pathetic. As a child, I equated my daily potty experience to that of entering an indispensable chamber of horrors that housed the boogeyman. Our outhouse tents were routinely pitched in some remote region at the edge of the show-grounds, so reaching them in time would present somewhat of a challenge—especially in a real bind. Adding insult to injury, the splintered wooden seats were abnormally large. (Possibly our ballooning boss carpenter had something to do with that.) Anyhow, within my gang of small fries, the worry of being swallowed down into the pit's stinky abyss made us downright paranoid. But luckily, my balancing genes helped me avoid the unthinkable.

In addition, those torn-to-tatters tents (devoid of toilet paper) were erected lopsided 99 percent of the time; supposedly, the unpleasant task was awarded with purpose to known boozers too liquored up for big-top duty. They were too drunk to care. Consequently, the tents were apt to fold pancake-flat, even on a calm day absent of storms that, God forbid, might've carried them off into the wild blue yonder. This dastardly scenario was of little concern to us damsels in distress, because each quick-footed loser who mustered enough courage to head in that direction had already exhausted every alternative. At that point, the best strategy was to scramble out before catching some type of superkiller virus or risking asphyxiation by the stench alone. Any seasoned troupers—like me, of course—couldn't escape the flashing mental picture of some illiterate, sloshed wino punching his way through the crisscross canvas opening after being bounced from the local bar.

Hoooo-ly shit! Damn, where go dat door?

Into the season, this menacing threat worked to peel away my defenses, especially when incapacitated on the punishing throne. Any rustling noise forced me to unscrew my courage from the sticking bench, levitate my hind end in midair flotation, and assume a rabid stance—a cruel indication that, when on the circus lot, there was hardly a stretch of dirt you could call you own. In circus lingo, those woebegone tents were called "donikers." Incidentally, if you should ever want to widen the eyes of an old-timer, just say that word.

CHAPTER 10

CIRCUS MAGIC IN MOTION

One can never consent to creep
when one feels an impulse to soar.
—Helen Keller

The Cole Bros. circus train was loaded with a variety of trained animals, troupes of daring entertainers, and an assortment of personnel involved in the talismanic process that kept the circus vibrant and alive. Riding inside the swaggering choo-choo as it whistled goodwill salutations past townships—neatly signposted on the verdant-pastured countryside—was spellbinding. During unavoidable delays, creatures large and small would turn their senses outward, wiggling their noses and whiffing the tempting bouquet of fresh-cut alfalfa. Most hysterically, the mighty elephants worked their twining proboscises through various vents— appealing for a peanut from the skittish mob of well-wishers. The gentle giraffes took turns stretching their towering necks around partially opened half-doors— maybe to relieve boredom, or perhaps partake in a little round of self-serving calisthenics while passing scenic, red-roofed dairy farms, golden wheat fields, and lush woodlands in the wink of an eye. America's heartland, known to be dependable circus territory, was an entity unto itself. The traffic often locked along rural byways and hamlets while peace-loving families filed out of their typically outdated roadsters and stared in charmed disbelief.

What a grand sight for a farmer, toiling in the soil or harvesting crops, to view with his young son or daughter at dawn! Townspeople were overtaken by the charismatic puff of excitement on circus day. This noticeable atmospheric change allowed a beam of titillation to touch each house, each occupant. It was a strange world those incredulous people came to see, for the circus way of life was not understood by most. But none could resist being part of it—at least for a day.

I am glad to remember now that the greeting offered by the townsfolk was just a courtesy of the times—an era when cordiality was in vogue. Even the familiar pack of bastard hounds wagged their tails and barked happily around the bustling town square—cozying up to the congenial party of city officials, as if they too had been promised a section of prime front-row seats. The scene was reminiscent of a Norman Rockwell oil painting as the mighty circus train whistled up to the welcoming station, bedecked with ribbons and doodads. This anticipated arrival attracted scores of happy spectators from across the county; they clustered together, peering with their necks goosed out, in hope of witnessing the first movement toward disembarkation.

At journey's end, the animals became wildly aggressive after an entire trip scrunched against each other like sardines inside boxcars smelling of dung and pee-soaked sawdust. Occasionally, one or two feisty zebras would rip away, kicking down the railroad track—leaving incensed grooms in hot pursuit.

Caustic animal chatter could be heard as the beasts nipped and kicked, bluffing one another in order to steal the lead. During the unloading process, looks could kill as they approached their roommates with combative intent. Their venturesome mood was spurred by a quickened ride to their spacious theater of cinematic action as they bullied forward, snapping at the bright sunshine and gulping down a mouthful of fresh air. What thoughts they must have had!

The circus lot was the one and only place where the animals could rest up in the comfort of larger stalls and receive preferential treatment before and after the show. Many were caught at the height of an unpropitious moment as they commenced down the wood-grooved ramp, twitching and quivering in short, mincing steps while passing gas, peeing buckets, and doing whatever it took in order to rid themselves of their own particular brand of smelly baggage.

*   *   *   *

As was the custom, the sideshow crowd, which included naughty hoochie-coochie dancers, authoritative barkers, and clannish freaks, coexisted in the same sleeping car—designed with either two or three-high berths on each side of the aisle. The sideshow curiosities were a quiet group, staying busy here and there, preferring to remain entirely self-sufficient by assisting any needy comrades with agreeable but wearing affection. For some reason, many people born with ugly deformities were happily married to normal spouses, blessed with sight beyond a physical shell. Ironically, those individuals—normally caricatured for being ignorant at best—not only thrived inside half-formed, half-developed bodies, but were considered reliable, honest employees—working with, and not against, management. And most important of all, they were known to have far greater empathy for people in general than those myriad individuals who examined them in disgust.

Christine, the alligator lady, was blissfully married to a happy-go-lucky band-leader named Dodo. She suffered terribly and yet withstood, with exceptional tolerance, unkind and cruel remarks thrown at her by the more indiscriminate individuals who paid to investigate the "human grotesqueries" of the freak show. Christine happened to be completely bald, and her flowing, reddened eyes had cold and mysterious reptilian characteristics—for one, they blinked from the bottom lid, which was strange in itself. Plus, her sore body was clad in rough, scaling skin that cracked and bled if not lubricated on a regular basis.

At least on the surface, the curiosities seemed at peace with their plight—ever willing to be received as an anomaly, welcoming the chance to earn fair wages for their efforts. However, receiving stares everywhere they went couldn't have been easy. As a group, they knew much sadness, an emotion they shared solely with each other. But on a bad day, their faces revealed to the world all the agony— and all the decency—one could imagine. Irregardless, they never stayed down for long. For all intents and purposes, they adopted the "life is what you make it" attitude and actually made a habit of recording a wealth of funny stories and self-deprecating witticisms from their favorite comedy shows, applying them to any given situation.

The sideshow crowd didn't always keep to themselves. By midseason, meal-time at the cookhouse could be a boring ritual, especially if there was nothing to discuss other than matters of dull concentration—devoid of juicy gossip to help the food go down. If the circus folk ever found themselves trapped in that frame of mind, and the chow failed to satisfy to boot, the sideshow crowd came to the rescue by livening things up. One particular example comes to mind. The more gregarious oldsters, wearing exaggerated expressions, drummed their table with forks, indicating they wished to summon our eager-to-please chef, so they could praise him for a job well done. But when the raccoon-faced ex-military chef graced the scene like a parading peacock, they proceeded to thank him (at the top of their lungs) for flavoring the food with their favorite toppings—specifically, crunchy rat droppings, tender spider parts, savory earthworms, and succulent horseflies. When the laughter subsided, the ringleader lowered his voice some-what and reminded the chef that latecomers might freak out if he didn't put some aside. The assertive chef ordinarily took these benign barbs with a grain of salt, while the regular number of finicky diners picked through their plates—already showing the sorry signs of extreme heartburn agitation.

CHAPTER 11

FAMILY FEUDS

No man lives without jostling and being jostled;
in all ways he has to elbow himself through the world,
giving and receiving offense.
—Carlyle

Even if my temperamental relatives were fiercely loyal as a family, scandal-riddled squabbles among themselves were commonplace. Interference was vehemently prohibited. Regardless, the almost daily war of words that raged between my relatives (who vented in Italian) were wildly laughable, especially to those not in the line of fire. For the right reasons, Daddy wanted me out of sight (and mind) during those *nose-to-nose* battles, so I usually journeyed far. If I dared disobey, it was at my peril. Though, remarkably, no matter how overheated their work-related quarrels became, the brothers claimed that they hadn't violated Nono's number-one commandment of avoiding intentional injury to one another since the riding act was formed. That may seem absurd in the minds of many, but in all truth I had never witnessed even one argument where the brothers actually came to blows in my entire life. The central reason for Nono's incontestable law was income security. Consider the consequences: if anybody was recklessly beaten out of commission, the Cristiani livelihood would be at risk and, with so many mouths to feed, Nono could ill afford forfeiting a single paycheck. Because circus performers are such self-aggrandizing creatures (the nature of the beast), disagreements, particularly on the road, are to be expected. And the Cristiani family never got a free pass from this stereotype.

Nono, satisfied that he hadn't sired a litter of sycophants, knew certain matters were beyond his control. Animation stemmed from the brothers' ethnic background. Waving arms and kicking dirt was as necessary to their steamed self-expression as it was for a team of seething baseball players protesting a bad call. Candidly, a more subtle reaction would've been against their philosophy. So if push came to shove, and outsiders flagrantly threatened the family's honor or turf, even Nono could not harness his double-fisted brood. Although some family tales are more myth than history, the Cristianis were indeed notorious and scandalized from countless brawls, but it neither spoiled their drive nor derailed their spirit. None can deny the troupe was obsessively flanked by a cult of fans—drawn into the fray by an intoxicant brew of uncanny talent, natural charisma, and controversial, flamboyant behavior. To a great extent, growing up the Italian way contributed to the men's emotional makeup. And because they were quick to comprehend the broad range of class differences within the industry, they acquired chameleonlike versatility that no doubt helped them survive.

Most intriguingly, the Cristianis were socially at ease among the elite. But when facing hostile, plebeian crowds (normally associated with show-related melees), they shed their northern Italian civility, backed away from no one, and fought at an equal level. When confronted combatively, the Cristianis were a powerful force with whom to be reckoned; if circumstances demanded, they battered opponents in the down-and-dirty style of a ruthless gang of Sicilian street fighters. The fact that dullness never followed in their wake only added to their mystique.

Aside from outsider confrontations, the family's work-related outbursts were really no different than most angry displays held inside the soundproof chambers of boardrooms worldwide. The marked difference for this ignitable family was this: the only available boardroom the Cristianis ever had on the road was the communal backyard of the circus lot. Essentially, they lived in one huge fishbowl, without the luxury of a private environment in which to iron out their differences. Family business, unique as it was, had the same contention points as any other corporation: budget, marketing, payroll, and profit and loss. Considering the strenuous itinerary of circus life, arguments were inevitable. Regardless, such ongoing spats gave the usual lowlifes reason to use the Cristianis' battlefield as an analogy for clashes beyond their kindred circle. Certain players referred to them as crazy wops or mad degos. The older brothers, at least, wisely dismissed most of the wicked inside jokes, believing the putdowns were the result of professional jealousy. The Cristianis were a hard act to follow. Much to the displeasure of competing acts, nothing could tarnish their reputation inside the ring.

On occasion, their confrontations were humorous, to put it mildly—particularly when Bogonghi (who was never the stooge) flew off the handle. Bogonghi was a chubby little guy with a pudgy nose. He had the shape of a potbelly stove; he wobbled when he walked, like a wound-up toy—mostly because his short, arthritic legs sagged from the overload. His temper was volcanic by any measure. Take heed: if Bogonghi found his iced six-pack two beers shy after returning from the cookhouse, he'd confront the suspected thief or thieves with the nerve of a man and a half. When such rage had seized his mind, people normally gave him all the space he needed. Oblivious to his physical shortcomings, he'd never back away from a fight, no matter what. That said, if Bogonghi felt threatened in any way, the knowledge that his vigilant Cristiani bodyguards waited in the wings gave him the arrogance that stoked the fires of his capricious behavior.

Scores of funny incidents involving Bogonghi and Uncle Daviso flit across my mind, but one particular story (on the Cole Bros. Circus) stands out from the rest. Though Bogonghi never took sides, he couldn't resist eavesdropping when the brothers' tempers came to a boil. Fly-on-the-wall Bogonghi often flaunted his boldest self someplace near the action, unnoticed. On one sweaty, hot midsummer day, however, Daviso crept up from behind the men's dressing tent and enunciated a very wicked wisecrack right in the barrel of Bogonghi's keen ear. Whatever was said made the petulant dwarf hoist a finger upward in hailing vulgarity—warning my uncle (in Italian) that Daviso would never outlive the fifty-year curse on his penis. Predicting the aftershock, curious show folks wrestled for a safe corner from which to witness the next scandalous episode of the Cristianis' ongoing soap opera. The brothers panicked the instant Bogonghi started shuffling his feet, with fearsome, yellowy eyes and nostrils rounded out like those of a goaded bull. No doubt, confronting Bogonghi's unorthodox method of reprisal for the umpteenth time—without the protection of a rock-hard suit of armor—stopped short of being funny. By force of habit, Bogonghi marched toward the dressing tent in typical military goose steps. As his muscles limbered, he gained confidence and began kicking his short legs even higher—aiming to render inoperative the lady-killers' most prized possession. Mogador, being caught in the crosshairs, ran out in his briefs and hid directly behind the (not-so-safe) cat cages ... and immediately flagged an apologetic truce with his towel.

Daviso wasn't laughing. "Bogonghi, *abbastanza* [enough] ... cut the shit!"

Young Pete, feeling the heat for his own share of abusive teasing, reached for the nearest shield. "Gentlemen," he advised soberly, "cover your baaaaalls!"

*   *   *   *

When Bogonghi was drunk on beer, he'd sit on the cool side of the dressing tent and belch the time away—repeating "*scusi*" [excuse me] after tapping his chest with the thumb side of his fist. But if town monkeys invaded his private domain to the point that he felt squeezed, they'd better be prepared to outrun the punch of his oversized clown shoe or the impact of his half-empty beer can. A caricaturist's dream, Bogonghi was—except when he went shopping in town. Then he'd go out of his way not to be noticed, which wasn't easy, given his head-turning measurements.

During one of our talks, Nono told me that Bogonghi's physically normal parents had been so ashamed of his dwarfed state that they became cruelly abusive. Among other despicable acts, Bogonghi had been locked inside a suffocating trunk for punishment, or so I was told. If correct, this bit of history explains why Bogonghi was stricken with so many phobias.

As a general rule, children have a unique ability to size up adults; they can tell in a heartbeat if a person is genuine. I felt a deep affection for this little man with a big heart, and for dear Fachini as well. Both men were kind to me in every conceivable way. I'll never forget how patiently they responded to my day in, day out gunfire of questions—the exhausting "but why?" questions that tend to infuriate many grownups.

Papa Cristiani
Circa 1905

Mama Cristiani
Circa 1905

Cristiani Family - 1928

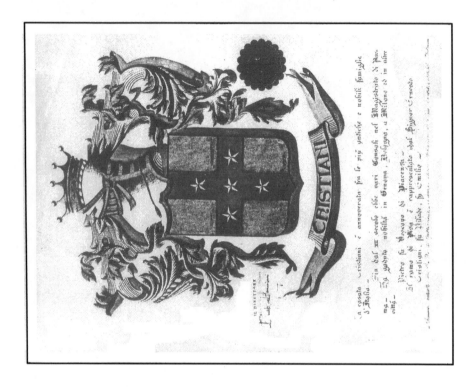

Daviso, Oscar & Lucio Cristiani

The Cristiani Brothers Band

Oscar, Lucio, Belmonte & Daviso

Cristiani Troup
Madison Square Garden Engagement
Ringling Bros Barnum & Bailey-1940

Carol Lombard and Clark Gable,
mesmerized by the Cristiani performance
1937

Hyman Fink

Marion Cristiani & Famous Clown, Lou Jacobs, at the Ringling Bros. & Barnum and Bailey Circus. At Madison Square Garden, NYC - 1938

Publicity Picture Of Lucio With Ringling

Wallace Berry (center) with (left to right)
Daviso, Oscar, Cosetta & Lucio - 1937

Barton MacLane (center) with Belmonte, Lucio, Oscar & Daviso

Fork Jump From Ground To Legendary "Polo"

(Above)
Fachini calms the Cristiani bareback horses just before "Spec" on a stormy day, in 1940.

(Below)
The attractive Cristiani troup, as they appeared earlier in the season at Madison Square Garden

Vickie Marion Cristiani Stateroom
Ringling Bros Circus
Mama 1940

Bonnie Corky

Pete Oscar

Papa

Mogador

Belmonte

RINGLING BROS.
1940

VICKIE BELLE

Oscar, "Vickie Belle" & Marion

Pendergast

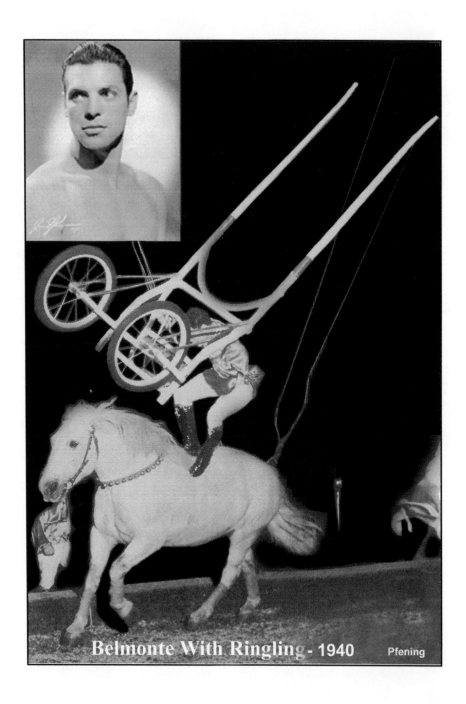

Belmonte With Ringling - 1940   Pfening

THE CELEBRATED CRISTIANI FAMILY
ACTION PICTURE TAKEN DURING FILMING OF Metro-Goldwyn-Mayer

Leo Carillo With
Lucio, Papa and
Belmonte Cristiani

THE CELEBRATED CRISTIANI FAMILY LEO CARILLO
PICTURE TAKEN DURING FILMING OF Metro-Goldwyn-Mayer

The celebrated Cristiani family
with George Raft and Jack Oakie,
taken in Hollywood, California
March, 1937

Cristiani Bareback Troup During Filming
Of MGM's "GreatPicture" - 1937

"Baby"

"Kansas"

Cristiani Photo Shoot At Old
Ringling Winter Quarters

Joe E. Brown With Cristiani Family

Edward G. Robinson With Louise And Daviso

Ted Allan, MGM

Hurrell, MGM

WORLD'S FOREMOST RIDERS ON GIGANTIC PROGRAM OF FEATURES PRESENTED BY GREAT HAGENBECK-WALLACE AND 4 PAW-SELLS BROS COMBINED CIRCUS

Celebrated Cristiani Family, Earth's Most Sensational Bareback Riding Marvels in Great Equestrian Display With Big Show

LUCIO CRISTIANI
Only Rider in the World Accomplishing Twisting Somersaults from Horse to Horse

Two Complete Performances are Given Daily by the Hagenbeck-Wallace and 4 Paw-Sells Bros. Combined Circus at 2 and 8 P. M., the Doors Opening in Each Instance One Hour Earlier to Permit Leisurely Inspection of Its World-famous Menagerie.

Daviso, Rio & Joseph Cotton

Mogador, On Finish Horse, "Alba"
And Oscar In Ring

Marion & Corky Cristiani
"Old Lady In The Shoe" Float
Cole Bros. Circus - 1947

Marion Cristiani

Marion On Mother Goose Float

Ortans Triple To Chair - Cole Bros, Cincinnati - 1947

Ortans - *Among The Greatest!*

Ortans & Belmonte

Ortans & Corky Cristiani - 1940's

Louise, Baby Antoinette & Daviso Cristiani

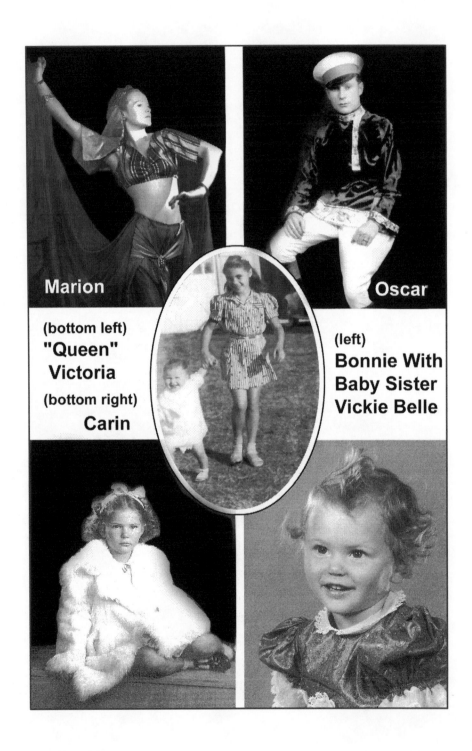

Marion

Oscar

(bottom left)
**"Queen"
Victoria**
(bottom right)
Carin

(left)
**Bonnie With
Baby Sister
Vickie Belle**

Vickie Belle & Circus Pal, Curtis Genders

Vickie, Tina & Friend Joanne
Cole Show - 1947

Ben Davenport lifting a three-day old, 400 pound "punk" elephant

Ben Davenport (above)

Eve & Norma Davenport (below)

"Born In A Trunk"
Norma Davenport On
Dailey Bros. Circus

Eva Davenport as "PRINCESS IOLA"

Norma Cristiani

Young Norma
On Dailey Bros.
Circus

Pete

Jane, Marion & Corky
Visiting Bogonghi At
Clown Alley

Bogonghi & Lulu

(above and below)
June, Lucio and Baby Baleine

Anchorage Daily Times

READ BY ALASKANS EVERYWHERE

| PHONE 56201 | ANCHORAGE, ALASKA, WEDNESDAY, JULY 7, 1954 | 16 PAGES |

CIRCUS ARRIVES IN TOWN

Bringing Circus To Alaska Dream Come True

Snakes Alive And Large At The Cristiani Circus

'Alaska Nellie' Sees First Circus Acts In 45 Years

"Alaska Nellie" Lawing came to Anchorage yesterday to see her first circus in 45 years. The last one she saw was in Leavenworth, Kan., before there were any cars to make transportation easy.

"I enjoyed every minute of it. It was just wonderful. If I could I'd run away with it," she declared. "Alaska Nellie" will be 83 years old a week from Sunday and is famous for her collection of trophies and Alaskana at her home at Lawing on the Kenai Peninsula.

She got a lot of thrills yesterday in addition to seeing the circus and plans to stay several days so she can "see television" and all the improvements made since she visited Anchorage five years ago.

"When I first came here in 1914 there was just a large log house and two tents next to Ship Creek, and the thing grew," she declared.

The tourist business on the Kenai Peninsula has also undergone tremendous change, she said. "This is the first year the trains don't stop at Lawing, and all the visitors now come by car." She has had visitors from all over the world.

Although she fractured her wrist a few weeks ago she has "nothing to complain of—it might have been a leg."

Alaskans are especially fortunate she thinks, just because they are Alaskans.

'ALASKA NELLIE' LAWING

"SNAKES ALIVE"—It takes a lot of blanket to cover the 26-foot python which arrived today from the Washington, D. C. zoo especially for the circus. Elaine Reinfield (right) is the "charmer" who handles the huge snakes and its smaller specimens. The snake is kept under wraps between shows so it won't get too cold. Assisting in the unwrapping are (left to right) Larky Crossieri, Al Dennis, Mogador Cristiani and Ben Davenport.

Memories Of Alaska's First Circus

THIRTY-NINTH YEAR

Charles Van Doren, Corky And Gene Rayburn

Charles Van Doren
And Corky On Set
Of "Roll Out The Sky"

Ortans &
Husband
Freddie

NBC "Roll Out The Sky" Wrap Party At The Colony - Sarasota, Florida

Interior Big Top   **Papa 1959**

Cristiani Circus Layout (above)   **Street Parade (below)**

Corky
Emma & Oscar

Daviso

Praise for David Budd's Paintings

"...in spite of his nutty simplicity it is really work of Mandarin subtlety." John Ashbury, 1962

"The image, in other words, is a mirror of the viewer's sensibility. It can be dull and blank. It can brim with sensations and ideas. It is you." Thomas Hess, 1977

Dave Budd

Corky On Siesta Key Beach, Sarasota, Florida

Pfening Jr. - Columbus

Vickie Cristiani At Chicago's Soldier Field Lakefront

Pete & Norma's son, Tony, Riding Eva The Hippo

Marion & Oscar With Elephants - Carrie, Babe, Shirley and Emma

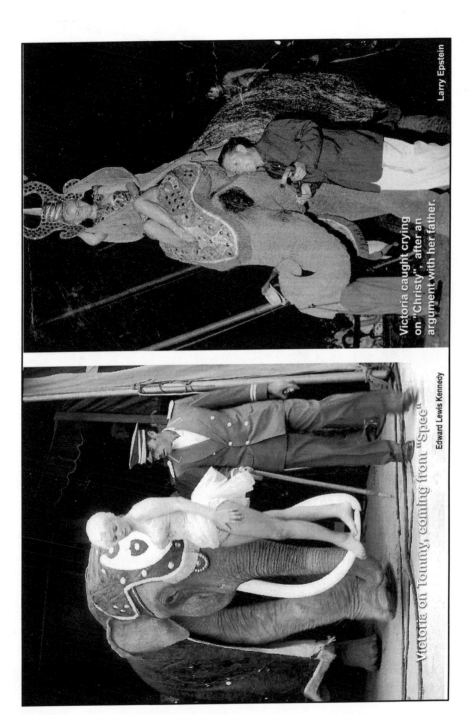

Victoria caught crying on "Christy," after an argument with her father.

Larry Epstein

Victoria on Tommy, coming from "Spec"

Edward Lewis Kennedy

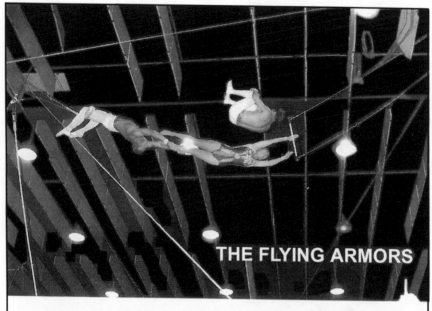

THE FLYING ARMORS

Reggie, Bill Kay (Shriner), Bonnie & Paul

Corky As Doris
Day Double In
MGM's "Jumbo"

Corky During Performance

Jane
Cristiani

Antoinette Cristiani

Lucio, Daviso, Writer Friend, Oscar & Belmonte

Belmonte, Delia & Daughter, Mia - 1964

Shecky Greene (above) with Jane, Victoria & Corky

**James Garner With
Hadassah Sponsors
L A - 1959**

Hollywood Celebrities

**Mama Cristiani Meets
Bob Cummings**

**Caesar Romero Looks On
From Under The Big Top**

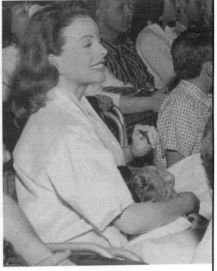

**James Garner
With Sponsor's
Hedassah Queen**

**Jeanne Crain Enjoys The
Cristiani Bros. Circus In
Los Angeles - 1959**

Benny Rossi

Trick Rider & Trick Roper

(above)   Rex   Roy Rogers   Jimmy

Mark And Rex   Mark In Army -1944

Marion & Baby Carin

Carin, "Shirley" & Husband Pete At Disney's Epcot Center Circus

Benny Rossi

Victoria Rossi

CHAPTER 12

▼

WINDING DOWN

When you define liberty you limit it,
and when you limit it you destroy it.
—Brand Whitlock

Once again, August was drawing to a close, and my happy summer days on the Cole Bros. Circus were almost over. The summer from then on was a haunting time—mostly spent awaiting my fate like a poor ladybug on its back. School-age circus children, other than those who performed in family acts, left the show around the same time—albeit traveling in opposite directions. Looking back, winding down was never easy. Obviously, we each handled the heartbreak of separation in our own particular way, so I can only speak for myself.

After the final blowoff (the time everybody exited the big top), when the circus began to pull up stakes, a handful of zealous fans stayed behind. Many huddled together, reflecting quietly on the sidelines; others walked, pensive and alone, reminiscing until the peek of dawn. For reasons that eclipsed even the most pressing matters, these wonderful people—among them, perhaps, creatures of mere aspiration—were unable to say farewell to the pageantry of events that had turned their sleepy community upside down. What a shift in spirit! To think that only hours before, these same small town folks had entered the big top clowning around and talking it up with the enthusiasm of a child opening presents on Christmas day. In those simple days of yore, our tented city truly created a fantasy world with which they could not easily part. But as soon as the last piece of equipment smoked off into the horizon, they headed home, satisfied and happy, having fully surrendered their heartfelt wishes to a dreamer's mind, where imagination afforded them the vision that the nakedness of the circus lot denied.

I truly empathized with those dear souls, for at this late date, it couldn't be more obvious to me that my vacation days were numbered; shopping for school supplies was just around the corner. I had no lifesavers left.

The hours drained away as I bid farewell to every person I had befriended in various departments. I couldn't help but linger when I gazed at the big-top flags blowing freely, as if signaling a parting message of their own. Lastly, I moseyed inside the menagerie, giving my animal friends a loving pat. The course was important; I simply wanted to say good-bye in the halo of light, so I could register the entire day for future recall. Regrettably, the moment arrived when I had to leave the protective egg of my universe, where the glory of my vagabond spirit thrived. It was most difficult to contemplate returning to a place where I had been slighted—that certain pallid dungeon where none gave more notice to me than to a boring plate of cabbage.

It wasn't a nice day, that day!

Sprinkles dampened the cow pie-littered lot in the outskirts of Richmond, Virginia, while a bank of dark clouds raced overhead. Word of an early show gave Mommy little time to prepare for spec, so we hugged and smooched outside the women's dressing tent until Daddy gave us the final nod. *Miss you, my Mommy, miss you* … Daddy then carried my bags up to the midway, where we met the grim-mouthed cabdriver. Shucks! There he was, on schedule, sloping over the hood—with meter running and sockets poppin' out like eye stalks on a crab. Gobs of mud had collected on the soles of my newly shined penny loafers, but I didn't care; it was circus mud, and nothing whatsoever could make me scrape off the perfect memento to carry back to Cardome. I cringed when my feet landed on the floor of the cabby's revved Chevy, thus sundering mortal ties with my circus home.

"Well, scalawag, got your walkin' papers?" he squeaked, with a note of sarcasm embedded in his voice. A vexed frown was my only reply. Besides, what kid can trust a person who smirks? Instead, I narrowed my eyes and time-traveled back to Cardome, when Sister Margaret had called me "scalawag." The inference was negative, all right—hardly a revelation to me. I despised the word! Regardless, I was in no mood to respond to the wisecracking cabdriver—who, much to his credit, knew enough to wear black. All I wanted was to purchase another hour of wild disruptions, crammed with circus mayhem, but that wasn't likely. The deluge came moments before the taxi sped away to the airport, tailpipe rattling like mad.

My glad summer flashed before me while I sat inside with Daddy, quite dry and deafened by the rain. The mocking barbs of separation had me spinning around like a pin-stuck mule, but the fogged rear window obscured my view.

Directly, I blotted the vapor with my coat sleeve and watched the circus evaporate—poof—as if it were a tiny snowflake caught in the cavernous mouth of a blast furnace. Bam! Alacazam! Gone! The posters along that loathsome drive were the only remainder of the world I'd left behind, which made me consider the notion that my holiday had been purely an optical phenomenon—one summer-long mind trick.

It was impossible to escape the farewell chorus of orchestrated wails and doleful telepathic signals broadcasting from the circus behind me. Thinking hard, I hung low, crouched in the backseat, hugging my knees and bobbing my head with indignant passion, struggling to stay centered in the tangles of its squeeze. The dimension of anguish, blazed by a zoo of animal sounds, was encompassing—as if, in galvanized oneness, they mourned the loss of a sibling. I wanted to interfere somehow—to lend my forbidden shadow to bandage the hurt.

I was in some sort of knowing, melancholy freefall, about to land in an awfully familiar scene. As time sped by, I screwed my mouth sideways and imagined a hostile battalion of convent gargoyles dragging me down deeper and deeper into a hideous vortex. At this neurotic moment, I was irrational enough to grip at anything: a leaf, a feather, or even a droplet of rain for buoyancy. *Shame on you, Vickie Belle*, I said to myself. *Soaking in self-pity won't help!* Sheer practicality helped me overlook my predicament for the time being.

Straightaway, I pictured Mommy gluing on her false eyelashes, halfheartedly, in her maroon flannel robe before probing her trunk for rainwear and galoshes—all the while praying for my safe flight back to Cardome, and for Daddy's return in time for the web production number. And there were other images worth pondering: Mimi, the baby orangutan, caught rolling the bare foil from a box of Ex-Lax; Daisy, the aging donkey, ailing with a split hoof; Peanut, our darling midget horse, who, the day before, had ripped a bag of sweet feed and was down with colic; the bandleader's gorgeous Siamese cat, Minerva, rushed to the vet after licking a jar of fishhooks … and, gosh, what would become of poor Fabby, the exotic-looking sideshow belly dancer, sent packing because a watermelon seed was growing inside her stomach—yet again!

Then came two sobering words from the cabbie: "Airport ahead!"

Daddy looked down at the floor, as if he had been dreading the call. "OK. It's Eastern Airlines."

Unable to postpone the inevitable, he kissed my forehead ever so lightly before handing over Mommy's surprise gift: a perfect four-leaf clover, pressed flat and wrapped up like a present in red tissue paper. He then tickled my nose with the end of one of my long braids and uttered, "Love you, Spino," in a soft, broken voice. "Tell me, are you OK?"

I wilted under his gaze and pillowed my face on his leather-padded shoulder.

"Love you too, Daddy ... but no ... *I'm not*!"

*   *   *   *

Although I missed my dear friend Jenny in the worst way, I got the feeling that she was watching over me like a phantom guide, urging me to ward off the wolves and stick up for myself—which I learned to do. Most of the school year passed uneventfully, except for a chilling ordeal that reminded me of the scary plot from *Jane Eyre*: the apparent suicide of the certain nun who allegedly jumped to her death from the bell tower. Even if the circumstances of her death were kept secret, one fact couldn't be denied. At early sunrise, on their daily march to flag duty, two seniors made the gruesome discovery near the edge of the walkway.

Although the incident was handled in the hush of silence, rumors traveled campuswide that Sister's crimped hand was spotted poking from under a rise of bloodstained snow. Some even claimed that her holy habit had been stiff and stinking with blood and gore; within days, the story had a life of its own. The uncertainty continued. No one knew exactly what to believe. Supposedly, the visibly shaken girls had observed a trail of crystallized blood around her nose, with even more passing from her grayish, open eyes and misshapen blue mouth. My imagination went wild; a body falling from such a height had to have left an unsightly stain in the snow. So I believed every word—truths, half-truths, and total fabrications. I vehemently opposed going to the funeral mass and actually schemed to hide someplace where I couldn't be found ... but the ramifications of such obstinate behavior scared me far worse. *Jesus, Mary, and Joseph, please order them not to make me go!*

As expected, not one student was excused from attending the somber, drawn-out high mass. Consider the mood as Sister Agnes gave our class explicit instructions—which did nothing to bolster my morale, presently at rock bottom. Accordingly, after the priest gave his blessing and said the opening prayer, everybody left their pews and circled around to the rear of the chapel, only to file down the center aisle, past her pale, withered corpse. We were prodded from behind by a morbid procession of chanting nuns entering from the shadowy, candlelit corridor.

Seeing as I had never before set eyes on an honest-to-goodness dead person, I was completely intimidated—so much so that when I knelt before the altar to receive holy communion, I dared not open my mouth too wide, lest her damned spirit jump down my throat and possess my mind forevermore.

First off, I must admit that it was more than shocking to finally associate a face with the disembodied screams that had haunted the school night after night. What's more, Sister's skin had the dreadful hue of leaf mold, which gave off such a stale odor I almost gagged—yet, most surprisingly, I gathered enough courage to pause long enough to see if her eyelids moved. They didn't. But in a moment's time, I saw what I deemed real: her pupils, dilated with fright, boring through the flesh like two blazing coins cast in hell.

I spent many days dealing with her untimely death. Maybe I felt guilty because I hadn't prayed hard enough for her salvation when she was alive. Ghoulish appeals from the undead inhabited my mind in recurrent nightmares for weeks thereafter. An evolution of fiery red and green eyeballs pelted my body like a legion of devilish monsters in pursuit of my soul. The presence of Sister's contorted figure forced a closer study of her solidly waxed face in the plain wooden coffin. Her ghost, twice the size of her mortal body, reappeared over and over as she lay beneath the arduously gathered silk cover. She came at me—mad, and mum with secrecy—cloying, reaching, and tearing with bony fingers, attempting to draw me near.

I took solace in my secret place outdoors, the embodiment of which was conveyed in a language I was born to understand. To my gratitude, that sanctuary offered a spectrum of color celebrating life. It carried me over the rainbow, and managing to stave off my achromatic existence. No wonder I fled to my shrine of friends; they were my emissaries, faithful custodians of my wishes who never let me down. Whenever I took solace beneath nature's canopy of continual growth, I felt assured that its tether of energy would cradle me. Mostly, I'd walk away feeling as replenished as a newborn full of its mother's milk.

*   *   *   *

As it happened, 1947 was my family's last season on the Cole Bros. Circus—for no other reason than sore bones and overall disenchantment with the business of performing season after season. The Cristianis didn't want to end up crippled in old age. Everything has a life, and it was about time to map out a future apart from performing, which up to then had been the motive of their lives. In between working spot dates to cover living expenses, the brothers investigated various business opportunities. At this point, thank goodness, there was no reason for me to continue my education at Cardome, which was cause for celebration. As a result, I lived with Nona and Nono, who had decided to stay behind in Sarasota rather than bounce around the country for no good reason.

The following school year, I attended Sarasota's exclusive Out of Door School—known for its flexible and innovative approach to education. Naturally, I was all for it. The school was located smack on the heavenly shores of Siesta Key; it was surreal, paradise found. Morning recess included a swim in the warm, frothy Gulf—or, for a dollar a day, students had the option of horseback riding down a tight-winding nature trail of blooming tropical forestry. Imagine. Not surprisingly, I saw myself on center stage, sitting throne-high on the crust of an academic oasis—kicking through Sarasota's famous flour-white sand with the pluck of a squirrel crossing the road. Know, too, that I felt deserving, especially after my stretch at Cardome.

But I dared not make any sense of it as I cruised along on the private school bus every weekday morning, sipping Nona's fresh-squeezed orange juice with my prissy white sunglasses securely in place.

Meanwhile, another Cristiani milestone was within reach.

CHAPTER 13

▼

THE MACON YEARS

Every man is a volume,
if you know how to read him.
—Channing

By 1948, the Cristianis were in pursuit of a long-lasting dream. Motivated by Nono's entrepreneurial seed, which had been implanted at birth, the family set out to produce an American circus of their own, intuitively assembled through the wisdom of gained experience and personal taste.

As performers, they were a living legend, with nothing more to prove. Greatly in need of an elixir for their fixation, the tented circus, the Cristianis crafted a plan to invade the shark-infested waters. My family hit pay dirt when introduced to Floyd King, owner of the lackluster King Bros. Circus out of Macon, Georgia, with whom they formed a most lucrative partnership. Mr. King, who kept his pretty young wife safe and pregnant, was short and barrel shaped. Nonetheless, he was a wise old hoot who borrowed his owlish look from the build of his no-neck body and gold-rimmed Benjamin Franklin spectacles, evenly perched on a beaklike nose. Yet, upon those droopy shoulders rested the head of a circus-routing dynamo. Soon after the formal handshake was announced in 1949, when I was nine years old, the title changed to King Bros. and Cristiani Bros. Combined Circus. The union proved to be an ideal pairing of creative minds. The Cristiani affiliation gave Mr. King enviable prestige, instant recognition, and a celebrated management team that would attract the best sponsors. Mr. King, in return, offered his methodical booking skills and ready-made circus, which was in dire need of revamping. The partnership seemed to be the perfect professional marriage. Notably, the totally refurbished King Bros. and Cristiani Bros. Combined Circus beat the competition right out of the starting gate, so the partners were in the winner's circle from day one.

The next five years were some of the happiest and most memorable years I had growing up. I fell in love with Macon and the people who lived there—especially those venerable Dixie charmers who, with gallant pretense, dallied in the white-glove fakery of their so-called picture-perfect lives. Few things escaped me. I marveled at their natural finishing-school manners, ultrafeminine gestures, and sophisticated raw nerve—detecting a deliberate shroud of secrecy in their eye-batting conversations. These women were superb teachers—the best. When interruptions were next to nil, I would rehearse their Loretta Young-like holier-than-thou attitude, deportment, and stride.

Adolescence took hold. I was maturing overnight, and I accepted the change with cool logic. Southern women were pampered, I noticed, using honey to their advantage. There was a method to their madness, I surmised. If I had to ripen, Macon was the place to do it. I'd study with an eagle's eye and learn from the pros. No one could deliver insults with more charm than an authentic, home-grown southerner. Yankees couldn't decide whether to thank them or poison their tea. The perfectly accurate quip, "Enough marshmallows, properly placed, can be lethal," had to have come directly from the cherry-painted mouth of a wise old southern matriarch—if not I'd be terribly disappointed. In time, I became a magnolia-sniffing, peach-eating Georgia gal, who derived much joy from the laid-back way of life ... and the food. I ate grits with my eggs and licked my chops. On one school outing, I consumed so many peaches that I broke out in a fiery peach-fuzz rash; even that didn't stop me from indulging.

Our model circus winter quarters was located practically in the heart of Macon, at Central City Park. The spacious fairgrounds, reminiscent of the countryside (and bordering the murky Okmulgee River), had enough brick buildings to house all the animals and equipment. On sunny winter days, the wooden fence corral gave horses, zebras, and camels a chance to buck and nip to their hearts' content. Workers had sufficient heated shelters, which they were obliged to scrub down every day; however, the trailer-park facilities were strictly maintained by the city. And the generous mayor offered the performers and other employees free trailer space and utilities in the camping area next to the public bathhouse. Besides all that, immaculately kept stables sat across the way, filled with thoroughbred harness-racing horses that exercised daily on the dirt raceway before dawn. The professional trainers shared the grounds in fine spirit, so everybody managed to live together in blissful harmony. The trainers became good friends with old Fachini and jotted down many of his remedies.

The Macon Chamber of Commerce was entirely supportive of the arrangement, because its members knew how much circus people contributed to the local economy. Automobile and tractor-trailer dealerships felt the benefits from financially responsible customers forced to update their road-battered vehicles yearly. Also, other area businesses thrived on the steady revenue in an otherwise lean winter period. Unquestionably, there was a mesh—a perfect blend and genuine exchange of friendship between the circus and the community. Daddy laughed the day away after his well-caffeinated policeman friend made a straight-thinking prediction. "Oscar," he said, cocking his head convincingly, "ya'll soon be speakin' Eye-talian with a southern twang."

What a bargain: all these wonderful perks in exchange for merely posting a welcome sign seven days a week. Life couldn't have been better, and taxpayers seemed content. During the layoff period, the winter quarters doubled as the city's only zoo and free cultural compound—advertised as a village of complex activities, where the common folk could break the monotony of after-church humdrum. Before long, scores of families adopted this picturesque site as their very own protected place of privilege—the winter home of strange people, wild beasts, and objects of bizarre enchantment. Understandably, the hospitable townspeople were in no rush as they passed through the coal-heated buildings, absorbing all the action in southern stride. They'd stop to feed peanuts to the elephants, watch performers practicing daring tricks indoors, and then cruise over to ogle Bonnie and Clyde (the strange-looking anteaters) or the glass-encased polar-bear exhibit (still under construction). Others ventured outdoors just to fraternize with gabby old-timers, busy patching canvas or stitching storm rips in some warm, sunny corner.

Canvas patching was an art form the oldsters perfected with great pride. Their callused fingers worked tirelessly, seaming together torn canvas with beeswax thread and large, curved needles. While stitching and guzzling down the proverbial ninety-nine bottles of beer, the brick-faced chaps exchanged farfetched tales ranging from weird UFO sightings to their Granny's prize soul food recipes. The more ornery ones, like Halfear Scotty, regularly relived bad times in the slammer, although his version of the story at hand became more questionable with reduced sobriety. "We 'ave to let orf steam somehow," he'd say. "Booze makes the tellin' a bit easier."

Delusional Scotty, who could barely scratch out his name, owned a great pair of tap shoes, along with a tattered silk top hat that folded up flat—when it wanted to. He claimed the heirlooms, kept in a dusty knapsack, had once belonged to his "rest in peace" daddy. Anything could touch him off. Many a sober night, when liquor was scarce, Scotty went sliding perilously down the dark path of paranoia;

he'd fly off his army cot in a funk … threatening to slit the throat of any man who tried to steal his belongings. Now that was one statement everybody believed.

On weekends, Maconites generously opened their jam-packed picnic baskets and spoiled workers with ample helpings of southern dishes such as fried chicken, corn bread, salt pork-flavored veggies, and sumptuous pecan pie. While the brawny crew unhesitatingly fingered the remains of their foil-wrapped feast, they could experience the joy of being included in a real family get-together for the afternoon. Regardless, most of these men (destined to wander until they were dropped into unmarked graves) existed in a halfway state—neither here nor there. They never planned more than a day ahead and had not a clue of how their lives would end; they knew only that life would end, at some time or other. One or more recruits appeared gifted in select fields, but like any idiot savant, they were also impeded with troubling flaws that made it downright difficult to hold down regular jobs. All things considered, a warm bed, camaraderie, three square meals a day, and enough dough for tobacco and scanty needs would suffice.

Alice and Mona were a pair of potentially killer elephants owned by Floyd King before they were grandfathered in with the partnership. These elderly Asians were notorious in the business. Besides the elephant boss, only one handler was expert enough to supervise their care, which happened to include on-the-hour dung shoveling (dubbed the shit-kicker job). Apart from exercise outings, the sinister-looking pachyderms stayed double-chained at the far end of the cordoned-off elephant section, which displayed the necessary sign:

DANGER! KEEP OUT … BAD ELEPHANT!

Curiously, under normal conditions, the aging rogues were dependable workers while performing their duties of setup and tear-down. But beware, for when these animals were idle within the boundaries of their compound, they were most feared. Alice was the worst of the two. She invoked a morbid awakening in onlookers through her blind left eye, which appeared macabre at first sight. I swear the eye itself had a kind of mysterious milky white glow that stabbed through the darkness—emitting a frightful caveat to anyone who stumbled upon her chilling presence. When foolhardily approached on her blind side, Alice would use her destructive trunk to swipe out in hunt for anything to crush and destroy. In contrast, Alice's strong right eye had a black, penetrating stare—one that anesthetized voyeurs captured in her focus. Her behavior was cunning: sensing her prey, she'd wait for a blundering mistake and calculate her maneuvers with the cold-blooded stealth of a crocodile.

Railroad shows were slowly becoming history, with only a handful operating—and operating in the red, at that. The King-Cristiani Bros. Circus was a truck show—also known as a mud show. Basically, house trailers provided humble abodes to the show folks. We owned ours until Daddy found that pulling that clumsy tank of a trailer around the country wasn't worth the risk of a bad accident that was bound to happen. In those days, hardly a week went by without house trailer mishaps—mostly caused by out of control swerving, busted hitches, rollovers and blowouts. Ultimately, as a preferable option, we lived out of hotels and motels when on the road.

The partnership had the Midas touch, yielding a treasury of gold each season. The circus broke sales records practically every day—weather permitting—and the Canadian tours were a smashing success. In addition, we all enjoyed a delightful summer diversion when the entire circus was transported by ferry to Prince Edward Island, off the Canadian coast. The island's curious citizenry, combined with assorted worldwide travelers and accidental tourists, walked the midway, drawing in the odor of hot heartburn grease while gripping the tiny hands of apple-faced youngsters engulfed in wonder at the extraordinary events. Preschoolers trailed behind their siblings, biting down on frozen strawberry or grape snow cones, unconcerned that streams of syrup had already left permanent stains on their freshly laundered playwear.

With management and general show operations in the competent hands of the Cristianis, and Floyd King bossing the booking and advance sales department, what could go wrong? What could go wrong when net income soared beyond expectations—which enabled the partners to triple their savings in the very first year, invest capital, and luxuriate in the best cashmere clothing, high-priced automobiles, eighteen-carat-gold Rolex watches, prime property, fur coats, and first-class cruises abroad in the off season? *Hmmmmm* ... Nono, Daddy, Lucio and Daviso were the primary investors. Off season, Lucio and June traveled extensively and, rather flagrantly, enjoyed the fruits of their labor. Daddy, being a cautious spender, saved every penny. Eventually, he took Pete's advice and purchased a herd of four young Asian elephants with personal funds: Christy, Carrie, Babe and Shirley—Emma came along later. Nono and Daviso wisely invested in safe real estate back home in Sarasota, Florida.

No doubt, the financial watershed left the Cristiani family independently rich, and the future looked as bright as the North Star. Daily, the big top filled to capacity, and the blues (end bleacher seats) were packed to the rafters. Acrimonious tiffs were downgraded to weighty, businesslike discussions, but middle age was telling. The long-awaited question of just when the family could ease out of their traditional performing roles—which, through the years, had inflicted a gazillion body-punishing blows—was resolved. The Cristianis counted their blessings, believing that they were amazingly fortunate in escaping serious injury thus far—with the exception of a broken nose or two. If only for the sake of sanity, the family agreed that performing as a group would clearly be limited to special engagements. Unfettered at last!

At this point, a transition was in the making: the brothers turned their thoughts to other avenues of achievement. For instance, Pete managed the concessions; Mogador sharpened his skills in booking and advance sales with Floyd King; and Belmonte served as big-top superintendent, as well as performing in some capacity. Daviso purchased a pair of gorgeous stallions and trained them for his (dancing horse) dressage act; Daddy, with his love of elephants, studied their daily habits with mounting interest and eventually supervised the department. And although Lucio was appointed general manager, he never lost sight of his comedic talent and continued to put his skills to use throughout the show.

By now, Nono, like any sensible aging father, knew it was time to loosen the reins. He encouraged his capable sons to make their own calls—after they heard him out. I might add that he was never out of touch, and his advice was rarely overlooked. This sea change in family government, embraced by both of my grandparents, proved to be the cure for many nagging personal attacks and sudden outbursts. Suffused with a newfound liberty—to which they rapidly became accustomed—the Cristianis achieved another goal: *la dolce vita!*

Though I never took part in family discussions per se, I took in everything, and—for whatever reason—stored it in my head under lock and key. Most often, envious showpeople—lost in the delivery of their poisonous speeches—made the mistake of ignoring a child standing within earshot. And because kids are blessed with the uncanny gift of sizing up adults, I usually had them pegged. Daddy and I had always engaged in limited conversations about certain people in the business. Sometimes he seemed surprised at my assessment; other times he wasn't. Family sympathizers, I noticed, were elated at the Cristianis' success; ultimately, faithful devotees and clingers-on shared in all the glory. But their detractors (and there were ever so many) were markedly imprisoned by envy.

CHAPTER 14

▼

MOUNT DE SALES
ACADEMY

A more perfect race is a more soulful race,
a more soulful race having greater capacity for love.
—Ellen Key

The Sisters of Mercy, a refreshingly outgoing order, ran Mount De Sales Academy in Macon, Georgia. The location was perfect ... except we soon discovered that the elite boarding academy admitted high-school students only, which left a child of ten out in the cold. Nonetheless, when—out of sheer desperation—Daddy presented his ideal plan to the affable Mother Superior, Sister Mary Elizabeth, she agreed to bend the rules by welcoming me as a part-time boarder. What a coup!

Except ... during Daddy's initial parlor talks, Sister's actions caught me unawares. The impetus of her flirtatious assumptions boosted my brows like twin rockets. Up until now, I had figured that all religious orders were the same, so I couldn't digest this shocking revelation. Actually, it was quite a relief when, on second thought, I disregarded the entire episode and decided to defer judgment.

Since St. Joseph's parochial school was one mile down the hill, Sister Mary Elizabeth suggested that I ride to class with the nuns in their black, chauffeur-driven limo—provided by some wealthy parishioner. Of course, when I recalled the infamous limo back at Cardome (with Ichabod Crane at the wheel), I perked up. Now I'd be a passenger, like Madame—that was, at a cost. It was a fun ride, I'll give it that, but sitting sandwiched among a carload of nuns, suffering from morning migraines (probably caused by wearing those stiffly starched wimples), was about what I expected: awkward. That's why I was glad my boarding would be limited to about two months in early fall and equal time in early spring. In the interim, I'd triumphantly live the cushy life of a regular day student.

To my astonishment, Sister Mary Elizabeth proved to be special. She had a real head for business and, as I witnessed, was afflicted with a great deal of vanity—the unconscious exposure of which made me imagine far more about her than she cared to divulge. Even her unflattering habit couldn't hide her curvy figure. Besides, I had studied Sister long enough to grasp that she cut every corner with style. Definitely, she had a rare quality that made people take notice. What was it?

By hook or crook, I had to find out whether she had showbiz connections, so I investigated with the stick-to-itiveness of a Sherlock Holmes scholar. In no time flat, I concluded that Sister Elizabeth must've been a dancer; she sure moved like one. Her carriage had an indefinable flow—rather unique, especially for a nun. Some smooth detective work on my part verified that she was a close personal friend of Arlene Francis, the sophisticated and impeccably groomed celebrity panelist who appeared on the weekly TV show *What's My Line?* Later in the week, my not-so-wild hunch was substantiated in the activity room. "Miss Francis calls Sister Elizabeth often," a needlepoint-happy freshman confirmed. "They must be related." The young gossiper's friends, lost in their own preoccupations, nodded casually, as if that were common knowledge. So there—our intriguing Mother Superior did have a tangible tie to show business, even if she wasn't actually related to the actress. Although the details of that tidbit remained a mystery, the link had been established. Case closed. Naturally, the discovery made me crowingly proud of my perceptiveness. The whole time, Sister Mary Elizabeth left no room for doubt, for her commitment to her vocation was crystal clear to all who knew her radiance.

In the beginning, I was apprehensive about boarding with high-school girls who were years older, but at the same time, I was so elated with being done with Cardome that I put my worries on the back burner. Mercifully, my concern was unwarranted, because the girls took me under their protective wings from the get-go—and I made certain to behave myself in order to maintain the status quo. I felt grown up being included in all activities (well, except the scheduled proms). Participating on an adult level brought about a new awareness and feelings of acceptance. Therefore, when I returned as a boarder in early spring, the transition was far less agonizing.

Mount De Sales Academy was a multistoried, red-brick structure adorned with ivy—a lovely sight. The building itself had an inviting southern elegance, so my first impression left me aware of how vastly different it was from the intimidating presence of Cardome. Also, a diverse excess of trees, including prized magnolias, decorated the entire woodsy acreage. Georgia's enormous, breathtakingly beautiful magnolias stunned me. Every day, I'd stop to caress their outrageous blossoms, breathing in the lemony fresh scent ever so slowly.

The first semester had been great, but the second semester got even better when I was selected to lead the procession to crown our Blessed Mother "Queen of May." Soon after, the nun who taught homemaking class fitted me for the most beautiful white chiffon dress I had ever laid my eyes on. In time, I learned to crochet, embroider, knit, iron, and even sew a little, as we watched Bishop Fulton J. Sheen, Eddie Fisher and Ed Sullivan on our private TV in the recreation room. We had to complete an item of choice before each grading period. I excelled, surpassing everyone's expectations.

I didn't find the same joy in my piano lessons, which I continued at my parents' insistence. My fingers did just what they had to; anything more was pure drudgery. Further, Sister Lucia's fat, tapping foot interfered with the clicking metronome, and it drove me nuts. So I refused to rehearse until a recital drew near, forcing me to put forth special effort on behalf of my hopeful folks—and my rosary-clutching music teacher.

Local teenage boys caught up in the frustrations of puberty, with their slicked-back hair and harmless line of garbage, would climb the tall, ivy-covered brick wall behind the recreation area every weekend after work. The Brylcreem brigade, who crossed every shade of faith from Christianity to Judaism, balanced themselves on the narrow edge specifically to engage in flirtatious dialogue with their favorite gal—until rebuked by Sister Mary Rowena's tattletale surveillance squad. At night study hall, the aged Sister Rowena paced the floor with enormous energy, fondling patches of wiry facial hair before she went into a lengthy dissertation about Lucifer's knavery. Even if Sister were there to assist students with their homework, who would dare to ask with glad-eyed eagerness? Sister Rowena had her own agenda: making students paranoid over wicked contact with the opposite sex. She acted as if girls could become pregnant by touch, which affected me in a big way. Honest to goodness, while watching her in the throes of her delirium, I sensed that she'd lop off our heads if we didn't obey her doomsday warning: beware of the long-haired ducktails!

The enclosed activity area was lined with graceful weeping willows, towering sycamores, and umbrellalike elms. Lush pecan trees stood majestically against the inner wall that faced the competition-size tennis court. Our plentiful harvest of soft-shelled pecans had students in competition with sharp-whistling birds that continuously dived for discarded leftovers. After school, we'd rest on the weathered benches just so we could watch a brigade of assertive squirrels bobbing about, reckoning with nut-crammed jowls.

The scheduled dances were memorable occasions at Mount De Sales Academy. Every time one would near, I became a Pollyanna who reveled in an emotional high. I would attach myself like a crustacean to Beverly Brady, my favorite senior belle. Mostly, I busied myself by brushing her wavy, chestnut locks, sorting her matching accessories and fluffing out her floor-length pastel gown, which she herself had designed and stitched. Every task was a kick. I gladly volunteered for the job of lowly handmaiden, giving all assignments equal attention. None were considered minuscule or inconsequential. In my estimation, it was an honor to be run ragged. I even served as a courier, skimming stairs and delivering corsages with gusto. In between my draining runs, I'd wash down Snickers bars with icy Coca-Colas to win back some needed stamina.

On the evening of each event, the halls rang with giddy excitement and exhaustive attempts to emerge as flawless as a select Georgia peach. The lovely tulle gowns, swelled with crinolines, flowed as each Cinderella left amid nervous chatter. However confident they seemed, the prom girls were never satisfied that they were pretty enough. They were so wrong! I had spent many hours of the day studying their highly cultured poise and elegant reserve in mum exile—wishing and pretending that someday I too would look as dazzlingly beautiful. When preparations were complete, I'd watch with anticipation as every cascading debutante alighted the spiral staircase to receive the tuxedoed gentleman callers who waited in the front parlor, alongside the bejeweled and watchful statue *The Infant of Prague*. The statue's liquid eyes possessed the room, and once visitors acclimated to his presence, they appeared visibly inspired. The Blessed Infant's regal attire was rotated monthly by a worshipful nun who spent countless hours hand-stitching his vast wardrobe with adoring scrutiny.

*   *   *   *

Plainly, convent life had many downsides. By this time, I had experienced it all, even having my backside lambasted and fingertips jammed at St. Joseph's by Sister Mary Bernadette—notorious for her baton-twirling tactics. For good reason, I called her Sister Bee. Although she accepted my pet name with a dimension of humor, I have no idea if she ever made the connection to her stinging wallops—as I hoped she would. She seemed to soften up back at the convent, when school was not in session ... but this was an illusion, I learned. She must have fooled me into believing she actually had a beating heart. Anyway, I so desperately wanted to identify a single humane trait somewhere on her fossilized frame that I probably invented one out of sheer fantasy.

Sister Bee was ashen faced and tall, built straight like a stalk of celery—invective and reed thin, with narrow, banana-boat feet. And, most appallingly, her odorous spittle slapped across my face whenever she zeroed in, emphasizing her *p*s and *t*s. Honestly, I presupposed she manufactured the foul-smelling spray for further punishment. If anyone tripped Sister's alarm, she'd march full tilt, aggressive as a grizzly. Her crooked finger and mad look directed students to the wretched scullery—for stings in the tail from the vertical thrust of her swift ruler.

One regrettable morning, I raised my hand repeatedly to be excused to the lavatory. Each time Sister Bee refused me, she got angrier. For fear of being clobbered on the head, I gave up the plea until my uncontrollable bladder burst, and I wet my pants. Imagine my hurt. A slight groan escaped my lips as I grappled with the pressure of imminent ridicule. The room was agonizingly noiseless as the flow cascaded onto the wooden floor and flowed, serpentine, down the aisle. A few students cringed involuntarily, but none jeered. I held my breath until blue, resisting the lifesaving need for air—verily unable to partake, as if drowning in the sea. I nearly fainted trying to muffle my crying moans. This was one rare occasion when I wanted to be completely ignored. Only God knew the full extent of my mortification ... St. Joseph's parochial school was coed!

As if such humiliation weren't bad enough, I had a mad crush on two Italian brothers named Ralph and Don Genatasio. The popular, olive-skinned athletes studied downstairs in a higher grade. I was equally smitten with both, not caring which one paid me heed. Egad, I recall feeling somewhat relieved that neither one knew I had a pulse after I found my image literally in the toilet. Of course, my classmates knew that any one of them could be the next scapegoat, so the majority blamed Sister Bee for my mortifying ordeal. Although my need for a shower and change of clothing was reason enough for my crestfallen trek back to Mount De Sales, I'm quite certain sheer punishment was Sister Bee's intent. If so, the joke was on her, for I had prayed for nothing else.

After visiting the restroom in tears, I hobbled the long, barely walkable mile in pee-logged shame—all the while sobbing over my soaked penny loafers and sorely blistered heels, trying to think up ways to reinvent myself. Upon arrival, I blurted out my side of the story to soft-spoken Sister Francis—a much younger, sympathetic nun who was mindful of the consequences of Sister Bee's overdue retirement. Despite good grades prior, I completely lost focus, and my final report card said "Failed" in bold type. I never got over the stigma attached to being held back. To my friends, it didn't seem to matter that much—at least on the surface. But as far as I was concerned, I was destined to remain a scarlet-lettered child for life.

Most kids are phenomenal rebounding wonders, but I'm stymied still by the particulars of that broken-dike trauma. Catholic schools were awash with this sort of anxiety. But there is reason to believe this much: I was also indoctrinated with values that became symbols to which I still cling. Then again, since I had no monopoly of spirit in the schools I attended, I must assume each student was left with varied insight.

*   *   *   *

Since Mommy was due to give birth mid-June of 1951, Daddy thought it advisable for her to stay off the road until after the baby's delivery. Naturally, this was exciting news, so I grudgingly accepted *partial* blame for my bad marks and finished the remaining school days responsibly, while caring for my mom in high glee. At least I wouldn't miss much of my summer holiday, especially if the baby arrived early—in fact, I counted on it. (But what did I know?) On the plus side, Daddy was able to extend the lease on our apartment, which provided a perfect fit for our family. With little prodding, Daddy had agreed to lease a fascinating second-floor apartment from the Leaptrot family for the entire winter. I was living out my lifelong fantasy of residing in an immense three-story home, situated on a picturesque street crowded with stately mansions.

Our sunny-side, one-bedroom suite had a red-brick fireplace inside its lavishly appointed living room. I didn't mind not having a separate bedroom, because I loved the novelty of having my own Murphy double bed that pulled down directly from the living-room wall. And while nodding off to never-never land, I could hear and smell the crackling embers in the fireplace—something I'd never before experienced. The fresh, pale yellow kitchen that opened to a wraparound porch was equipped with a tricky outside pulley used to drop our garbage down to the alleyway. Using it became a fun chore once I got the hang of it.

Seeing as this particular summer was unlike any other, I woke up feeling like a lost soul. Ordinarily, the last day of school triggered my summer furlough to the circus. But now I had to stay put for an inestimable amount of time, while my classmates left for camp or took fun road trips to much cooler mountain homes—a prickly thought, need I say, so any reminder brought me down a notch.

The following weeks were warm, peaceful, and boring. While I'd tried in vain to cast aside the selfish notion of deprivation, I ended up wasting dull time with waning tolerance: kicking stones down the sidewalk, playing jacks, and tracking sailing clouds or runaway kites—heavily dependent upon the extemporaneous for cheer. Sundays were much different—a refreshing diversion, actually. After dark, we'd dine with our special Methodist friends, Pat and Tom Walker, at the fashionable Moose Club, located in downtown Macon. The private entryway at the top of the staircase pointed to a rather plush, windowless room that boasted the best roast beef in the entire state. Moreover, the provocative smell of to-die-for peach cobbler summoned reverent inhalations, even from the highbrow, martini-stoned diners.

Most southerners back then, as decent as I found them to be, were quite comfortable in their prejudices against black skin; even our good friends the Walkers exhibited this racism. Georgians were dead set on protecting their southern customs and weren't about to change old habits. As tradition demanded, blacks had no place in their social pyramid—other than as workers who allowed the white folk to sit back in their rockers and enjoy the pleasantries of life. Although I recognized the wrongness, I cannot claim total innocence. For instance, I drank from those separate water fountains and said nothing; I watched crippled old ladies and blind old men struggle toward the back of the bus—old men and women who were often left standing in plain sight of all too many vacant seats up front—and said nothing. I remember the discrimination, the separate swimming pools, the smiling pickaninny merchandise, and the obtrusive "coloreds not allowed" signs (swinging on chains) outside every eatery there was. Threadbare little black kids played in the street, delivering a string of winded compliments while admiring our sporty Chrysler New Yorker, politely asking if we needed our shoes shined. Then they would follow us in a skip to wherever we were going, saying, "Mammy does ironin' and laundry *cheep*."

I heard and saw for myself how they were portrayed and demeaned and laughed at.

"Negroes can sing, and tap and cook and clean, I'll give 'em that … but drop 'em in water and watch 'em sink, just like a dang Sherman tank. They're plain different from us white folks … different as night and day." This last bit would be punctuated with a snicker.

Yes. I can remember all that, and much more—and simply disliking it was not enough.

*   *   *   *

At dawn, an elderly black woman would proceed down our street, pushing a vegetable and fruit-filled cart. She made little headway as she cried out in lyrical Dixie jive, "Mornin', folks. Strawberries … blueberries … fresh-picked fruit!" Cheered, I'd spring out of bed, dance into my glad rags, and fly aerobically out to her, cash in hand. Even when I offered, she never kept due change, carefully counting every penny back into my hand and making sure my fingers were closed tight. But in compliance with the racial climate of the day, she swiftly moved on, as if it were illegal to engage in any type of small talk with whites.

Because this proud old woman seemed possessed by that hurt, I became all the more determined to win her over. In trying, I was able to read beneath the burning silence of her unvoiced belittlement. For the very first time, I understood what it was like to have the burden of weeping for the kind of freedom I had enjoyed all my life. From then on, I recorded every interaction with her, as though on a mission. As an independent human being earning her own keep, she demanded something better, something finer: a communion with life's basic entitlements and the common birthright courtesies I had taken for granted. Still, her social guard stayed up until I was adequately appraised by the set rules in her suspicious mind. This struck me as particularly sad, so I became fixated on her friendship; with all my young soul, I wanted to be her friend. *Here's my chance,* I told myself, but I really had no hint of what to expect.

After a spell, she freely chuckled at my tales of adventure at the circus and annoyance at St. Joseph's—overly dramatized with mimicking outtakes of Sister Bee's cruel physical intimidation. Before rolling away, she'd always break to inquire about my mother's delicate condition, convincing me wistfully in her delightfully slow southern drawl, "It takes uh-while, dear child. Gospel truth … birthin' sho duz take uh-while."

Sometimes I'd ask if I could help push her cart as she wheeled forward, vocalizing her marketing approach, but she insisted she was healthy and strong and not a bit frail. "Pushin' da heavy cart—y'understand—helps me keep dat way. Gospel truth!" I called her ma'am, never knowing her real name. She called me missy. This remarkable elder was skeleton-thin, with a very long neck that was nicked with scars. Her very long, crooked fingers clutched the cart handle determinedly. A floppy straw hat spared her lovely dark face from the morning sun, and her shabby shoes were cut out on the sides—to relieve a painful corn or bunion, I assumed. I wanted to help solve the problem, but didn't know how to broach the subject without seeming rude.

On one occasion, I worked up the courage to ask if we might help replace her walking shoes. "No child, Looord no," she said, quite emphatically. "Don't you be worrying your little head 'bout that!" I took it her wink excused me for asking. "My feets jus needs the breeze, missy," she confided. "They don't cotton to being closed no mo … soos I don't argue with 'em. Anyways, when ya does as much walkin' as I does, and ya's tired-old as I is, they's the boss. Y'understand my thinkin', little missy?" Ma'am stopped her cart momentarily and smiled broadly, snapping her fingers twice to garner my full attention. "Y'understand what I mean, dear child?" she asked in a coy, fainthearted way. "D' you hear me, sweet thing?"

Obviously, she was referring to a particular story I had repeated so many times—the one about my sore pee-logged hike back to the convent, caused by my hateful teacher, Sister Bee. But what impressed me most was the clever way in which she set me up for the punch line. Her delivery was so perfect, I wondered if she had rehearsed the whole thing beforehand. My nifty lady friend—whose spirit, it seemed, had not grown old—never ceased to amaze me. She had me in stitches until I got full control and coughed out, "Yes, ma'am, I suuurely do!" Amply satisfied by my reaction, she buckled over and slapped her leg … and laughed as I'd never heard her laugh before. Oh goodness me, at last, the seeds I had sown had borne fruit.

Weeks later, on one typically lackadaisical Saturday morn, Mommy and I were taken by speechless surprise. At the very instant the fruit-cart lady accepted a flowered silk shawl gifted by my mother, she (by no coincidence, mind you) waltzed about our tree-lined street seemingly without inhibitions—distinctly regal, as if she were a highbred Ethiopian queen. Perhaps the floor show was her special way of telling us that we were no longer under a cloak of suspicion. Mommy and I waited, our eyes following her in eerie sync as she excelled in fluid native dance—encouraged by a rare, intense moment of artistic self-confidence.

Her feet—what about her feet? I wondered. *How did she do it?* Just then, as if I were standing in Ma'am's shadow, I pictured her speaking with that same all-knowing wink: "No child, Looord no, don't you be worrying your little head 'bout that!" Mommy was as flabbergasted as I was. "That woman is an absolute marvel," she remarked.

Neither one of us could've scarcely foreseen that we would never see her again—ever. For many days, I rapped on every door on the long block, asking if anyone knew her whereabouts. No one did. No one even cared! Beyond doubt, my proud-hearted friend, sealed in memory, had just taught me one of the most meaningful lessons in life: never flee from the responsibility of caring for others less fortunate, for the rewards are great.

$$* \qquad * \qquad * \qquad *$$

Mr. Stork was late. My sister wasn't born until July 6. Hmmm … it seemed the lingering odor of smoky fireworks was portent of things to come. Alas, I was banned from the maternity ward, because I was only eleven—underage, according to hospital guidelines. Regardless, whenever my babysitters, the caring Walkers, offered, I tagged along—only to camp below my mother's room the whole while, blowing kisses from my supposedly germy hands. "Mommy, tell the nurse I scrubbed all over, and I'm not infectious!" I begged.

Even though I knew both Mommy and baby were fine, I felt perturbed at the silly idiosyncrasies of adult reasoning that shut me out of the entire blessed event. However, the day before my mother and new sister's homecoming, Pat Walker looked me square in the eye. "Sugar pie, I'd better warn you," she intoned, leaning into my face in a delicate, ladylike fashion. "Your baby sister has a reeeeeal bad case of the colic, and her cryin' might test ya'll's sanity for a while." Then she pulled back.

Being stubborn, I wouldn't budge until she explained further. So I stood up straight as could be, holding my hands at my side—inordinately interested in what she had to say. After all, I was already half-blind with worry. You see, I'd never heard of this weird colic condition before, so Pat had a problem convincing me it wasn't deadly contagious by breath or touch. While she sorted out a reasonable answer, it dawned on me. Without pause, I posed the one vital question.

"Pat, you said a while … how long is that?"

At first sight, my squealing newborn sister looked so breakable—analogous to a porcelain angel. I couldn't comprehend how her tender little lungs could hold up for long. So, while Mommy catnapped, I stood watch over the crib, wiggling my handpicked supply of scintillating articles. In next to no time, I would trick her into taking at least forty winks. When Daddy phoned, I gave him the latest news about his waiflike daughter, Carin.

"Daddy, she has spider legs, curly blond hair, and a perfectly featured little face—only with a real crabby expression," I said, pausing for effect. "But don't worry, it doesn't matter, 'cause Mommy says her scary look will go away in a few months."

In truth, we never mentioned the bummer—meaning Carin's colic problem, to Daddy.

"Why be a spoiler?" I asked Mommy with grown-up confidence. "He'll know soon enough." She agreed entirely, so that was that!

CHAPTER 15

▼

CHRISTMAS AT THE OLD PLACE

Certain thoughts are prayers.
There are moments when,
whatever be the attitude of the body,
the soul is on its knees.
—Victor Hugo

Every Christmas, we'd drive from Macon to Sarasota for a festive holiday gathering at my grandparents' house; Christmas 1951 was no different. We never missed taking our happy detour to Florida's ultimate attraction, the pristine Silver Springs—if only for the privilege of riding in those fabulous glass-bottom boats. The highway was overrun with billboards advertising various roadside cafés, girlie bars, and native rattlesnake and alligator farms. You name it, they sold it: cypress knees, gator meat, seashells, coconuts, fresh fruit, pecan rolls, guava jelly, and flamingo-pattern bedspreads—hung under moss-covered pine trees. Once, for laughs, we investigated a questionable establishment promoting Big Bruno (the world's largest two-headed bull). Daddy reckoned that head number two must've been engineered, hastily, by some retired carnie hoping to keep a finger in the business.

Traditionally, the circus season began in early spring and usually ended sometime before Thanksgiving. Although Nono and Nona were not entirely retired, they had gotten into the habit of joining the circus a month or so after it hit the road, then heading home at the first sign of fall, so they could get the house in shape and prepare for the holidays. Christmastime was a staged event, held on a grand scale, with fabulous food and mountains of presents under the tree. I was filled with admiration as my favorite aunts, Corky and Ortans, transformed the house into a Christmas wonderland. They took charge, decorating the ceiling-high tree with bubbling lights and old-fashioned, spun-glass angel hair. The fun holidays had me under a spell. The aromatherapeutic blend of live spruce and my grandmother's ever-steaming caffe latte made me weak at the knees. The yummy smell provided the perfect pardon for a biscotti recess in some secluded corner after I assisted my Nona in the kitchen.

Corky, the youngest daughter, was beautiful and slim. She exemplified fine taste and always managed to look ravishing—never ridiculous. In my own view, she wore the tag of a classic thoroughbred on her sleeve. A year earlier, in 1950, Corky married David Budd—a talented abstract painter completely detached from the business. After many years' strife, David was honored with the distin-guished Guggenheim Award in Venice, Italy. April, their only child, was pretty much a loner, often fleeing off into her own creative corner, but never offending anyone.

Corky and my godmother, Ortans, were the closest of the four sisters, and were protective of one another. Petite Ortans, hands down, was the most versatile performer of the four Cristiani girls. Although she had the face of an angel, I was told she was full of the dickens in her social life. But all of that was a mystery to me, so she was nothing other than an angel in my eyes. Following Aunt Louise's dreadful thirty foot fall from the swaying perch-pole act (she and Uncle Daviso performed together) that had left her with a broken back, skilled and fearless Ortans had filled in literally overnight. As the star of the Cristiani acrobatic act, she never got the credit she so richly deserved. Above and beyond, Ortans, not given to jealously, was totally without airs—and therefore never corrupted by the ephemeral limelight of circus celebrity.

Aunt Cosetta, looking sun burnt as a gypsy, was an outstanding tumbler, strong of will and frame, and highly capable of taking the "pants role" of steady-ing her brothers on her muscular shoulders. She was branded the family bully; she bickered incessantly with her siblings with the grit and stamina of a steel-belted tire. Moreover, she wasn't hesitant to box the ears of either gender until they were raw and bloody. Blatantly forward Cosetta ofttimes slung poison-ous accusations at targeted foes—enemies who had been judged and tried, of course, according to her faulty perspective. But my softhearted grandmother always blamed Cosetta's problems on the bad concussion she had suffered at the age of nine, back in Italy, after being thumped on the head by a boat oar.

(Hmmm … I wonder if devilish Daviso was around.) Though Aunt Cosetta was intimidating, with her smooth, loamy voice, her onstage personality was spiked with wit … probably so she wouldn't betray the legendary charm of her ancestry. Her sun-bronzed face was stunning, classically European in richness—the painter's and sculptor's delight.

Aunt Chita, being the oldest of the four sisters and quite beautiful at that, was a remarkable horsewoman in her generation, but I was much too young to track her act, about which everyone raved. It's common knowledge among circus folk that John Ringling North was lovestruck by her regal beauty and showered her with gifts and constant attention. Clearly, they were seeing each other for an indefinite period. Then, in a sudden shift of affection, Aunt Chita married her first cousin, Tripoli. Now I understand that there had been much talk at the time—privately, within the family circle—that Chita's first son may have been fathered by Johnny North. But Chita remained tight-lipped on the subject so out of respect, I suppose, the book was closed. Still and all, the question burns in my mind because the physical resemblance between the two is absolutely stunning— in more ways than one.

On the other hand, I was much more familiar with Aunt Corky's performances. She always set the tone in the big top by flashing her signature "I have arrived" smile. In the minds of many binocular-equipped observers, Corky had the gilded look of a fairy tale ballerina—one who could be photographed from any angle. Second of all, her broad shoulders and petite, short-waisted form guaranteed a camera invasion as she baited a mob of admirers with her photogenic playfulness and coquettish charm. Her femininity was fluid; her figure was akin to that of a dancing figurine made of fine china. Watching her work was a joy, she projected the perfect image of the ultimate enchantress on horseback as she entered the center ring—side-mounted on her favorite bareback horse.

Few were blessed with the total package. Privately, Corky declared a guarded sense of self with a tad of mystery, identifiable even by those who knew her best. Circus fans might wonder if Corky had the Cristiani temper; she did, but less intense. Just like Pete, who was only three years older, she wrapped my grandparents around her finger. Regardless, as the youngest bambina, Corky was given much latitude—after all, my grandparents were acutely aware that she would be the last sibling to join their noble empire. Over ten years later, in her prime bareback riding days, Corky was contracted by MGM to double the ever-popular singer and actress Doris Day in Billy Rose's *Jumbo*. Wise choice, she was perfect. (Incidentally, this 1962 musical extravaganza was choreographed by the multitalented genius, Busby Berkeley. Sadly, this project marked the end of his movie career).

*   *   *   *

As far back as I can remember, my grandparents' house bustled with people. Both were always happy to receive visitors without notice, and would surrender elegantly as their ongoing tide of guests paid respect. When the Cristianis accepted a person as their friend, it was done in totality. From that day forward, they would trust that person almost to a fault, scarcely realizing that some so-called loyalists wouldn't blink if my uncles' pants were aflame. Yet, during the holidays, Nona and Nono's caller-friendly residence—strung with flashing lights, swags of holly (snipped from outside shrubbery), and poinsettia plants set in moss-stained terra-cotta pots—opened its tinseled doors to the world. Not a soul was left hungry. All these niceties and more filled the house with the usual heady Christmas scents that universally make kids dream, laugh, and whistle—and subsequently, ignore persistent pleas to hit the sack early.

To everyone's credit (and by everyone, I mean the Cristiani men in particular), quarrelsome debates desisted with a temporary truce ... unless something unexpected touched off another round of heated debates, in which case all bets were off. In any event, holidaymakers, all looking alike to me, convened daily at the lively compound, presenting bottles of aged wine that suited Nono's epicurean tastes. Tables and counters displayed a succulent cornucopia of hors d'oeuvres, swelling with the prevalent Italian fragrance of rosemary, garlic, and olive oil—and nothing but the best balsamic wine vinegar, made in Nona's hometown of Modena. In fact, the award-winning blend tasted so wonderful that I became addicted to the flavor—so much so that I'd run off and guzzle it straight from the bottle, falling asleep with an ache in my stomach and the occasional aftertaste of regret in my mouth. This was mild mischief ... but once upon a time, on one scorcher of a Florida day, I got the not-so-smart idea to put Nona's listless tabby cat in the icebox, so the poor thing could cool his graying whiskers. Having just consumed more than a few swigs of wine vinegar—which always made me drowsy—I overslept and forgot about the cat. Some while later, when Nona opened the icebox door, the stunned creature screeched out, attaching its frosty claws into the flesh of her tender bosom. *Meee-ouch!*

"*Madonna! Madonna!*" she hollered, looking heavenward. "*Papa, venga subito ... miei povero gatto!* [Papa, come at once ... my poor cat!]" Afterward, when the incident was safely over and my grandparent's were satisfied the cat had survived the trauma, I told the whole guilt-ridden truth of what I had done—in part blaming my "forgetfulness" on Nona's intoxicating wine vinegar.

Although everyone contributed generously to my grandmother's ongoing holiday festivities, few could resist cleaning out my mother's smorgasbord of

Christmas cookies, cakes, and pies. Within seconds of unveiling such an array, my mother was surrounded by a ravenous pack of nieces and nephews, who approached, surreptitiously, with swarming fingers itching for a little larceny.

I tried to forget the bloody stump out by the chicken pen as the Christmas turkey was hoisted to the table, along with sugarcoated ham, roasted duck, antipasto, dreamy risotto, chard gnocchi, and Nona's specialty: rosemary-seasoned quail. My grandmother took great pride in her table, so pilfering even a tiny sample ahead of dinnertime was risky business ... but her grandkids were crafty enough to evade the nip of her reprimanding sneer.

Nona and my aunts had prepared for the feast as least two weeks in advance. As always, the pasta was made from scratch, hand cut, and frozen for meals throughout the holidays. Undeniably, the holidays served to fortify the family link—and yes, every member got involved in the true spirit of yuletide, without the typical family conflict. Ahhh! What a relief!

Visitors probably chuckled at first sight of *Custer's Last Stand*, the larger-than-life oil painting that hung smack-dab on the foyer wall. Frankly, I was forever mystified as to why it hung in such a prominent location. I often stopped to study its morbid landscape—very bloody, I recall, with General Custer about to be scalped by an enraged Indian. Nona loved to barter for collectibles ... however, whether the reproduction had been a real bargain or not was a matter of opinion.

Left of the foyer was a rather curiously decorated parlor—or, more explicitly, an ego-gratifying hangout that offered *some* objects of rare antiquity. However, Nona's happy finds, with the exception of a dandy print of the great Marcellus Coolidge's anthropomorphic art, named *Dogs Playing Poker*, were mostly a queer mixture. The room featured snapshots of the family posing with Esther Williams, George Raft, Wallace Berry, Jimmy Durante, Mae West, Jean Harlow, and many other recognizable actors (but lesser stars by comparison). The antique Victrola that crowned the tall mahogany cabinet played endless arias of *Pagliacci, Puccini*, and *Madame Butterfly* as my grandparents reminisced, their heads elevated in thought. Such music was fine for them, but those depressing melodies were not for me. At that quirky phase in my life, I'd rather have ingested a quart of castor oil than sit through that stretch of misery.

After breakfast, Nono ordinarily retreated to his acre yard to check things out. With the exception of fishing, gardening was his favorite escape. He nursed lemon, tangerine, orange, mango, and pink-grapefruit trees with fond dedication. As expected, my grandfather used a different form of Miracle-Gro: his own mix of ever-so-potent circus fertilizer. And it worked.

When single, Corky and Ortans had occupied the corner bedroom; now it served as a boudoir for the holidays, wherein Nona could be enticed to lend out her cache of gold jewelry. The closet was stuffed with fancy party clothes and fur stoles, plus one uggg-ly mink shoulder wrap—probably conceived by some sicko. How cute … five angry little critters, all smelly-dead, arranged in a row—linked butt to butt, tails floppin', jaws glued shut, and eyeballs gouged out to be reset in glass. Once I got in deep doo-doo for spraying that thing with half a bottle of Corky's eau de cologne. Really, her fury was all about the wasted cologne! Even if the wrap hung unworn after that, Ortans came to my defense by announcing that her genius goddaughter had in fact created the most unique air freshener in town.

Outside Nona's kitchen was an old-fashioned hand pump that drew water from a well. The cool water had the odor of putrefied eggs—though, if left to stand overnight, the yucky smell would disappear completely and ended up tasting pretty good. To the right of the pump, Nono's rusting semitrailer stood unapologetically in the background like a once-admired icon. It happened to be another great escape spot; my active, restless mind enjoyed the time I spent there, pretending I was inside the illustrated pages of a dusty circus storybook about the Cristiani family, traveling through some whimsical land of myth and rhyme.

The old trailer was stuffed with every kind of junk conceivable: discarded harnesses, pulleys, ringcurbs, ropes, poles, rusty teeterboard parts, and all else. Whenever I cracked open the cre-ee-eky, cobwebby door, daylight reflected off the anointed costumes strewn about, emitting a ray of resurrection that danced off the walls. I imagined that I had invaded a mysterious attic filled with over five generations of circus history, and that I had been left wondering what each demoted item would tell, if it could. The paladin appeared to be my grandmother's worthless taxidermy fox, cursed with a pair of shiny eyes that glowed yellow, like traffic lights. For ages, that roach-chewed varmint (frozen in a toothy snarl) patrolled the stowage—while perched on the crimp of an enormous rolled-up canvas ball.

Some time ago, my uncle Pete kidded through his version of the funny tale behind that stuffed fox. "It was me," he boasted. "I shot that murderous fox right after he butchered two of Mama's chickens. But after I nailed my trophy up on the wall, alongside her old boyfriend, General Custer, she threatened me with a knife *this* long. Hell, the little bastard was lucky he even made it to the semitrailer!" My grandmother doted on her gorgeous youngest son, and usually relented to his overaffectionate persuasions. But housing that mummified critter inside her home was taboo, so she wouldn't have any part of it (an amusing inconsistency considering the unfortunate little family of glass-eyed minks hanging in my aunts' closet). Regardless, superstitious Nona held her ground regarding Pete's monkeyshines; otherwise, she rather enjoyed his obsessive teasing and was radiant in his presence.

There was a duality in Pete. You had to learn how to read him. He was full of piss and vinegar and could turn on a dime. Frankly, he flickered somewhere between Godzilla and Prince Charming.

*　　*　　*　　*

It was disheartening when Nono decided to sell the property and move closer to town. As it was, the old place, the home of so many memories, felt safe. Aging Fachini and his wife actually lived in the small cottage located behind the semitrailer. Visiting with him after he exercised his horses around the practice ringcurb fixed on the back lot had always been a treat. Exiting our housebroken quarters was such a sad occasion, especially after the place was emptied out. I mourned for years.

All in all, the move taught me a traumatic lesson: the one certain thing in life is change. "Change" is a scary word for some children, and I suffered for it. Dramatic changes scared the heck out of me, but as a child, I had no say. I suppose my grandparents' relocation represented a timely move, because bordering homes were in decline and ripe for repair; for many, the area had lost its pleasurableness.

The move went slow as snails, as I recall. The house was rented for a year or more, but eventually, the abandoned homestead (guarded only by a flock of loyal egrets) was sold.

I proudly recall the old ring 70547, and the PO Box 105.

Ortans lived next to Nono's new property. Pete and his young family remodeled a place two blocks down the street, while Chita and Cosetta built homes on the opposite side of the old train station. Soon after, they constructed duplex rentals down from Nono's two leased fixer-uppers. And investment-smart Daviso acquired several properties, including prime acreage with a cozy cottage home and rental units on glorious Orange Avenue, near Sarasota Bay. Sightseeing tourists could spot circus contraptions throughout the area: teeterboards, empty lion cages, flying-act and high-wire riggings, practice trapeze bars—and perhaps one or more silver cannons in rehab.

Since the Wallendas and Zacchinis, longtime family friends, lived within hollering distance, cards were dealt well past daylight, or until my Nona could retire happy. My grandmother's inner circle of card-shark friends were the usual peevish bunch. During coffee breaks, the cranky oldsters would rant and rave (with a puzzling amount of energy) over sensitive issues. Finally, in the wee hours, they'd help tidy up and wave good-bye with their jewelry-loaded hands and meaty arms, boasting in Italian, "Nothing gets past us. We're the real circus insiders!"

Everyone cheated! Everyone! But shhh … it's a secret.

Most performers hobnobbed at circus-related events and off-season hangouts, competing in the annual winter sport of dicing one another up into savory bits of gossipy relish. Naturally, they excluded any prospect of error. Besides that, at the bottom of the season, jealous performers were stricken with competition phobia. A predator always loomed large—someone who posed a real threat. Especially feared were performers with similar acts who brainstormed a new theme or routine that outshone someone else's presentation—a familiar workplace jingle. What with one thing or another, ego clashes were shelved for the holidays, replaced with slobbery kisses under the mistletoe and stretchy, boring, sappy anecdotes.

CHAPTER 16

▼

RELATIVE OBSERVATIONS

Every man loves two women;
the one is the creation of his imagination
and the other is not yet born.
—Khalil Gibran

My uncle Pete, the youngest brother, was born exactly twenty years to the day after Daddy. His smooth, baritone voice and other dynamic signatures never failed to command the scene. As an uncle, he was exceptionally generous, affectionate, jovial, and fun to be around. It was obvious to me that Daddy had a soft spot when it came to his baby brother, and I suppose his affection for Pete rubbed off on me. Fortuitously, Pete had won the genetic lottery; he boasted sandy-brown hair, fair skin, an athletic build, and a radiant smile—attributes he bottled, corked, and labeled "catnip for the broads." Sensual masculinity was a basic trait of all the Cristiani men, but my testosterone-driven uncle was riddled with it; he often scripted his devilish quips to make women blush. Pete presented a polarizing figure indeed—women either worshipped him as a God or hated him for kissing them off. Of this I'll give him credit: Pete was an incurable prankster not a braggart—all the same, his flippant attitude toward women in general suggested that he might be showing off, just a little. Babes were not just a passionate sideline; they were part of Pete's daily menu. Life in the shoes of the youngest Cristiani stud had its rewards: the girls swarmed.

In business, Pete was a tough turkey: he ran on empty and never burned out. What's more, he expected his employees to do likewise. If not, he'd pounce like a junkyard dog, often firing out sharp appraisals with a direct underlying message that rattled teeth or brains, depending on the level of harebrained behavior. Pete's language was unique in that he had a shocking way of driving in the nail—which, by the way, did not transfer over to the rest of the family. His indulgent siblings never denied that he could be downright ruthless and totally irreverent in the wise-guy Italian tradition, but said little more. When their favored kid brother behaved appallingly, they mostly looked the other way. Behind all the artifice, they saw him as more of a prankster than anything else—one who'd sacrifice all to guard his kin. This assessment was accurate enough, but Pete kept that part under wraps, preferring to bask in his villainous "chew 'em up, spit 'em out" reputation. Although not exactly primed for the College of Cardinals, Pete was a fairly committed churchgoing Catholic ... off-season, that is. In traditional mafioso custom, Pete dressed to kill for every funeral.

It was the talk of circusdom when, in 1950, Pete up and married his mentor's smart and sassy daughter, Norma Davenport. Norma's father, Ben, a hopeless skirt chaser himself, owned the notorious Dailey Bros. Circus. Ben Davenport was a stocky, square-jawed mercenary who could digest railroad spikes for breakfast and never suffer for it. He was hawkish and dogged—the ultimate flimflam showman who could sell a mouse a ticket to a cat show. Beneath Ben's bristly brows was a face of unabashed confidence—implying that he could take the world, if he wanted it. As the master of schlock art, Ben ran his show with an "anything goes" style. The sizable Dailey Bros. railroad circus encouraged lascivious play. The show itself was infiltrated with pocketknife-carrying thugs, unsavory grifters, drag queens, and kowtowing cronies.

Seasonally, Ben hired a mixed-race line of suitcase-ready harlots from local red-light brothels to satisfy the male needs of those under his employ—all of whom were keenly aware of their indebtedness to the master and therefore understood that they might be asked to return the favor down the road. If double-crossed, Ben would attack with hard-core one-liners that grabbed hostile attention pronto—driven in with a knockout smack in the jaw of the sorry hombre who had wronged him. When necessary, Ben would fraternize with his worst enemy in a cool, manipulative manner—then strike like a spitting cobra at the very arse he had so cunningly cavorted with. Sinister yarns were rampant, including rumors of Ben running down office thieves with a semi and later warehousing their decomposed cadavers in stored canvas spools at his Gonzales, Texas, winter quarters. Strangely, the cajoling slicker was a congenial man, his darker side notwithstanding.

Ever armed with aggressive flirtation, Ben was fairly branded for his womanizing and salacious tone—which impressed the same handpicked buddies who shared his "go for the jugular" philosophy. His loyal cult of true believers regarded him as some kind of sacred monster who best championed their "screw him before he screws you" creed. Others looked at him with half-vexed adoration—unable to escape the wicked tug of Ben's intoxicating he-man charm, regardless of his begrudged prosperity.

However, when caught at his own game, Ben was hard to pity. Compassion for one in league with the devil didn't seem right to some individuals with a conscience. On the other hand, it's only fair to point out that Ben's fire-and-brimstone upbringing had been so brutally enforced that he totally blacked out his childhood. At any rate, he demonstrated a softer side when it came to his much-loved daughter, Norma—a redeeming side in direct contradiction to the Ben Davenport everyone thought they knew. Only on rare occasions did Ben slip out of character to recall (with much acidity) the extent of religious abuse he had suffered as a child. Objectively, I contend that Ben's reluctance to live by the golden rule is self-explanatory.

Norma's mother, Eva, had been convent-reared, with no intentions of enlisting. A glib fox in negotiation, she had escaped through a window at sixteen only to return to her parent's medicine show and ended up rich from trading and hawking elixirs in gypsy guise—under the alias Princess Iola. Charitable Eva happened to be an easy touch for anyone in need, so she had a forest of friends in the industry. Her precocious little girl was a genuine trouper—and already a bit of a showbiz sage at seven, having performed in some capacity from a wee age. Though long separated, Ben and Eva were never legally divorced. Having never lost the genuine love and respect they felt for one another, they remained lifelong confidents and appeared most content when fusing over their only child together—the bonding jewel in their relationship.

Tawny-skinned Norma had exotic good looks. She appeared poised and casually garbed (tastefully, nothing too fancy), and her naturally golden face inspired envy. Her ability to slip into surprisingly intimate conversation slowed men with double takes. It would doubtless be an understatement to say that Aunt Norma grew up on the wild side. To be sure, she knew all the ropes and was no fool to Pete's antics—but she worshipped him and never strayed. The controversial couple managed the concessions on the Cristiani Bros. Circus with innovative minds and boundless energy. Even so, Norma, who could hold hard liquor better than most men, never lost sight of Pete and kept one eye on "the swarm."

Above all else, both Pete and Norma were known to be affectionate, hands-on parents. Their curly-top kids—son, Tony, and daughters Eva and Desi—were exquisite looking. They resembled tiny cherubs dropped down from a Michelangelo ceiling. As parents, Pete and Norma excelled. As husband and wife, they lived under a roof of phenomenal pressure. Eventually, Pete's scandalous womanizing and Norma's obsessive drinking flooded the gates of privacy and became fare for gossip fiends.

My godfather, Mogador handled bookings, advance ticket sales, and supervised the publicity mostly on the smaller dates. He was handsome like the rest, quietly reserved, and poker-faced in business. These traits were combined with a bright visionary mind, off-the-wall humor ... and gambling fever. Conclusively, he was classy, polished, and cool.

Jane was his wife, and together, they had three children, all girls: Valintina, Linda, and Laura. As a performer, Jane was fit, competent, and versatile. I'd describe her as having an adorable Kewpie-doll look—curt hint of a nose, full lips, pouty mouth, and curly, almost-black locks. Both Jane and her sister-in-law, Norma, battled severe alcoholism. It's puzzling to everyone that they were even able to function under its hazy influence, but they did—though Jane's bipolar swings worsened the problem. As it turned out, these swings created a core of imbalance in her marriage, and since Mogador only drank socially, the pair often mixed like oil and water.

Even though my mischievous Auntie Mame, an appropriate nickname, was a singularly strong and caring person, her raucous nature either raised brows or left people incensed with red-faced laughter. If life didn't go Jane's way (and it usually didn't), she was prone to brazen flare-ups. Specifically, whenever Jane had issues— major issues—she reacted with the brooding sadness of a spoiled child and hit the bottle. At least once that I know of, she bathed her half-naked body in vodka at a strip-poker game in the women's dressing tent, then boogied into the wee hours, along with a few boozing musicians, concessionaires, and scumbag performers— until rescued by some sober pal (who, in this instance, knew to keep his or her mouth shut). Ultimately, Jane's drinking problem—which was passed down from her alcoholic father, who'd hanged himself in jail when she was a small child— made her increasingly blind to Mogador's needs, which may well have robbed both of a healthy atmosphere in which they could redefine their relationship.

*   *   *   *

In many ways, the Cristianis were no different from any other charged Italian family. That ethnic climate negated my Norwegian side. Even my full-blooded Norwegian mother became half Italian; however, she refused to give up the other half. I was a member of a focused, ambitious family preoccupied with the business that gave them status. They had style; they walked with a swagger; and, though sometimes misled, they were never pushed around. Unwavering rebels, the Cristianis isolated themselves by choice. Illogically, they never exactly fit into the stereotypical circus-performer mold—therefore, they belonged to no specific group exclusively.

From my unique perch, I had been offered a wild ride by virtue of birth. Most regrettably, I made no contribution whatsoever to my family's success or fame; their status was just something wonderful I was able to enjoy, shoulder high. Putting aside the many faults all human beings have, I'm secure that my aunts and uncles had a sensitivity and devotion that ran deep, though often veiled. Each showed their affection in different ways—some more, some less.

Four Cristiani cousins remain comrades to this day. We were the first set; therefore, we can recall the good years, when the Cristianis were still in full reign. Though poles apart in every respect, we hardly argued. My two older cousins, close in age, are Antoinette (Louise and Daviso's daughter) and Baleine (June and Lucio's son), called Chris; my younger cousin is Mona Lisa (Ruth and Belmonte's daughter), nicknamed Tina. And, of course, there is me.

Naturally blond and knockout beautiful, Antoinette was such a gifted pianist that she could've played professionally. She was that good. While pursuing a fine-arts degree at Wesleyan College in Macon, Georgia, she dropped out of class and left for New York City to follow her dream of becoming an actress. Talent alone bought her way into the elite Actor's Studio, where she studied method acting with master coach Lee Strasberg. While Antoinette, whom I adored, was mostly even-tempered, she had a wildly headstrong personality—and, in my opinion, derived much joy from being a maverick, sometimes to the point of conflict. Moreover, my articulate cousin wasn't a carbon copy of anyone I ever knew: loyal, deeply complex, and frightfully outrageous.

Daviso had an unusual ability to connect with kids, and he sought quality time with his nieces and nephews. Plagued by a failed marriage to Antoinette's mother, Louise, that tore his family apart, Daviso continued his life with hidden feelings we will never know. There was a mystery in his eyes that made one mindful of past scars. From what I gather, after they formed a breathtaking perch-pole act—their greatest triumph—Daviso and Louise's matrimonial venture turned abruptly sour. Louise herself, a fine and lovely aerialist of German descent, worked at dizzying heights atop a thirty-foot sway pole, balanced on the brawny shoulders of her husband. Even near the end of her performing days, gutsy Louise, a legendary star in her own right, continued working her death-defying single-trapeze act with the elegance of a swan. By all appearances, she soared to the crest of the big top with no fear of danger, and hoodwinking the crowd into blissful ignorance of the negatives in her personal life. On the ground, however,

Louise was emotionally wired—in part due to her embittered marriage. And due to her complicated childhood, Louise battled a range of personalities that burst forth in various degrees. But I often observed a touchingly compassionate side of her that, regretfully, was smothered by the ravages of a woman scorned. The torturous stress she and my uncle engendered eventually fostered barriers in their once-coveted relationship. Although, strangely, I do believe that even their lame level of fulfillment sustained their sanity until their relationship got way out of hand. Daviso, not without fault (and regularly pestered by women), was also coated with layers of complexity. All too many years, he stayed trapped between two emotions: passionate love for his two children and a rupturing desire to be free.

I loved Chris more like a brother than a cousin. I enshrined his total makeup, every tender quality. My selfless cousin was unusually bright and uninterested in following his father's path. Instead, he steered his academic mind and business sense in other directions. While I shadowed him regularly enough to be considered a pest, I know he loved me back. His father, Lucio, was philosophical and charismatic, with a closet full of guises.

Lucio never settled into the temper of one persona, yet his conversations were rarely absent of witticisms—upon which he almost seemed dependent. The brothers gave Lucio much slack in his business decisions as general manager; some of his calls were right on, and some weren't. Growing up, I detected a certain distance in his affections that (I prefer to believe) even he was unaware of. Because I somehow understood that his coolness was never intentional, I accepted that circumstance without malice. For unknown reasons, Lucio's marriage to Aunt June lacked warmth. And, if I'd dared to delve a bit deeper, perhaps I would have discovered that Lucio shielded himself from that of which he felt most deprived. Like many gifted souls unable to cope with the highs of performing genius and destructive, intangible lows, he seemed to take comfort in solitude, preferring to keep his personal troubles from those closest to him.

Young June, who wasn't at all afraid of bruises, sought the widest possible knowledge regarding the circus. She participated in every production number possible, finally earning a part in the very tough Cristiani riding act. But the fact that June was a resolute mold-breaker, with no limitations, caused many problems down the road. As expected, she was never content in the traditional woman's role, so the germs of resentment multiplied—along with the level of her involvement in the very touchy matter of family business.

My dear cousin Chris worshipped his father, ever proud of Lucio's artistic achievements. But until very late in life, Lucio was helpless to give his son the love he so desperately needed.

My younger cousin, Tina, was a genuine horse lover. A gorgeous little darling from birth, Tina had been blessed with an ivory complexion, a circumspect smile, and a generous mane of chestnut hair—and beautiful eyes, dark as Nona's espresso coffee. However, I'm reminded that she often appeared sad, displaying the pout of a misplaced fairy—although she was never a bit awkward, and she rarely misbehaved. Her father, Belmonte, though offhand about his looks, was drop-dead, movie-star handsome—and though he had every reason to brag, incredibly talented as he was, there wasn't a swank bone in his body. He had a way with people and connected with them instantly; he put everyone at ease with a genuine, fraternal touch.

Tina's mother, Ruth, a classic New Orleans beauty, fell hopelessly in love with Belmonte—but not with circus life. I theorize her mind-set stemmed from her mélange of weird neuroses. Germs were her worst enemy. She couldn't handle even the thought of germs—especially nasty animal germs—which incited her sanitization of all things to an irksome degree. On necessary treks across the lot, she would tiptoe around any suspicious source of microorganisms. Then, seemingly without volition, she would jump back, outstretching both arms in defense, as if fending off an invisible foe hosting the bubonic plague. Aunt Ruth, as I saw it, took pleasure in obsessing—playing the misfit. And, since traveling aggravated her condition, she preferred to remain holed up inside her germfree Sarasota home (situated conveniently near the hospital), where she spent the humid Florida days working crossword puzzles, testing uncontaminated city water, and dousing mosquito bites with prescribed solutions before they turned septic.

Meanwhile, girdled by an inundation of devoted suitors, Belmonte hardly missed a day polishing his routine between shows, clad in a very revealing French-cut swimsuit. After his intense workout, he generally cooled off in the grandstand alongside one of his beautiful showgirl admirers. Naturally, Ruth did what she could, but nothing could salvage the soured remains of her unworkable (though time-hallowed) marriage.

Sadly, marital problems were begging to surface, not only for Lucio and Daviso, but also for Belmonte. By the mid-fifties, the waters were being tested (with caution), but it was clear that permanent separations were inevitable. Fully aware of the situation, I'd stir in midnight darkness and envision my cousins' dreadful apprehensions as they lay rigid in beds of torment. The bad state of affairs made me as vulnerable as a spring leaflet. I lived in constant fear that the slightest uncivil word between my folks might turn my stable home topsy-turvy, making me the latest divorce victim. Although neither of my parents warranted suspicion of infidelity, I couldn't exclude the prospect. Daddy was a Cristiani, after all, and since Mommy more or less favored the exploratory path of a flamethrowing free spirit, an isolated affair had to be in the realm of possibility. Regardless, here and now, I might as well announce, to anybody who might find joy in producing shocking evidence of such a tryst ... for what it's worth today, I couldn't care less.

Let it be said that the Cristianis' philandering escapades were never, by any stretch, nefariously motivated. Not for one minute were they proud of their guilty pleasure. But the fans' hot pursuit made their fixation all the worse, thus furthering familial furor. The men had an intrinsic weakness for women—plural. *That* was their monkey! When obvious adulterous favoritism got in the way of family business, as it often did, all hell broke loose. Although I often looked at my uncles' philandering actions with a disapproving eye, I loved each and every one, individually, for different reasons and in special ways. And so, as their loyal niece, I wouldn't permit an ill word about any of my relatives in my presence—ever.

One day, expressly for those not yet born, I'd like to have this supplemental tag inscribed on their epitaph: *These skillful riders were known to be notorious, skirt-tailing desperadoes and incorrigible mischief-makers—forever toying with the feminine heart.*

CHAPTER 17

▼

A NEW VENTURE

The highest and the most lofty trees
have the most reason to dread the thunder.
—Charles Rollin

The King-Cristiani relationship ended in 1953. Multiple factors contributed to this breakup, but the decision to split came midseason, shortly after my uncles smelled a rat in the ticket wagon—the root of evil, where the money flowed. As in any business, such disputes had to be worked out, but the Cristianis were already planning their next move—only now, their entrepreneurial aim was much higher. Although discord was obvious to outsiders, total unanimity regarding their goal generated a behind-the-scenes ambitious solidarity that had the Cristianis salivating in the hunt like a nest of spiders, looking to spin the fabric of their next enterprise with a common thread.

Emboldened by a string of incredibly successful seasons with Floyd King, the brothers congregated regularly at Nono's Sarasota roundtable—examining a gamut of exhilarating ideas over pasta and red wine. The Cristianis were never a family who lent much time to sitting back on past laurels—even if, during the past five seasons, they'd never experienced the anguish of a vacant seat. Overall, the brothers were proud at this point, but not boastful. In a way no dolt can overlook, they hungered for the greater, unforgotten vision of total independence ... one that had never really deserted them.

Looking to a bright future, both personally and professionally, the Cristianis purchased new homes, pricey automobiles, and investment properties, all in the heart of Sarasota's unique white-sand community. Daddy even seriously considered placing a fair bid for the old Lynn Hotel, an ailing, low-rent facility smack in the downtown district. The hotel's need for extensive renovation could be discounted somewhat, for the repairs were such that they could have been proportioned over a suitable period. Backing out of this prime real-estate transaction was one of Daddy's lifelong regrets.

Feeling a little too invincible that winter, I suppose, might've clouded the Cristianis' business sense ... but who's to say? After computing a hellish row of digits, the budget-conscious men ended up biting at the wrong bait (within weeks after the final King/Cristiani breakup). God almighty, they hooked up with Big Bob Stevens, an ill-mannered character who never failed to leave his calling card of cathartic wizardry at every turn. My perception of the man was that of a slick, uncouth, nose-picking promoter—in whom my family misplaced a degree of trust. Mr. Stevens was to book an outdoor circus designed to play ballpark stadiums or various other outdoor arenas. With reservations, the idea seemed a clever angle, and supposedly the new "Bailey and Cristiani Bros. Circus" outdoor concept originated from this cost-saving premise. Not unlike most promoters, the baggage Mr. Stevens brought to the table was little more than the idea itself—together with his inflated reputation of racking up a healthy profit by filling the stands with free-spending circusgoers.

Although they were confident, the Cristianis knew that starting over would be difficult. The headline circus-news attracted promoters, like Mr. Stevens, who sugarcoated his proposal with the guile of a Venus flytrap during haggles with Floyd King. The elimination of the exorbitant cost of purchasing a new big top sealed the deal, so to speak, and ultimately swayed favor of a buyout. Gossip relative to this new enterprise was circus-tabloid dessert. The Cristianis felt that if Stevens was as adept as reputed, they could easily stay in the black.

Meanwhile, back in Macon, Mr. King and his new partner, Arnold Maley, prepared for the next season. Mr. Maley had been the office manager on the King-Cristiani circus for the entire span of the partnership. He was a pleasant-bellied, middle-aged man with falling cheeks and spidery wrinkles who in my opinion operated under the facade of honesty. Apparently, Arnold and his matronly wife, Esma, had a penchant for a self-indulgent lifestyle. The childless couple's ascent from humble means to prominence surfaced conspicuously after season one: brand-new Cadillac, designer garments, fine jewelry—the whole lot! Once, when I mentioned to Daddy that Mr. Maley must be very rich, he just smiled ... strangely.

Apparently, Mr. Maley's fastidious wife, Esma, being a beneficiary of the profits, had knowledge of the tomfoolery act taking place twice daily inside the front office—while the brothers stayed occupied supervising the show and screwing around, hitting on gals who hit on them. Although the signs all but plastered my babe-oriented uncles in the face, business was great. Why rock the boat? Privately, the heat was on—and no one liked being duped. Take into account that back then, credit cards were basically nonexistent, so dunes of hard cash collected faster than dust in old Tombstone ... but an untold amount went directly into the pockets of opportunistic slimeballs out for their own gain. Money rolled in and money rolled out as each date struck it rich. By all indications, Arnold Maley (freighted with every gimmick in the scoundrel's guidebook) had a hand in it. It's my contention that, by the time family members gathered to compute the figures, Mr. Maley had somehow managed to pigeonhole enough money to finance his bargain with Mr. King. Sure enough, he was confronted, but the sleight of hand was impossible to prove. Consequently, *the* jackass—with startling luck— had escaped the barn.

Here it should be noted that the Cristianis could and should be vilified on many issues—nevertheless, they'd always earned their money the hard way. I'm comfortable with this notion: if the Macon-based enterprise had included old man King, the Cristianis, and a reasonably honest front-office staff, the partnership would have continued years longer without too much hassle. In retrospect, I believe that everyone could have enjoyed a cushioned ride—blessed with lasting success befitting the ethical exchange of those involved.

Ironically, the King-Maley partnership collapsed in record time, ending in bankruptcy. Within months, Floyd King (a decent man overall) and Esma Maley were struck with degenerating health. As for old Arnold Maley ... well, he landed another office job with some carnival, where I'm inclined to believe he played at the game he was best at until he passed on.

Shortly after the deal with Mr. Stevens (a deal the brothers hoped and prayed would work), problems increased exponentially. Sooner rather than later, the long-term image was mentally axed—with a sigh of relief. Reasons were evident from day one, but the Cristianis' sudden realization that they had been sweet-talked into bankrolling this reckless venture took an ugly form. The brothers bared saber teeth tout de suite—not a good sign, even for humans! Alas, the debates began; it was tragicomic, sort of. Used! Bamboozled! Suckered! The family wanted out, but knew better than anybody that they could ill afford a hasty breakup. (Ironically, bad judgment clobbered both Mr. King and the Cristianis alike.)

Naturally, egos were bruised and, though my family was far from broke, months of scanty crowds had siphoned off a good chunk of their well-cushioned bank accounts. In hindsight, the outdoor show had been a dumb mistake. The brothers allowed themselves to be slimed in a willy-nilly direction that stripped the varnish off their pride. The Cristianis detested mediocrity, so they pledged to return to the colossal blue big top of their dreams, whatever the cost. But at present, they had a puzzle to solve: how to get out of this helluva mess!

I've always bought into the theory that *some* good comes out of every bad experience. As it was, the single atoning decision that directly resulted from that windy relationship matured into a significant drama—a drama destined to inscribe a unique chapter in the archives of the American circus: the unprecedented Alaskan odyssey. This was one slice of history no one wanted to forget. Whatever occurred up to then helped the brothers realize that, even though Bob Stevens would officially remain in the equation, the Alaskan tour would definitely mark the end of their alliance. Mr. Stevens may not have been fully aware of the situation, but that was his problem. The Cristianis' anger at having been dumbly dazzled by the supposed economic perks of Bob's canvasless proposal turned the tide against him.

Energized by the temper of strategic thinking, the idea of touring Alaska climbed skyward. What power our imaginations hold! Although the brothers agreed solidly in principle, the unanswered questions were mind-boggling. Never before had even one circus dared undertake such a risky enterprise—and since the devil lies in the details, the baby steps toward preparedness evolved into a logistic nightmare. Uncle Mogador debated the subject, vigorously, with knotted temples and sound logic. "Granted, Alaska is a visionary leap," he reasoned, "but if it brings home the gold, the tour could be a lucrative bailout, offloading our debt."

Lucio, riled over the family's declining fortune, stood up in his normal macho posture and emptied his pockets of loose change. "Good point, brother! Maybe I'll get my roll back." Contempt for failure made everybody a little crazy. Mired by indecision, they trudged through a complicated maze of impossibilities until solutions inched forward. Murphy's Law, which states that if something can go wrong, it will, became the Cristianis' eleventh commandment; consequently, the convoy was trimmed to a bare minimum. Everyone agreed with Mogador's plan: mechanic trucks would be interspersed intermittently between a maximum of fifteen trucks—plus the Zacchini cannon, and maybe twenty cars and trailers. Reasonably, heavy equipment and animals were to be mounted on flatbed railcars at Laramie, Wyoming, for the 1,485-mile journey to Dawson Creek, British Columbia. All were in agreement that the advance crew should fly directly to Anchorage, except for one volunteer who would follow behind the caravan— basically for tracking noteworthy publicity.

Everything was coming together nicely. That is, everything except the still-unsolved elephant dilemma. "Let's address the elephant situation," Daddy fretted. "The stakes are high!"

There was no easy way to transport our five elephants on this forbidding odyssey … and no easy way to make provisions to leave them behind. The science behind Daddy's agonizing decision was that the herd would be much safer traveling with us, remaining under his personal supervision. The news rid our publicity agent of gray hairs. "A circus can hardly be called a circus without elephants. I'm relieved as hell!" he said with jubilant bounce. "They'll bedazzle the Eskimos and prove a spectacular draw."

What an unerring statement!

*　　　*　　　*　　　*

While the riveting topic of Alaska was tossed around the Sarasota quarters all winter long, I was enrolled at the Academy of the Holy Names, on scenic Bayshore Boulevard in Tampa, Florida. In Tampa, life was better than good. After completely shedding the nagging awkwardness of adolescence, I was on a productive roll—feeling very grown up at fourteen—empowered by that unstoppable force indicative of the dawn of womanhood.

Further, all the do-or-die personal issues that loomed before this precariously balanced stage of youth were negotiated with few traumas, chiefly because of the softhearted wisdom of my favorite teacher, Sister Joan Theresa—and the companionship of a wonderfully bright and stimulating class of students at Holy Names. Though gone are the days, this chapter brings clear and dear memories of my semiprivate room, which faced sparkling Tampa Bay. From my command of view, I pondered my forthcoming Alaskan adventure, as well as the silhouetted backdrop that opened a portal to the most amazing summer of my life.

CHAPTER 18

▼

THE GREAT ALASKA TOUR

Eternity is in love with the productions of time.
—William Blake

Long before the circus opened its doors the Cristianis won the admiration and friendship of all Alaskans: Admiration for their courage in such a gigantic undertaking and friendship for the warm and congenial spirit in their relations with local residents. Alaskans are going to accept the circus people into their hearts like long absent members of the family. From now on, the Cristianis will be full-fledged members of an exclusive and somewhat mysterious fraternity of Alaskans.

—*Anchorage Daily Times* (July 7, 1954)

Intricate plans for the great Alaskan tour were in place by late spring 1954. Our journey up to the land of the midnight sun, the enchanting territory where night and day coexist, remains *the* most treasured story of all. That the pure memory of that historic event chokes me up even now is truer than true.

We arrived in Dawson Creek barely in time to see the colorful convoy of circus trucks roll off the rust-stained, flatbed railcars. The day was dismal, I recall, because the sun chose to retreat permanently after playing hide-and-seek with a reluctant sky. Drivers appeared skeptical as they gazed into the haze-hung distance of the wild and forbidding Alcan Highway. Of course, breakdowns and

blowouts were inevitable, but every engine had been completely overhauled and tuned to brave the brunt of the unapologetic wilderness.

Every person involved knew the untold risks—that danger lurked around every bend. Surprisingly, we tackled the Alcan in a most impractical style. Our brand-new car had impractical white leather seats and air-conditioning that flowed through clear plastic tubes extending from the rear corners. The year had been chaotic; Daddy had had no way of knowing we'd be heading for the rough Alaskan territory at the time he traded his sporty Chrysler New Yorker for this stunning 1954 powder-blue and white Cadillac DeVille.

We spent two great nights in Dawson Creek, a storybook town with evocative remnants of past days. Sure thing, I expected to meet Sergeant Preston in the flesh (straddled atop his horse, Rex) with his faithful dog, King, trailing behind. Our comfy attic rooms overlooked a crowd of dutiful citizens busy shoveling the muddy street for the pending parade. The newlywed innkeepers treated us like celebrities as soon as we told them we were with the circus. Their extraordinarily large mutt lay at the base of a stone hearth, worrying a meatless bone. Even though trusted voices activated his bushy tail, his drowsy eyes stayed camouflaged under a shaggy mass of fur thick enough to keep him warm in the worst snowstorm.

Nothing short of a catastrophic setback could keep the Cristianis from fulfilling their promise to the cooperative Canadians. Enthused merchants had been assured of one scaled-down performance before sundown, so the rangers got busy posting the schedule for an inquisitive crowd, equally obsessed by the details of our operation. Merchants, being experts on the dangers of the Alcan route, told disturbing tales, but they only meant to warn us.

"Few mistakes go unpunished," one tall and skinny clerk advised Daddy, after expressing the absurdity of anybody traveling these parts in such a fancy vehicle. "If ya wander from the Alcan, you'll soon wish ya hadn't."

Next, some tobacco-spitting character—who'd missed hitting Daddy's shoe by a hair—offered his two cents. "And cover up outdoors. Exposin' a body to Alaska's bug society could turn nasty. They're part vampire! Some of 'em buggers actually survived the ages by the nifty trick of keeping their blood from freezin' over. Best sleep with one eye open, 'cause our party-lovin' skeeters celebrate the season by lunchin' on the veins of any creature within reach."

∗   ∗   ∗   ∗

Finally, on July 1, we had the wherewithal to tackle the barely passable road on an adventure that proved to be the envy of anyone with a palate for the unknown. It was a testing, rutted journey between Laramie, Wyoming, and Anchorage—approximately 3,085 miles. Most notably, the 1,522 miles of the meandering Alcan (known in military circles as "the road that stopped the Japs") had been neglected and really all but forgotten since shortly after World War II. Consequently, the gravel road had badly deteriorated. It was a minefield of gigantic potholes, made worse by the hammering force of frequent downpours.

My father, a zealous history buff, had read that President Roosevelt gave true life to the Alcan after ordering hasty maneuvers to 10,607 troops in a race against time. In actual fact, 3,695 of these amazingly fit and competent men were black soldiers from the Ninety-Fifth Engineer Regiment. The troops only learned of their (top-secret) historic mission—which was to carve out a ribbonlike track from Dawson Creek to Fairbanks, Alaska—minutes after departing by train to an unknown destination. Many underprivileged southern black soldiers—housed in miserable segregated quarters—sacrificed their lives to complete the assignment in eight months, despite extremely cold temperatures known to plunge as low as minus forty degrees Fahrenheit.

I took in an eerie sight, watching our convoy trudging up this legendary highway at such an uneven pace while sucking in clouds of dust and airborne debris. The great fear of abandonment was ever present. Nevertheless, everybody had full trust in our competent mechanics, who faithfully policed the rain-splashed highway. A popped hood signaled anything gone wrong: broken axles, overheated engines, and untold blowouts. A hood would fly open about every twenty miles or so up the lonesome trail. It was *not* a trip for whiners!

When Daddy stopped to investigate problems, he was barely noticed by show mechanics as they tooled through smoking-hot motors with tar-black faces, on less than an hour's sleep, with their noisy stomachs hurting from their shrinking stockpile of tasteless canned food. Rest stops were planned ahead of time so animals could be fed, watered, and exercised. It was a sight to behold as the grateful creatures stretched their limbs to the limit while passing choral exchanges of relief. By the look of it, they enjoyed bathing in the eternal drizzle the most, especially if the wind was still. We'd gather in an emotional reunion, exchanging driving tips and a wealth of sightings that included distant glaciers dating back thirteen million years.

The spectacular, snow-capped mountains exuded an implied calmness—effectively veiling the treachery of careering elements that stalked our caravan. The mountains were in fact the draw of everyone's attention; they instilled a sense of exhilaration, and of soaring above the roof of the world. Lovely wildflowers carpeted the flatlands, and ghostly gorges knifed the mist, electrifying our senses.

The magnificent scenery had such an impact on me that, even when napping, I stayed dimly conscious of its splendor. My mind retains imprints of a wonderfully inviting log-cabin café, gas station, and grocery combined. It blended into the surrounding shield of glacial calm. A cool, gurgling stream ran furiously behind a small wooden lean-to, only adding to its serene beauty.

"Look, Mom! Look how beautiful!" I was in such awe that I almost whispered.

"It's *all* beautiful," she replied, savoring the view as if it were only a dream.

Yes, everything *was* startlingly beautiful—seemingly incorruptible and at rest.

Not surprisingly, the fast-running stream was alive with plump and healthy rainbow trout. From my plane of view, the crystal-clear water thrashed about the assortment of smooth, mineral-shaded rocks held captive against its flow. Salivating fish lovers watched from the elevated rear porch, pointing to the unlucky pod netted for the grill. A few sporting workingmen carried sugarcane fishing poles and took pictures before releasing their prize catches back in the stream. With no refrigeration or cooking resources, it was the thing to do.

As we advanced, the famous bush telegraph communicated with a host of antsy natives who had hiked from far and near. The dropped airplane messages kept residents informed of the convoy's latest station, so they could position themselves well in advance. Caribou, deer, and moose lifted their heads from the verges of grass, but they stood their ground amid the sounds of rumbling trucks and spitting gravel.

My mother, the muncher, hid snacks in every pocket to satisfy sudden hunger attacks. She carried assorted nuts, dried apricots, hard candy—anything that wouldn't spoil. Sketching scenery kept her occupied, and she was mostly unaffected by distractions as she directed her soft-lead pencil across the pad. My vigilant father stayed focused on the gravel road, which often jarred our teeth; his mind worked to anticipate the torrent of obstacles in our remote path. A chilling aura hung.

One late afternoon, my chronic car sickness forced us to investigate what Daddy thought to be a suitable lodge, snugly nestled in a clearing with four or more cabins attached to the right wing. We agreed it was near perfect. As a matter of fact, the cracked-open screen door gave us good reason to believe the owner was nearby, so we spoke loudly on purpose, singing "yoo-hoo" to make our presence known. What else could we do? Anyway, we relaxed the instant Mommy spied an open ledger next to a burning oil lamp (in itself a reassuring clue). After all, who'd dare leave an oil lamp unattended for long? The ledger stated, "Prices are posted on the door. Please leave your cash payment inside the top drawer."

A wealth of moose and antelope heads hung complacently on the walls. Each set of eyes seemed to follow us as we tiptoed in search of someone—anyone at all. I was positive we were being watched, and even Daddy couldn't use his wits to convince me otherwise. An imposing collection of bear rugs decorated the polished floorboards—all preserved in an eternal growl, with heads intact. I'll say they looked alive—a little stoned, maybe, but *alive*. Granted, I always had had a phobia about bears, but I certainly didn't take joy in the sport of killing any animal, bears included. Their senseless execution was a total waste, as far as I was concerned—even if their favorite main course was leg of man! That said, after a quick rug count, I was a goner. *Eeek!* The idea of sleeping alongside the flattened corpses of those predatory creatures almost made me break out in hives. On top of everything else, the lodge was immaculate. So clearly, somebody was caring for the place, whomever he or she may be—owner, clerk, or person in charge. It didn't make sense, but we didn't have much choice but to follow instructions and check ourselves in for the night.

The element of mystery heightened a tad when my father compared his watch to the slowly ticking grandfather clock that stood in the far corner. After noting only a slight variance in time, he made a really strange face—which translated to a spooky assumption that someone might be playing tricks. We never heard a human sound the whole night. Sunrise couldn't come soon enough for me, and when it did finally arrive, my sleep-deprived eyes reacted accordingly. We were out of snacks and starved to death. My little sister, Carin, was the only one who slept like a log. But when I jostled her awake, she was a dragon. Guarding my shins (as usual), I merely pulled her up by her shoulders and gave her the evil eye. She got another look as I wrestled her lanky body out the door, directly toward the safety of our car. And when at last my dad returned from placing his cash payment inside the top drawer, as directed, he split. Oh, yeah: the lamp was still burning oil.

About midmorning, sixty miles or so up the road, we spotted Uncle Daviso's sixteen-wheeler parked off the gravel road. His customized semitrailer had partitioned living quarters, with dual padded stalls in the rear. Since the hood wasn't up, we didn't suspect engine trouble. At first, all seemed in check. Nonetheless, we couldn't just guess—we had to make certain. But as soon as our car pulled alongside his giant tractor, we knew something was wrong. In broad daylight, we caught a glimpse of Daviso's curious profile—wearing a familiar black shirt, collar up as usual. His stare was nebulous as he batted a mad swarm of bloodsucking bugs. My uncle was bitten awfully—so badly I thought he was infected with chicken pox.

"Playboy's gone!" he said. His words were chilling. "See, his tracks go over there."

Daviso went on to say that he'd parked temporarily so the stallion could rest from bracing the bumps. After a tuna-sandwich lunch, short nap, and a shave, he parted the curtains only to detect the horse's busted halter hanging from the hook. While Daviso considered the vast wilderness, his emotions surged from within. As we stood there, he ran both hands through his thick, black hair and paced aimlessly, with head down, in a concerted effort to collect his thoughts.

"Oscar, how can I find Playboy in territory like this?"

We feared the worst: that Playboy, startled by feral beasts, had jerked loose. Or perhaps he had fallen victim to a mother bear or lone cougar and wouldn't be found alive. Back at Dawson, we had heard talk of unapproachable wolf packs, known to lurk in slumps or hollows—ready to charge easy prey. Travelers were told the burly grays were fierce defenders of their spring litter of pups so they lazed around on lookout. We traipsed into the middle of nowhere until Daviso insisted we leave. The trouble was, we were being attacked by the same squadron of kamikaze insects that had driven him to seek cover. They looked weird—otherworldly. I even entertained the notion that we had interrupted a colony of mutant mosquitoes, dumped on Mother Earth by little green aliens in flying saucers. Anyhow, in the space of an hour, Daviso blew inside the next pit stop—hysterically dressed in a box of Band-Aids and making quite a show of kissing the Sacred Heart medal about his neck. My uncle told a shortened version of his story in original witty fashion until he interrupted himself.

"Oscar, Playboy was only looking for excitement. He's a smart stallion ... like me!" Then, as if in pain, he changed the subject. "Marion, got some Camphor Phonic?"

"What was that?" she answered. Mommy, of course, had no idea of what he was saying.

Excitable Daviso then pointed to his bandaged face with both forefingers. "Marion, my *sore*! You know, Camphor Phonic ... for my *sore*!"

Mommy was quick to laugh. "You mean Campho-Phenique. Sure, it's in the car."

Everybody at the station—especially longtime circus troupers who were, for the most part, accustomed to Daviso's classic mispronunciations—stared in amused perplexity. Immediately after, we followed the guffawing gang out the door.

The long, drawn-out decision to transport the elephants to Alaska proved to be priceless. What would we have done without them? They were our blessed saviors—virtual heroes, rescuing every truck and trailer stuck on the lonely artery.

But at a designated stop en route to White Horse, in Yukon Territory, they caused a costly delay. While unloading the elephants for a much-needed water break, a handler was nearly trampled when three of the animals tore out of the trailer and rampaged out of sight. A qualified team of RCMPs (Royal Canadian Mounted Police) combed the territory on horseback for the remainder of the day without luck until a bush pilot spotted the runaway herd wandering near an open plain. Sometime during the gradation of nightfall, while rescue plans were still under way, trumpeting cries and rumbling brush were heard as a number of dappled human shadows scrambled around in the brightness of the moon's rhythm. A millisecond later, the missing pachyderms burst forth from the untamed wilderness—on their own. Ever creatures of habit, the mammals headed straight for the elephant truck in the distance, then sank their trunks deep into the wooden water barrels purposely placed below the loading ramp. After filling up on oats and hay, the herd clambered inside the elephant trailer in quite an orderly fashion, without quarrel. Even the mighty fearless Mounties were astounded by the too-close encounter. In the interim, the volunteers crawled out from behind the brush and headed back to the truck stop to collect their thoughts. Looking as if he'd seen a ghost or two, the grubby, hairy-faced organizer took charge for a quick head count after area volunteers gathered around the bonfire.

"Everybody OK?" he inquired, eyes bugging.

"Yeah, just shook," one husky fellow answered, squaring his shoulders.

Others joked back and forth in a convergence of happy and very relieved voices.

"Hoooo-ly mackerel, those devils can *move!*"

"You can say that again. I need a beer," said another, hard-pressed to keep a straight face. "For starters, gimme a six-pack."

*   *   *   *

The Bailey and Cristiani Bros. Circus (a title acquired at the onset of the Bob Stevens union) arrived at Mulcahy Park, in Anchorage, on July 7—not one day early. We were all covered with scabs and pus-filled sores—and flat out of "Camphor Phonic"! Anchorage was a city hewn out of arid wilderness; the summer's high was sixty degrees, and the low forty-nine. Hundreds of giggly kids took turns carrying buckets of water to our thirsty zoo. Planeloads of natives were scheduled daily to fly directly to Anchorage by special charter—all the way from Bethel, Seward, the Kenai Peninsula, and the Aleutian Islands. Headline news of the circus coming to town had spread over the region well before we set foot in Anchorage.

As circumstances predicted, Carin's third birthday was celebrated one day late, so I rushed to announce her merrymaking party between shows. Shopping for a birthday cake in downtown Anchorage was an awakening. Signs advertising moose, deer, and bear meat hung overhead inside the small markets, where locals usually shopped for household staples. Window-shopping along the creaky walkway broadened my perspective. We could see at once that most Alaskans were rendered hopeful by the day's splendor, for they depended on otherworldly communiqués from Mother Nature—a measure of how basic life was. Alaska was the only place I knew where the landscape seemed as vast as the mountain-anchored sky. It was as if I'd been drop-kicked through the gossamer vapor of the uncultivated Alaskan atmosphere and had actually landed in the fabled world of wonderland.

My mother kept a personal journal, and as best I can remember, the introduction was written during the layoff period right before we left Laramie, Wyoming. "Every incident needs to be recorded," she said in an uncompromising tone. "Who knows—one day we may want to write about this once-in-a-lifetime experience." (Thank you, Mommy!)

Nothing about this region was ordinary. We watched rugged fur trappers balancing six-inch Kodiak bear claws on their foreheads; outback characters right out of the pages of frontier storybooks waged bets on who could launch tobacco spit missiles with enough propulsion to hit the farthest cast-iron spittoon. "Those Alaskan men have to be inventive," Daddy teased. "Circuses don't come to these here parts every day."

*   *   *   *

On July 10, a special parade wound through the streets. The Shrine Oriental Band led the procession, followed by a succession of flatbed trailers decorated with circus stars and clowns. The parade was as much a treat for us as it was for the estimated fifteen thousand Alaskans who welcomed us with tots on their shoulders. Many were clutching war-surplus binoculars, jostling for a prime spot. The *Anchorage Daily News* reported that the circus parade drew the largest crowd Anchorage had ever had. Our elephants, nine in all, drew shrieks as sightseers collided with one another, obviously frightened to death at the sight of the herd of prehistoric mammals.

The antique calliope was a musical conduit of festive energy. Many old-timers had never before eyeballed real live elephants. Screams led to pandemonium in the streets! The mammals wowed the Alaskans' furry moccasins off. We were later informed that an emotional centenarian (accompanied by his tribal family) actually fainted on the spot. Other natives, many of whom were brought to tears, craned their necks like giraffes the instant they spotted the globally famous daredevil Hugo Zacchini (gladly blowing kisses from atop his shiny silver cannon). By all appearances, none intended to risk missing Hugo's 220-foot jump. "See you later, cannonball man!" they shouted.

In increasing numbers, Eskimo families camped on the showground in exquisite native dress. Their happy voices tolled the attainment of long-held dreams, for they loved the circus, and the circus loved them in return. All exhibited sweaters in tribal designs to an exclusive circus clientele. "You like? Stop and buy. We bargain good." In an odd role reversal, they artfully sold seal boots, fur hats, and every ivory trinket imaginable to obliging concessionaires and free-spending performers. To say our circus had a love affair with the endearing Eskimo tribes would be understating the truth. Their fine-lined faces shone with perpetual smiles—smiles that told stories of hardship and joy. Gentleness was their nature. They followed us everywhere, shouting, "We love the circus!" before giving us genuine bear hugs. How marvelous!

The most appealing feature in this barren land had everything to do with its people. In actual fact, Eskimos are a peaceable society—with no apparent earthly ambition except survival. Holding to Alaska's culture reflects their total span of interests.

The journey had had its pitfalls—yet, even the intense exhaling moments were relished in our memories. And when all was said and done, we had the satisfaction of knowing the fruition of our efforts had touched the hearts of every Eskimo. The natives erupted in belly laughs and clapped furiously as the powerful pachyderms paraded in spec, but whenever the mammals lifted their broom-like tails to unload their steamy droppings, the observers couldn't contain themselves.

The youngsters went bananas: "Hold your nose! Hold your nose!"

The elders in the clan locked their heads together and contributed to the hysteria: "How funny! Look at the dung! It's soooo big!" With complete authority, I'm bound to say how humiliating it was to sustain a glamorous pose after sensing that dreaded break … Plop! *Ohhhh noooo!* Believe me, begging for an emergency airlift from those wind-breaking dinosaurs was plain useless. Who'd venture to guess that I was never rescued—not even once?

The instant Hugo Zacchini was ejected from his silver cannon, the Eskimos froze with shock. They could not believe their eyes as they waved away the smoky aftermath. But if they'd only known the inside scoop, they would've had enough belly laughs for life. Hugo (bent with age and well aware his human-cannonball days were numbered) was an eccentric, bohemian character, somewhat lecherous in his old age and engrossed in abstract art. His Tampa, Florida homestead was molded into an art colony strung with statues, wind chimes, and an army of metal objects, all sculptural in shape—all beyond bizarre. He never paid heed to detail, preferring to live in another terrestrial sphere. His once-white leather jumpsuit, which he vowed to use until his (ever on the horizon) retirement, was covered with obvious patches. All of these facts go a long way toward explaining the extent of his idiosyncrasies.

Hugo glued a cheap toupee onto his bald (as a billiard) head before each performance. His tolerance of such an uncomfortable hairpiece was no doubt motivated by the fact that it cushioned his skull from the rotted-out lining of his vintage helmet. Hugo never bothered placing his jet-black toupee properly—or securely, for that matter. Sometimes, after Hugo removed his helmet for his final bow (which signified the show was over), the ragged hairpiece remained inside the helmet. Or, worse, half would be stuck on one side of his freckled head—with the other half flagging upward for a bow of its own. *Hot damn, the old man lost his skull-rug again!* However, none of this nonsense ever annoyed complacent Hugo, who walked offstage with his usual perfunctory statement. "Vel, vhat am I to do? Ve out tof glue!"

Currently, the popular inside joke—referring to the cannon man's final call from his dutiful assistant—was all the rage:

"Hugo, are you ready?"

BOOM!

"Noooooo …"

*   *   *   *

Ben Davenport, who dealt for coin, transported well over a hundred nonpoisonous snakes to tantalize Eskimos for the tour. Obviously, snakes, accustomed to a much warmer climate, couldn't survive in Alaska. Ben saw the novelty of snakes in Alaska as a vein of gold that needed to be mined. His exhibit, which consisted of a tent acrawl with slithery serpents plus a walk-through trailer that advertised a mammoth twenty-eight-foot rock python purchased from a Washington DC zoo, made a fortune. Except … this normally unaggressive reptile, who had arrived just in time for opening via airfreight, was not a happy camper.

The moment he was lifted from the crate, his lashing body knocked the team to the ground.

"Scary … the serpent bit into my boss handler's wrist right off. Blood gushed from his artery like a spouting geyser," Ben affirmed. "The bastard had the mean grip of a pit bull." Ben had bellyached to anybody who'd listen over having to jack up his initial bid for the monster serpent, so maybe a perceptual hunch that the snake would bite the dust before the date was over made him eager to recoup.

Sadly for him, his costly star attraction expired midway through the tour due to a faulty thermostat. Uncle Pete, unaffected by the loss, was cool and philosophical. "It's just a stroke of crapping-out luck," he teased, hoping to get his father-in-law's neck hairs up.

"What say you, Mr. Genius?" Ben barked, flexing his muscles. "Eat the loss?"

This lion of a man reveled in trickery. Ben plopped down on his canvas chair and thought hard. After taking a long drag from his freshly lit cigarette, he had it nailed: "That badass mother might be stone dead, but I'll be damned if I'm goin' to bury him 'til …"

"'Til what?" Pete questioned boldly. "OK, what bullshit idea do you have now?"

Ben collected his men. "Take a seat, guys! Here's sound advice from the General. Better forget walkin' around with the black ass, 'cause I'm inspired. Why in hell must we announce our little problem? Trust me … depriving them Injens is reeeal bad business."

Accordingly, Ben's zookeeper (who wasn't, by inclination, either resourceful or even mildly creative) draped the stiffening reptile around a suspended tree stump inside the glass-enclosed exhibit trailer, while mobs of unsuspecting Eskimos were reverently warned, "This deceptive serpent is in deep hibernation." How deep, they didn't want to know. Whether they felt duped or not, every person who weathered the wait came out laughing their heads off, and so did Ben—all the way to the bank. Having earned a proper burial, the reeking snake was laid to rest by Ben's masked crew on the final day of the tour. So now it seems Alaska has at least one snake … but who will ever know?

*   *   *   *

The engagement in Fairbanks, also sponsored by Shriners was received with equal fanfare at Griffin Field ballpark. The crowded corner café, frequented daily by the entire entourage, exhibited a colossal, snarling Kodiak bear—still looking cocky in his inanimate state. I don't recall his exact dimensions, although his record-breaking size was engraved at the base of the wooden gantry on which he stood. Not forgetting his forelimbs reached out with the longest, most evil claws I had ever seen, I avoided eye contact the whole time.

Unfortunately, rain plagued the entire Fairbanks run, but not one performance was canceled, so as not to disappoint thousands of loyal fans traveling from as far away as Point Barrow to experience a part of circus history. We showed Anchorage at Mulcahy Park about four weeks and Fairbanks three weeks. At the farewell dinner, Shrine members honored Nono with a bronze medal for the Cristiani family's courageous endeavor. The toast, which brought my grandfather to tears, went something like, "Mr. Cristiani, you and your sons have made an enormous contribution to the territory of Alaska and, at the behest of our indebted citizens, you have an open invitation to return anytime you wish."

Mommy's journal had it to the button: "Money-wise, the Great Alaska Tour was only a marginal success after factoring in the danger and fathomless expenses, but the negatives were leavened considerably because our lives were magnificently enriched." The *Anchorage Daily Times* paralleled our expedition with that of Hannibal crossing the Alps with elephants some 2,200 years before. (Kudos for our Caddy—it ran great, not even one blowout. Uncle Lucio's Hudson set the record in that department.)

*   *   *   *

Four years later, on June 30, 1958, news broke that Alaska would join the union as the forty-ninth state. When the Senate voted (overwhelmingly) 64–20, the Cristiani Bros. Circus was already on the road for the 1958 season. Honestly, the opus of that poeticized memory will never leave me. This release, hot off the press, inspired a time-out for quiet reflection, with no small measure of pride for our native friends. After a suspended moment, I imagined the aurora borealis flitting across the arctic night in silent salute to this historic event.

Nono and his sons gathered inside his trailer for a powwow to reminisce about their 1954 Alaskan odyssey. Speaking half in Italian and half in English, they discussed what statehood actually meant in terms of Alaska's economy, and the likelihood of the Cristiani circus returning. Some while later, everybody walked away uplifted, shaking their heads in calm accord, in the more placid climate of a clear and postcard-perfect circus day.

President Eisenhower officially declared Alaska the forty-ninth state on January 3, 1959.

CHAPTER 19

▼

IN THE CLOVER

It's good to have money and the things that money can buy,
but it's good, too, to check up once in a while
and make sure you haven't lost the things that money can't buy.
—Theodore Roosevelt

Diamonds are formed under infernal pressure, and the latest sparkling Cristiani venture was no different. By autumn 1954, Big Bob Stevens was history, and the word "Bailey," which was his bright idea and really meant nothing in the way of a draw, was at last dropped from the circus title. March whipped around our Sarasota winter quarters with spring madness. Daviso's novel idea became reality the instant his ingeniously designed seat wagons (with special emphasis on safety) arrived.

Each and every piece of equipment got the red, white, blue, and gold treatment, and the family crest was scribed on the new Cristiani Bros. Circus stationery. The constant drive of equipment plowed the earth, and the pixie dust of cast-off spangles illuminated the sandy soil—imitating the look of real gold in the glorious wave of Florida sunshine. Many members of the Circus Fan's Association of America visiting our family circus that particular year believed the Cristiani Bros. Circus to be one of the most beautiful big top circuses in America. Consequently, in March of 1956 respected CFA members Hank Fraser and Jack T. Painter formed "The Cristiani Tent."

As I got older, I spent my summer holidays working in the swinging-ladder production number and assisting Daddy in the small elephant act to relieve Mommy. I had never trained to do anything more, because a circus career was absolutely the last thing on my mind—Daddy made sure of that. Frankly, I never considered myself a true circus performer, although I enjoyed the glamour of the business, the animals—and the travel. I wouldn't think of dismissing that!

Venturing along the rural highways with a truck show had many advantages. Certainly, one benefit was the acquaintance of unassuming country folks who spent their evenings watching the golden simplicity of the vanishing sun. In a post-card-inspiring scene, neighboring townspeople gathered on scrubbed porches just to hear the welcome hum of our colorfully painted flotilla of trucks traveling toward the fairgrounds. Normally, flocks of playful tykes would bike alongside the drivers, laughing and gesturing with nods of confounded interest until they plumb tuckered out. Breaking for a home-cooked meal at any family café, situated off a trail that happened to encircle the heart of a farming hamlet, was priceless.

We really loved playing those friendly Mayberry-type towns, with dust-free grassy lots. The patched-up britches of little towhead sidewinders sneaking under the sidewall would catch my granddad's eye. But after hearing their tearful cases, Nono, the gatekeeper, would give each and every penniless rascal a dollar from his metal change box before making his way up to the marquee to greet the horde of regular paying customers. Still worse problems often resurfaced during the late blowoff. Underage teenagers were of course banned from the hoochie-coochie sideshow display, which was risqué by olden-day standards, but in truth was nothing more than bawdy bumps and grinds performed behind the rear canvas divider, which provided due privacy. Our star attraction, self-created Talla Ray, was billed as the only living hermaphrodite. Refusing to put anybody on the spot, I decided to go straight for the dictionary to determine whether the physiological handicap was fact or total malarkey, regardless of the scandalous pictorial-banner: MINI FLASH OF PROOF EXTRA! Fess up ... who wouldn't pay a buck or more to see *that* in a tent?

Talla was a popular figure on the show who never invited trouble. At the same time, she always flaunted her whorish appearance, as if auditioning for a starring role in some raunchy porno flick. "I'm just a barrel of laughs," she (or was it he?) joked, "a tight-assed bitch living inside a man's bod. Looove it! Bitches get away with more shit."

Catching punks, chaperoned merely by a squadron of lightning bugs, was a nightly ordeal. "Hey, Pauly," one kid would say. "You hide out 'til it's clear, then sneak under and tell us what you see!"

"No, maggot brain. If you're so brave ... you go first! I don't believe it anyway."

State and local fines against adult only sideshow acts were especially heavy, if caught breaking age restrictions, so the back sidewall was usually policed. Still, I won't deny that a few thrill-seeking preteens were allowed to slip inside—if only by way of underbelly riffraff or greedy sideshow barkers out to line their pockets. It's a sure bet to say that corrupt troublemakers needed to watch their bare backs or face Cristiani wrath after jeopardizing a possible law-enforcement shutdown. Of course, "making the daily nut" was vital to the cause, so any unanticipated loss of revenue had to be offset at some point in order to stay in the black.

For those not familiar with the term "making the nut," it originated at the turn of the nineteenth century. As the story goes, traveling shows ranging from solo snake-oil salesmen to the grand master of deception himself, P. T. Barnum, and his first full-scale circus, moved strictly by horse-drawn wagons. Most of these shows existed—or ceased to exist—on a cash-only basis. This meant that axel grease, wagon-wheel parts, animal feed, and a list of other general supplies (including life's bare necessities) were purchased with the trust of a handshake. Parties involved agreed up-front that all bills would be paid bright and early, before the show left town. And they were ... most of the time! Inevitably, when show owners were short of funds, they made a habit of sneaking away under the cloak of darkness rather than face hand-cuffs or the angry posse of shotgun-carrying merchants who had been stiffed by the owners' hooligan ways.

Not infrequently, the caravan was forced to flee through fog-filled byways in the midst of flooding rainstorms, which often left everybody marooned in the middle of nowhere. Needless to say, a sturdy and secure wagon wheel was worth its weight in gold. So after putting their heads together for the good of all, the band of disenchanted merchants reached an utterly ingenious and altogether harmless solution. Not wanting to deny hardworking common folk pleasurable entertainment, the merchants agreed to provide traveling shows with critical supplies. But in the bargain, town deputies would remove the axel nut off each and every wagon wheel—until fair debt was satisfied in full. So there you have it: the expression "making the nut" translated to "pay the piper, or else!" Thereafter, skippin' town became nothing more than idle thought.

Most circuses hired at least one official fixer. He was expected to be a sort of legal wiz who could handle all the nagging issues that might require his expertise—such as lawsuits, highway mishaps, insurance claims, lapsed tags, last-minute permits, and so on. Bud Fisher survived as the Cristiani show's fixer for many years. Why? He had the right constitution. Bud wasn't a bad guy overall—quite likable, actually. More significantly, Bud managed to keep the show rolling by ingratiating himself with the police officers; he was never overly pushy (the name of the game). Nonetheless, as I saw it, most show fixers had the same traits of any shyster lawyer you'd expect to see conspiring in some hole-in-the-wall office in Vegas. Though I doubt fewer than few ever passed the bar, I'm afraid they retained job security. By that I mean, "Where in blazes do you unearth these toads?" If you ask me, the beefy windbag schmoozers were as soapy as they come.

Who could forget the hypnotic manner of the steely-eyed sideshow barker pacing across the midway platform? Ward Hall was the master at his trade, he never met his match. His faultless "See it live!" spiel had the worst skeptics reaching for their wallets and pushing their way to the front of the line. Folks bunched together in a trancelike state while he presented the bearded lady, the hooded alligator lady, the fire-eater, the phony one-eyed giant, and the tattooed geek— plus a line of hoochie-coochie dancers, keen to shock the pants off any noticeably starched churchgoers.

Johann Svarfdaelingur Petursson, the 7'6" Icelandic Giant, was my favorite oddity. I never knew anyone as large, kindly, or obliging. His glandular abnormality didn't hinder his shrewd mind; eventually, he turned celebrity into coin in the motel business. Mr. Giant, as I called him, was also a tease. Whenever I'd place my hand over his mammoth palm, he'd scowl down at me and speak loudly enough to make the ground quake: "Vickie, now do you understand why only a fool fools with me?" Rendered speechless and seemingly shrinking to the size of a measly pea, I could only nod affirmatively, showing all the white in my eyes. Rest assured, I got the gist, because this gentle giant was mightier than the cannibal giant in "Jack and the Beanstalk."

The Doll Family, as they were known, gained worldwide attention with Ringling. But decades later, the still-attractive midget family worked in the Cristiani sideshow until full retirement. All four—Harry, Daisy, Gracie, and Tiny— appeared in the original *Wizard of Oz*, starring young Judy Garland. But clever Harry nabbed a feature role as Emerald City's most respected citizen and munchkin spokesperson of Emerald City. Diminutive Mr. Doll grew inches whenever he reiterated (in sordid detail) the backstage scandals on the embroiled *Oz* set— notably tales of the lewd *affaire d'amour* involving the testy, warble-voiced cast. Though always a gentleman, if rubbed the wrong way, Harry would argue with enough attitudinal posture to blow your hat off … and, as the only male in the family, he pretty much ruled the roost in munchkin land. Actually, he enjoyed fame like no other. "Remember, I wasn't a mere amateur actor back then," he cooed. "Before *Oz*, I had star billing in the cult classic *Freaks*." That's no lie! Look him up.

The start of the season was definitely celebrated with fanfare for the colossal blue and gold big top. The tent's newness was protected as long as possible, but even a watchful eye on the fickle spring weather couldn't prevent the sudden materialization of violent storms. Therefore, an old standby tent was kept in reserve to absorb the indignities of the familiar Georgia and Alabama clay that left its rusty imprint on everything it touched. While the Cristiani Bros. Circus upgraded its equipment, a list of other circuses folded. Existing ragbags neglected repairs—cutting back to such an extent that performers were demoralized. In 1956, the Circus Fans Association of America unanimously voted the Cristiani Bros. Circus circus of the year. Lucio proudly boasted, "Thank God—finally, we must be doing something right."

Fairly, because the Ringling show had already abandoned the big top years earlier, the Cristiani Bros. Circus held another prestigious title: the largest tented circus in America. (Circus enthusiasts partially credit the Cristianis for reviving the old-fashioned big top.) Pride was apparent at work and at home. Harking back, survival, much less growth, was an extraordinary feat in that Iron Age. Yet our circus (not so quietly) ascended in the industry to form a nexus of power. While reinvesting profits back into the corporation, the Cristianis were in the clover.

My family's success was the envy of ingrates who had chosen to squat and judge on a personal level—but, at the same time, had no shame in pandering for positions that should have been eliminated long before the storm. Any friends who were down on their luck—especially the usual bunch of fawning performers eager for employment—knew they could play on the brothers' compassion. Many needy workers went to Nono and Nona for favors. However, no one begrudged the hiring of the sophisticated tight-wire star Con Colleano and juggling showman, Massimilliano Truzzi—both beset with health issues. Such dear family friends were guaranteed jobs as long as they needed income.

Atypically, the show's huge generator (or plain light plant in circus terms) ran twenty-four hours, even on multiday stands. This extended privilege established employee comfort, but these policies were a departure from the penny-pinching practices of other circus owners, who reserved certain perks for themselves. The family was extremely sensitive to this issue and strove to please everyone, if at all possible.

The Cristianis were never cheap—something they'd learn to regret. To some extent, their reluctance to cut salaries, when necessary, decreed their fate.

*   *   *   *

The Cristiani Bros. Circus was peopled with a number of characters worth mentioning.

Kilowatt, our assistant generator boss—known for his candor, and no doubt the worst gadfly on the show—looked as if he needed to be dipped in a tub of disinfectant. This nocturnally programmed, jabbery stalk of a man with gangly legs stayed covered in grease 24–7 and would've gone unnoticed in the night if it weren't for the glare of his buttonhole-size eyes. Young Kilowatt, who looked forward to turning twenty-one, reddened ears with his infinite nitpicks … but he whiled away his free time bragging to any straggler willing to listen about the magnitude of his job and the buzzing light plant he called "home sweet home."

Lardo, our gentle, tank-sized waterman, lost weight in the worst way possible. Excess blubber came off when an enraged brown bear ripped his muzzle and made lunch of the replete folds of Lardo's flesh before spec. The sweltering summer heat and the loud water hose may have incited the attack. Lardo was back on the job weeks later, dedicated as always … and fifty pounds lighter.

Ole Otis, a dutiful worker, pounded stakes and rolled canvas onto the spool truck. He slept all day in any shady place he could find—usually under a truck— with his empty wine bottle nearby. Otis operated in slow motion but never missed a setup or tear-down. An aging black man he was; he resembled legendary Uncle Remus, with salt-and-pepper hair and saucer-size, cataract-glazed eyes. This cherished trouper spoke in a metronomic beat and strode jauntily around the lot with a happy sway. He loved telling the story of his humble beginnings, stressing that he had still been wet behind the ears when he left his sharecropper mammy and whippin'-mad pappy and hopped a rail to join some passing minstrel show. His belongings were kept in a handkerchief tied at the end of a stick. "Best thing I did fer myself," he said about the move. "Weren't nothin' fer me at home … jes nothin'." Ole Otis had no interests except the circus, his job, and his wine.

Shaky Paul, a stuttering man who was somewhere in his forties, was a former elephant handler before he switched over to the relatively safer job of pushing souvenirs for Uncle Pete. The reformed alcoholic had been on the wagon ever since he survived a near fatal assault from deadly Alice, the half-blind rogue elephant on the old King-Cristiani show. Boozing around elephants can be lethal: they catch the stink, and they don't have much tolerance for ungovernable behavior. This particular incident happened between shows on hectic July 4—of all days! Shrill elephant cries and siren voices traveled over to the boiling-hot cookhouse tent, sending me under the menagerie sidewall just in time to see berserk Alice swash Paul back and forth like a bloody rag doll. Those arriving, unsure of what to expect, got the shock of their lives: Shaky Paul, presumably, on the threshold of death was loosing consciousness; his limp arms—hugging a fragment of life—pleaded for help in flailing gestures. It was difficult to control the rest of the herd, especially Alice's constant companion, Mona, who, if given half a chance, would've joined in the assault with avenging force. The menagerie exploded in a cacophony of high-pitched jungle sounds ... warning less experienced animal handlers to flee under the sidewall. Notably, Uncle Mogador's swift, courageous actions rescued Paul from Alice's final assault—which, in all likelihood, would have been punctuated by the menacing crash of her head. During the struggle, however, one of Alice's sharp tusks slit Paul's stomach down the middle.

Bystanders, drawn by all the commotion, became ill as particles of entrails spattered all over the place. No matter—Mogador risked his life restraining the mad bull until Paul (looking more dead than alive) was carted off by an ambulance to a nearby hospital for repeated surgeries, which saved his left leg and right arm from amputation. Some unknown show person renamed him Shaky Paul because of his acquired tick and stutter, and it stuck!

Irish, the baboon and monkey keeper, had the hide, gamy odor, and curmudgeonly disposition of a wicked troll. He took exceptional interest in his hostile primates, never venturing far from their cages. As feeding time neared, he evoked shrieks of gladness from the always famished creatures by dangling over-ripe tomatoes, lettuce, and fruit beyond their reach. Soon after the feeding ritual, he'd press his head flush to the bars, mimicking their expressions in an affectionate round of "monkey see, monkey do" that bordered on the bizarre.

Irish had legs that bowed so badly, an overweight pig could tunnel through with room to spare. Two knobby canes supported his truncated four-foot frame as he trekked from place to place. When maddened, the crusty character mouthed a waspish sting of words that was grossly intimidating, so he avoided humans whenever possible. Occasionally, Irish was approachable, but *he* had to pick the subject. If I dared ask anything too private, he'd cut me off midsentence—leaving me with the distinct impression that I'd better wait to hear him out.

"No pryin', girl," he would snap. "Don't never talk 'bout back-home days. Dwellin' on the bad'll get ya trapped—in some confounded cage—jes like all them fool monkeys. Let say me, life started the day I hooked with the circus. Now get ... get!" Even if Irish's condition excused his infernal profanity, he never played the sympathy card. Old-timers who had known him for ages said he joined Ringling early on—aspiring to become assistant caretaker of the infamous acid-disfigured gorilla, Gargantua, and his life mate, Toto.

Did these men change the world? Certainly not! But undoubtedly, a vast majority of our faithful helpers were vital players in their chosen "field of dreams."

Really, as far as I'm concerned, these unforgettable characters should be commended—for they, and many others like them, did make a difference to the world of the circus.

CHAPTER 20

▼

CHICAGO

They say the nightingale pierces his bosom with a thorn
when he sings his love song.
So do we all. How else should we sing?
—Khalil Gibran

Lady Luck smiled on us in the Windy City, and Chicagoans gave our circus a
heartfelt welcome at the lake front (Soldier's Field). The year was 1958, and the
advance sales were off the charts. The publicity was unprecedented, inasmuch as
the entire population of Chicago was aware that the Cristiani Bros. Circus had
arrived for an extended run. The performance was exceptionally strong. As with
most prominent dates, our program was enhanced with a list of circus superstars,
including the great one-of-a-kind clown and family friend, Emmett Kelly.

As lovely Delilah performed high above the center ring at Soldier's Field,
Emmett Kelly's tramp character stood below and pantomimed his tearful concern for her safety—leading one to suppose that this exquisite, unapproachable
creature was the fullest thing in his sad life. The scene painted a poignant portrait
of Delilah's artistry and Kelly's God-given gift to convey his heartfelt affections
to a multitude of fans, who were in turn inspired by his masterful portrayal. His
hobo-painted face shifted with every graceful move, so spectators were forced
to swiftly decide whether to focus on the girl on the flying trapeze or Kelly's
faultless dramatization. The Cristianis loved and respected this intensely private
personality and truly believed that he represented the soul of the circus in the
most beautiful way.

I haven't dwelled on the thought until now, but I should disclose that I was
never an ardent devotee of clowns. I can't say why, exactly. All I know is that,

in my own view, the supremely talented Emmett Kelly (and a select few who nearly made it to the doorstep of his league) was unlike the rest. Perhaps my feelings were influenced by my ability to read the real personalities behind all those painted faces (a gypsy's art); perhaps this sight jaded me along the way. Whatever the case, my thoughts seem to have instinctively settled where they are, so I won't abandon my view; this simple explanation satisfies me best.

Uncle Belmonte, long divorced from his former wife, Ruth, changed his ways before he married Delilah Zacchini (better known as Delia offstage), a member of the Manuel Zacchini cannon-act family. Besides accomplishing much as a (head-balancing) trapeze performer, Delia had somehow managed to beat the competition by taming my physically fit uncle for life. Beneath her opinionated nature, Delia—schooled by her doting German mother—showed the needy dependency of a child, only with a well-rehearsed walk meant to draw full attention to the whip of her man-baiting derriere.

Delia's older and mostly overlooked sister, Flora, had performed the cannon jump until she landed wrong in the net and maimed her arm. After a tiff in which Flora accused her parents of exploiting her for their own gain (the truth, as I saw it), she left the business to become an airline flight attendant and wound up marrying an annoyingly bossy redheaded pilot who scheduled her day down to the last second. While together, Delia and Flora yakked at breakneck pace—the "yeah, right," know-it-all stuff that pricked at my nerves. Their tendency toward bouts of verbal gymnastics was entirely genetic, so attempts to resolve their opinion differences became a dull exercise in futility. At first, the ooh-la-la sisters wrestled over Belmonte's affections. The competition was quite lively, but Delia, at barely eighteen years old, won out. However, I've a hunch my uncle was ingested by his future mother-in-law before he could blink, without ever having a chance for pause.

*   *   *   *

Savvy performers eagerly volunteered for media interviews and events, including me. However, when asked to accompany our feature stunt-trapeze artiste, Gerald Soule, on Jack Eigen's *Chez Show*, I tried to opt out. My excuse, which got me nowhere, was legitimate enough: its legendary host had a reputation for dropping blistering remarks during his live radio talk show, held inside the classy (and purportedly mob-controlled) Chicago nightclub, the Chez Paree. While backstage, I overheard the buzz that my favorite movie queen, the gorgeous Chicago native Kim Novak, had been Eigen's celebrity guest the night before. The technicians were still on cloud nine over her appearance. How intimidating to follow her! Totally feminine Kim Novak (Hollywood's uncommonly voluptuous actress) was the reason I had dared to bleach my hair platinum blond earlier in the year, against my father's wishes. I even copied her classic hairstyle ... but, even though I'd tested every affordable cream, nothing could help me duplicate the look of her utterly flawless porcelain skin.

As soon as we were situated, the steely-eyed host looked us over from top to bottom. After knuckling his nose for an unbearably long moment, he shifted his weight and scooted his chair back. Then Eigen tipped his head slightly forward and asked my prepped partner point-blank, "Where, and *how often*, do you circus people bathe?"

He touched a nerve, all right! In defense, red-faced Gerald (who acted as if he'd been kicked in the groin) came back cleverly, wearing a stiff, deadpan glare. "Do *I* look dirty?" he asked.

For the record, neither one of us had a hygiene problem, nor were we in costume. We were dressed simply, in proper attire for our evening interview. Anyway, Eigen must have admired Gerald's sober comeback, because he moved his chair closer in and laughed heartily along with the roomful of rowdy drinkers. We joined in, mostly out of embarrassment. Don't think for a minute that I wasn't, somewhere inside, dying—but there was no other recourse. Surprisingly, after that "gotcha" abashment, the rather lengthy interview proceeded more gently and ended on a high note, with a great plug for the circus. As usual, wit had saved the hour. Regardless, my fuming companion was less forgiving as he left the club. And when I laughed out my iffy sentiments that Eigan was just doing his routine thing, complete with predictable chutzpah, Gerald slammed back, "The hell he was!"

The next day went much better. I was interviewed on a segment of local TV news. While I waited in the greenroom, a kindly gentleman introduced himself. "Excuse me, are you Miss Cristiani?" he asked politely, in his distinct voice, and I told him I was. Naturally, I felt flattered by the fact that he recognized the Cristiani name. He was enormously friendly and indicated that he knew my uncles Mogador and Belmonte, and that he hoped for a get-together before leaving town. I was thrilled to meet the very recognizable and beloved actor, Burgess Meredith, in such an unexpected way. I think I was blushing the whole time and hoped he hadn't noticed. He kept his promise to visit that same evening and bravely rode my lead elephant in spec. I was pleased to have had a hand in the happy reunion.

My uncles had befriended young Mr. Meredith years earlier, in 1937, while touring California with Al G. Barnes. But Belmonte had renewed his relationship with the actor during military service in 1942, when he was cast as the lead acrobat in the Irving Berlin production *This Is the Army* in Washington DC. As expected, the patriotic extravaganza was a tremendous hit. Rave reviews and national headlines launched a very successful campaign that raised over five million dollars for the emergency-relief fund.

*   *   *   *

The Chicago date was unimaginably glamorous. I remember it well. Kids squeezed in the blue section, leapfrogging over one another for every sold-out show. At dusk, our circus glowed in the cup of Chicago's illuminated hand. And when the cold lake breeze curled over my cheeky grin, it seduced me in an invitingly genteel way until my shivering skin became toasty warm. The bright lights of this magnificent Midwestern metropolis infected us all, but on this full-mooned evening, I was entranced more than ever by both the oneness and the madness of the entire circus scene. I experienced the perfect Cinderella moment as I daydreamed about all the marvelous things a true fairy godmother could bring into my life. My eyes rested on the rippling swells of the big top as it billowed proudly. Then, suddenly, without struggling to find a single word, I recorded the romance in my heart: *There's nothing more beautiful—if you are able to see—no scent as fragrant at night, and no sounds more stirring than the complex whisperings of circus animals set to perform.*

Because the success of the 1958 season was contingent upon revenue earned in major cities, it was difficult to gauge which cutbacks would least deprive circusgoers. To put this into perspective, the family worked hard to enhance the circus experience. The main show was their baby—the Cristiani badge of honor. The brothers were insistent upon preserving the architecture of a large three-ring circus without prostituting the performance.

Yet, despite the joy that came from performing before Chicago's gracious crowds, the laughter was coming to an end. From what we were told, the money earned had better be put to good use, because advance sales for the rest of the season didn't look promising. For that reason alone, we were overcome by underlying sadness and strange melancholy—generated by the all-too-real premonition that times were changing faster than anyone could have imagined. The circus, as we knew it—as millions before us had known it—was slipping away. I could see it in the lackluster eyes of the performers, the crew, and even the animals. The winds of change were swirling, and I had the feeling we were disintegrating in the mammoth tornado.

I watched my father, seated with boxed hands in quiet repose, wearing a mask of impassivity in front of my mother. Though he was doing his best to uphold her "not to worry" philosophy, he failed. In spite of everything, some sort of impetus was at work—an unstoppable spirit driven by nothing more than the common need for survival. Our business outlook was not exactly desperate at this juncture, but privately, there was real cause for concern as the Cristianis meditated on the quagmire of bureaucratic red tape raining down.

It appears to me now that that memorable date in Chicago was pivotal for me. Something strange was happening inside my body. The sexuality bug kept biting me on the neck, so I was experiencing a kind of thrilling wooziness. Naturally, I had changed a great deal from the little pigtailed girl who had been sent off to that isolated Kentucky academy so long ago. I couldn't avoid reflections of myself. When I stood naked, the truth was plain to see. That alone, though I say it myself, was worth dwelling on. After all, I'd matured into a full-busted young woman of eighteen—reaching out for life and kissed with so many dreams that to focus on one would've been a bore. Even if my family were about to do battle with the harbingers of doom, I had real expectations for the future. Regardless, the answers simply weren't there. Although I believed I had many admirable qualities, the knowledge that I'd never excelled in anything up to now presented somewhat of a problem. The harsh realization, I suppose, gave me an excuse to convince myself that I was still finding my way; more or less deciding what to do with my life.

Despite my insecurities, I sensed that something very special or very unusual awaited me. The opportunity to be an effective player in the exciting lap of our family circus and the glamorous city of Chicago had fulfilled more dreams than I deserved. Still, my inner voice told me I had more … many more.

CHAPTER 21

▼

ROLL OUT THE SKY

Oct. 19, 1959—Faked emotions, rigged questions and phony games of chance;
the tangled web of television quiz shows began to unravel today when
Dan Enright gave subpoenaed testimony before Congress.
… Charles Van Doren, a distinguished
Columbia University professor who won $128,000 on "Twenty-One"
did not respond to the invitation to testify before the committee and a
substitute teacher has taken over his classes.
—*The Chronicle of the 20th Century*

New Year's Day dinner of 1959 felt like old times. The business horizon was astir in Sarasota—a stupendous development was in the works. Uncle Mogador had just signed a much-envied contract for the family to star in NBC-TV's pet project, a documentary called *Roll Out the Sky*. We understood that the Polaroid-sponsored Kaleidoscope project, to be narrated by the infamous game-show celebrity Charles Van Doren, would be the network's first videotaped project shot entirely on location. Besides the much needed boost of free nationwide publicity, the idea of being involved in a ground-breaking television event was in and of itself exciting.

Prior to this uplifting news, my family had been living in a house divided. Emotionally, the weather was stormy. Everybody stayed in a foul, werewolf state of hyperawareness—placing ridiculous blame that hit far below the belt. Cataclysmic rifts were unavoidable. Arguments, sometimes over nothing more than "a look," erupted like Mount Vesuvius. This timely contract calmed vaulting moods and crystallized the air overnight. What a transition! The news prompted a string of Sunday get-togethers where family members assembled to toast the probability that the buildup of national publicity could reinforce respectable status—and, therefore, increase chances for a healthy recovery. Once again, the brothers dined at the same table, reasonably respectful of one another. More importantly, they returned to the cultured habit of actually passing the pasta—instead of throwing it. There was a general consensus that this particular windfall could be the right patch to keep their raft afloat—that is, waiting to be saved by yet another miracle.

Bear in mind the present state of affairs: by then, the circus graveyard was full. Soliciting funds for a circus in arrears was next to impossible. Even solvent, heartland-routed animal circuses were hurting, and they were basically traveling zoos that hired mostly fat, has-been performers—all of whom bellied up to the ring, huffing and puffing. Budgetwise, the Cristianis had been taking it on the chin for the sake of the public. No matter, for they had been trained from conception to roll with the punches.

Everyone was pleased with the concept. The script (written by Gene Wyckoff, and to be directed by John Goetz) was designed to chronicle the Cristiani family's history up to the present day—describing the difficulties they faced while preparing their large tented circus to hit the road in uncertain times. Hopefully, the public would learn much about the pressure-cooker atmosphere of the coming season, and at the same time gain knowledge about the Cristiani philosophy, which was lodged in an age-old system of belief. Mr. Van Doren would begin by reviewing the Cristianis' rich and storied past, tracing their achievements from their European genesis up to their current efforts in America. The director intended to capture the men in a din of raised, convivial voices between the regular humming cycles of business and practice at the winter quarters. One segment would be videotaped at Nono and Nona's residence for a lively and *somewhat* realistic reenactment of our quasinormal family life.

The Cristiani homestead had always been the setting for traditional pasta din-ners—the nerve center where the family gathered regularly to engage in typical Italian colloquy. A hint of gladiatorial debate was encouraged to illustrate discussions of family business. No acting classes were needed! After the staged feast, we took a break until the table was cleared. Then the handheld camera followed the younger grandkids as they demonstrated simple acrobatic stunts, while Lucio and Daviso strummed their guitars in the background.

My father and uncles Daviso and Lucio (all born with a special ear for music) were performers by profession, but frustrated musicians by passion. In fact, the talented trio formed a comedy band early on and found success at booking popular basement clubs around Europe for "carousing" pocket money—that is, if food was on the table and Nono gave the nod. (For many years, Daddy kept his gold-plated trumpet handy for the bugle call. There were usually two calls: one for doors and a second call to line up for spec).

The taping was surprisingly fun, with very few hitches because (thank goodness) the confident director, John Goetz, had a special talent for easing anxiety—and, even more importantly, he knew exactly how to get the best performance out of everyone in the cast. Gene Rayburn, the sharp-witted game-show host, was present almost daily—he was affiliated with Polaroid. Mr. Rayburn's hilarious, though slightly off-color perception of our circus lifestyle contributed to the cooperative attitude during the rigorous shooting schedule. His great timing even made Nono laugh. Spontaneous crack-ups were unavoidable, as most dialogue was improvised.

Charles Van Doren, with his lack of pretense, was a hit. His timid demeanor combined with intelligence was a pleasing mixture. Everyone was drawn to this very gracious Ivy League man, including myself. Charles lounged on the cool terrazzo floor in my grandparents' home after hours, sipping espresso while eyeballing oceans of archival circus footage and old photographs. He seemed to catalog every word of the family's colorful, juiced-up tales about traveling the dusty back roads of Europe on their father's wagon-caravan circus.

While ducking Nona's evil eye, my uncles even dared to reveal one or two stories about Nono's promiscuous past, then downplayed their fistfighting history by blaming it on the frequent crossfire of cultural warfare.

One story, which involves my grandfather and the daughter of an archrival gypsy circus owner, must be told. The incident took place in 1925, somewhere in France, when my grandmother was pregnant with Pete. It was hardly a coincidence that Nono parked the Fratelli Cristiani Circus blocks from the next show town. Well past midnight, my father and my uncles Daviso and Lucio ventured into the wooded area to investigate the chorus of jubilant voices, the festive music, and the proverbial bang of tambourines booming from a clearing. Upon identifying the loutish clan of Parisian circus gypsies feasting around the bonfire, the brothers decided to leave well enough alone—until they heard an ominous beastly growl and, at the same time, Nono's "rescue me quick" call as his bottom half dropped down (or rather, tried to) from a wagon window across the way.

Apparently, my grandfather's lover's snapping pet wolf (leashed to the rear wheel) had just enough leeway to swipe at Nono's oh-so-private parts. Since Nona was the only person to nurse his agonizing wounds, nobody could say exactly whose claw mark it was that made my naughty grandfather walk funny for nearly a year. Regardless, I understood that little Pete would've never made it had he not already been in the oven.

*   *   *   *

I only knew Mr. Van Doren as a game-show supercontestant and had little knowledge of his extensive academic background. After researching his scholarly family history, I understood why he was so wide-eyed over my family's history. Although his stable scholastic environment was polar opposite from that of the Cristiani siblings, I could envision a common ground—a patent link that had everything to do with my grandfather's "rule of thumb" philosophy. In my view, Charles Van Doren's own father, Mark Van Doren (the legendary Pulitzer Prize-winning poet, and one time professor of fellow classmates, Thomas Merton and Bob Lax, at Columbia University) had instilled the same unremitting drive for perfection and competition in him. And regardless of the fact that his goals were distinctively contradictory to ours, I've come to believe that Charles Van Doren not only recognized, but rather enjoyed the ironic truth of it all: that he *was* raised in similar fashion.

When the production wrapped, the director seemed pleased with what he had in the can, as he put it, and he openly expressed his gratitude. All in all, it was a fun shoot. Consequently, the videotaping proved to be the one therapeutic break everyone had hoped for. Although old age had gradually slowed my Nono down, he never lost focus. After we voiced our good-byes, he raised both hands for effect and commanded everyone to concentrate on the more serious business of the day: "*Andiamo!* Back to work!"

Preparing to open took priority, but we left Sarasota with a gleeful understanding that this promotional vehicle was the season's trump card. Before the special aired on May 3, Mogador received word from his NBC contact in New York City that they had a winner. Anxiety mounted, and we were practically assured that there would be a rerun, which would provide another round of free publicity. When the telecast debuted, everyone was elated. Once again, the Cristianis had reason to celebrate.

The fact that NBC was happy with the shoot felt great. The project's success established our faith that possibly a follow-up or even future projects could be in the works ... but the optimism didn't last. Everything seemed to be going so great, so we didn't have a clue about what the future held. Besides, Charles appeared totally relaxed and hadn't shown a single sign of stress—so who would've guessed the trouble he was in? I suppose, the instant the bombshell (having to do with Charles Van Doren's credibility) became public, the network VIPs had no choice but to wipe his image off the television screen.

Consequently, the successful Kaleidoscope documentary that had given the Cristianis such a lift was among the casualties. So much for that windfall; however, what difference it would have made in the scheme of things is anybody's call. Advance sales for the once hopeful 1959 season were already falling way short of its mark. Thrown into immediate despondency, the Cristiani family circled the wagons in a last-ditch effort to seize the moment and come up with an alternative plan.

The Van Doren scandal quickly impregnated the airwaves. The nation was stunned. Producer Dan Enright had eight shows on the air, and now he was the person sitting in the hot seat! The carefully woven facade was unraveling overnight. All the adulation Charles had enjoyed from his $128,000 winnings on *Twenty-One* came to a screeching halt. His once irreproachable reputation was sullied beyond repair. Obviously, his followers couldn't hide their bitterness and feelings of betrayal. Charles Van Doren became a haunted figure, living with the knowledge that every household in America felt trounced by his reckless slip. The global stigma attached to this particular game-show scandal changed the history of television.

The entire episode was personally painful for the Cristianis. We had spent weeks getting to know this seemingly upstanding person, and the tenet of his involvement in such a scandal was inconceivable. As a group, the family had a great deal of empathy for him and the ruinous hit that invaded his life. However, there was no denying that he had willingly participated in the hoax.

Yet, my initial perception was that Mr. Van Doren had been victimized—fooled into believing connivers had honest intentions. Entrapment with no way out! According to Freudian psychology, we all have an id—an inner idiot that sometimes overrides wisdom (not to mention out-and-out common sense). For that reason alone, it's easy to imagine that even someone with the cerebral clout of a Columbia professor could indeed be had by network vipers. Sure, he should've been wise to the game-show charade, but it appeared to me that socially timid Charles was a hittable fellow. From what I could gather, he had the gentleness of a fawn, along with a measure of vulnerability that was noticeably exposed. Evidently, game-show executives had another opinion of the man in the soundproof box—arrogant and greedy, if you will—but quite honestly, we never saw that side.

As expected, the press followed Charles around until he finally broke from the pressure and admitted the crime. But saddest of all, the front-page headlines almost brought down his principled New England family as well—bang, like a shot between the eyes. After his public confession, Charles was so emotionally crippled by his reckless sojourn into show business that he went into permanent exile. I wish he hadn't, for we all shelter an Achilles' heel to some degree. Charles Van Doren was no different. His upbringing had carried heavy burdens, forcing him to vie in a nest of academic superachievers. I've often thought, and very reasonably so, that maybe he hadn't been lured by the money at all, but rather, a lack of recognition within the Van Doren family circle. Perhaps that need had propelled his deception. I for one wasted far too much time in life trying to measure up and went on with the mistaken notion of what made me happy. Perhaps lack of recognition was my Achilles' heel as well. Contrary to what the general public was lead to believe, Charles never stopped teaching in the familiar domain of advanced education. For my part, I don't think the felled quiz show media magnet could have survived without that option—and, the solid support of his family and straight-thinking wife, Gerry (who opposed her husband's participation from day one).

*   *   *   *

After Charles Van Doren left the Sarasota area, we had some correspondence over a short period … but, understandably, it ceased. Meanwhile, the Cristianis were inundated with real problems of their own, so laughs were hard to come by. And frankly, no one felt like telling jokes. The Cristiani Bros. Circus was on life support, and the nearly critical situation had to be dealt with as such. Beyond that, the Cristiani siblings had been cobbled together since birth—shepherded in one direction. In addition, they were staring old age in the face and were traumatized by the idea that their lives were about to be inverted evermore. The foretelling lyrics in the old Judy Garland song, "Better Luck Next Time," rang true. This cognition posed a knee-jerking question at the close of one somber family confrontation. My uncle Lucio summoned my feisty grandfather, who was still clearheaded in his eighties, and spoke to him in Italian, with all the fight in his heart. "Papa," he said, struggling to interject more of a positive tone in order to camouflage the extent of his concern. "It's not what *can* we do … but what *must* we do?"

After a moment of stillness, Nono, being a man of few words, looked at each of his sons lovingly. "*Lo alzo la mano,*" he said in a strong voice. "*L'unione fa la forza!* [I raise my hand. In union, there is strength!]" His faults meant nothing to me; there was never a time that I didn't feel privileged to be called Papa Cristiani's granddaughter.

Metaphorically speaking, the Cristianis had to suck the poison from the wound before it put them six feet under. Vultures were circling while persistent rumormongers whetted their appetites; the jaw-dropping cowards were already dive-bombing, eager to nibble at the edges of the Cristiani Bros. Circus obituary. Heads were counted. The vile predators were identified from miles away, and the brothers refused to pander or shake their clammy claws.

At long last, with the family think tank in high gear, the men agreed on a practical plan and doable timetable. Most appropriately, they pushed aside the very thought of failure; victory was paramount. Nothing else mattered but achieving their goal, which was to defy the odds of survival. The Cristianis weren't about to throw in the towel just yet. Regardless, the rapidly changing world predicted more difficult and uncertain times ahead for this determined circus family, who was fraught with mounting debt. At this point in time, neither circumstances nor youth was on their side.

CHAPTER 22

▼

WEST COAST HOPE

When you reach the end of what you should know,
you will be at the beginning of what you should sense.
—Khalil Gibran

An exhaustive fight for survival was under way by midseason 1959. The circus was poised in battle mode for a very promising agenda that included several plausible and attractive options. Nono and his sons borrowed all they could borrow on show assets and, as a last resort, mortgaged their personal nest eggs of real estate holdings in order to meet their crucial objective. By a long shot, their plan offered no guarantee—on the contrary. The family was relying on the gamblers' luck of the draw. Nerves were frayed; the course bared them to the bone.

The Cristianis declared their alert readiness, barring no expense in delivering that razzle-dazzle element to expectant LA crowds—hooked by the intoxicating octane of their old-fashioned blue and gold big top, designed to enchant the child within us all.

First-rate promoter, Tom Parker, thank heaven, (a true professional who had promoted most of the Cristiani show's major dates in past years) came to the rescue. There was absolutely no one in the business better prepared to promote major circus dates than longtime family friend, Tom Parker. He knew precisely what needed to be done and could be trusted to handle the job with utmost class. With the help of our powerful *Hadassah* sponsors, Mr. Parker prescheduled as many promo spots as possible: Our clown spokesperson (former school teacher) Tom Kelly was set to appear on *The Art Linkletter Show*, (Mexican aerial cloud swing star) Manuel Barragan, agreed to plug the show on *Truth or Consequences*, and plans were made for the Cristiani elephants to empress viewers on the *The Dick Clark show.*

Up with the arc lights! On with the show!

The future, after all, was dependent on California—especially the gem of the western tour, Los Angeles. Once the torch was lit, so to speak, magic reappeared with meteoric splendor. The strategy after Los Angeles was logical: downsize to build revenue while playing moderately populated California towns, then snake down the southern route to Sarasota—hopefully with a stash of money to last the winter. The Cristiani Bros. Circus (sponsored by the Hadassah Women's Organization) was set to deliver, so the best available center-ring acts were contracted for LA only. During our necessary break in Texas, show painters were given the green light to restore the colorful lettering on every piece of equipment—to make darn sure our forty-truck fleet would be candy to the eyes of spectators as our battle with destiny got under way. If we lost, no one could say the Cristianis yielded the sword.

Upon arrival in Los Angeles, the pace accelerated to a scary heart-attack speed. Finally, our mammoth big top—enlarged with rented sections—was spectacularly sited in the midst of the Pan-Pacific Auditorium's asphalt parking lot. In our heart of hearts, we felt we were engaged in a worthwhile struggle. Thanks to the precise calculations of big-top boss and overall superintendent Bill Hill, the Cristiani Bros. Circus looked fabulous ... quite magnificent in silhouette against the famed backdrop of the glamorous Hollywood jungle.

My mom and eight-year-old sister, Carin, were due to fly home after the opening to make ready for school. Mommy, poised to spring into action herself, wanted to stick around to witness the outpouring of energy behind this mother of dramas. At that time, I was a stereotypical teenager in the sense that I either woke up riding a wave of optimism or faced the day trapped in the deep, dark trenches of despondency; there was no in-between. Here, I did what any sensible girl would normally do on those rare walkin' tall days: I erased the word "defeat" from my vocabulary, knowing it would surely wreck my emotional high. Regardless, I appealed for divine intervention: *We need a triumphant win, Lord, and we need it now!*

Magic filtered through the California sunlight, and as the golden rays settled on the big top, they kindled a warm glow that surrounded the area. Astonishingly, the entire circus lot became infatuated with its own stardom. Uncle Mogador, fighting for composure but nonetheless smug in his conviction, revisited the front door to emphasize the importance of professional courtesy before Nono's ticket takers opened the floodgates under the marquee. He made it by a hair; sleep deprivation had him ready to ignite like coals in the grate. Tick, tock!

Spectators jammed the midway, attuned, with money in hand; they rushed between menagerie and sideshow, sampled cotton candy, and ignored the sugary web stuck on their clothes. I can still appreciate the particular look of those smiley-faced kids carried on the shoulders of an enchanted multitude—busy skirting around quarter poles, ropes, wires, and other trappings just to see circus performers defy logic and gravity.

Momentarily, the warmth of some very dear memories transported me back in time. I felt like an excitable child again, dealing with the same stomach butterflies I had had before leaving Cardome for my summer vacation on the Cole Bros. Circus. I visualized my former classmate, Jenny, washed in sunlight, and looking just as I'd last seen her. She separated herself from the crowd, moving closer frame by frame, then finally becoming smaller and receding in slow, cinematic motion—all the while beckoning me to recognize her familiar face. Back in first grade, our talks had often revolved around how much I wanted her to see me perform. Somehow, it struck me as funny that, even now, I yearned for dear Jenny to give in to a whim of her curious mind, just so she could physically experience the thrill of my circus world. Yet, before her picture dissolved—as phantom images always do—I shut all else out and enjoyed her sweet pleasure. If only she could appear for real on this glorious opening day, I'd christen her grand empress of the circus—worthy of royal treatment, held high in the midst of a phantasmagoria of sounds, lights, and sequined motion for the next fantastical hours. She'd be mobbed by adoring fans, all of whom would give a king's ransom for her autograph. Imagine!

The rubber man, alligator lady, soothsayer, sword swallower, pinman, and tattooed snake charmer mesmerized the addicted assembly from the sideshow platform. Queen Carlos, the fire-eater with repulsive gasoline and taco breath, dripped with hexing Santeria amulets, overawing the throng of squeamish patrons with his vulgar, effeminate gyrations while he danced barefoot on a pile of filed-down broken glass.

"Look at that weirdo! He's crazy as a loon."

"Wait, it's got to be trickery!"

"Oh no, it's real!"

The golden sun, which threw its beams every which way, was fixed directly above us, in a cloudless sky that stretched to infinity. The crowd stood in awe; the vibrations coming from Charlie Roark, the sideshow manager and pitchman, produced a novel form of behavior— permitting their vulnerabilities to be exposed. Mumbo-jumbo and hocus-pocus is fun for a day. Come one, come all!

Abracadabra: a legion of fans, skeptics, and die-hard disbelievers arrived as one, primed to be swallowed up willingly—even those *least* likely to be carried away by emotion. That was circus day in LA—the way I remember it, the way I loved it.

*   *   *   *

Ole Otis and his men walked the track, checking this and that—and every measure of ground—for debris. Belmonte grabbed the microphone. "Doors! Doors! Packed for both shows!" Lucio gave the ushers explicit instructions not to seat kids on the track until after the electrifying trick-riding presentation. Guests stampeded into the big top, clambering for the perfect panoptic view. A strange type of childlike lunacy manifested itself throughout the audience, revealing their liberated side as they temporarily freed themselves from the bondage of structured behavior. Laughter and merriment were audible, blending melodiously with the tinseled sound of the calliope. Candy butchers worked the stands at a feverish pace.

The flavor was pure circus, and the taste was grand.

On some incidental errand to the concession stand, I had no trouble recognizing George Sanders, the exceptional and notoriously pompous English actor (once married to the ageless Hungarian beauty Zsa Zsa Gabor), looking rather debonair and quite tall, standing beside the marquee—seductively framing my form with a come-hither look as I wiggled by wearing short shorts. I deliberately recorded his lecherous gaze out of the corner of my eye and nearly stumbled over my own feet trying to suppress a bigheaded smile. I remember mouthing these very words: "This is way too cool, Miss Smartypants!"

California weather lived up to its reputation as if it felt obligated, aware of the weighty role it played in this frantic drama. The stars were out, too, at least figuratively speaking; for David and Ricky Nelson, of *Ozzie and Harriet* TV fame, the lot became home. Few knew that circus blood came from the former Harriet Hilliard's side of the family. Consequently, the heartthrob brothers had grown up with a spray of circus magic and yearned to observe its wonder from the inside out. Only, most refreshingly, they wished to be treated just like regular guys, unmoved by the idea of celebrity. As everybody saw it, they hadn't been miscast in their role of ordinary circus employee, for they did appear awkward living within the artificial warmth of Hollywood's ecosystem.

Superstar Lucille Ball brought her two children, Luci and Desi. They charmingly befriended Pete and Norma's son, Tony, who was their age. Friendly Tony, who'd never missed an episode of *I Love Lucy*, had a dynamic personality, much like his dad, so he gave one of America's most adored families the grand tour. Tony must've made a fine impression, because he was invited to the gracious comedienne's home for the weekend.

Gilbert Roland, the handsome matinee idol from another era, arrived early to pay respects to his old mustached lookalike friend, Uncle Daviso. Mr. Roland scanned the grounds with commanding visage—still looking every bit the star, for his rugged manliness shone through his weather-ridden face. The Latin lover's appealing squint (matching that of Clint Eastwood's) could still raise temperatures. James Garner, who crashed the back door in western attire, was perhaps fresh off the set of his TV series, *Maverick*. An admirer of this modest Oklahoma charmer, I spied through a slit in the dressing tent and swooned.

Beneath the canvas sky, the woodsy smell of fresh sawdust, raked to perfection, greeted our guests as they perused the advertising banners that bordered the hippodrome track. Propmen, suffering nicotine fits, engaged in verbal quibble. The long jump over the sweltering desert, coupled with the mad vein of LA traffic, had put them in a state of near collapse. Iron-jaw Jake, our openly gay, hobbit-size prop boss, was also a frustrated drill sergeant. Outwardly cool but trembling inside, he told his travel-fatigued team that they'd better be shaved, clean, and sober before doors, or they were dead meat.

"Attention, you pissants," he commanded, "I'll ax ya once, so use your empty heads. Howsever ya wants ta do it, get it done! This is D-day—the troops is landing. Oscar says hard ground, so shit, triple the sawdust and lock them ringcurbs tight. Oh, fat mystery here, Reggie's unglued 'cause he's missin' a couple of them flyin'-act stakes. Big Slick Valentine, the catcher, says they best be found, or my ass is grass. If that's the case, soooo is yours! Let's say you smart college grads dig 'em up in half a shake."

"Yes, sir. We're on it!"

Iron-jaw Jake, who made a habit of stacking rubber lifts inside his army boots to appear taller, reached down and rearranged himself before he hitched his pants and squealed, "Teee-riffic!" But after he studied his notepad, he called out, "More shit, guys. Better tie back them stray guy wires. Don't forget! Hear that good-lookin' Okie trick-rider dude really hauls ass."

Bandleader Ramon Escorsia swayed with the lively tempo while his fine group of musicians played on with resounding impact—all looking sleek in gold-corded hats and double-breasted, gold-buttoned uniforms. Red curtains decorated every bar rail in the house. To borrow a direct quote from Fred Pfening Jr., the honorable Circus Historical Society president, "The Cristianis had the most innovative and comfortable reserved seating in the history of the circus." Bright red nylon seats and backrests were framed in lightweight aluminum, then combined in easy-to-fold sections of three.

My father, known as a manqué organizer under the big top, avoided small talk when engaged. Nothing was more important than the business at hand; every detail had the signature of that "special Cristiani touch," and it showed. Basically, the family had a natural flair for melding European and American customs, which assured each and every guest that they were welcomed into a privileged magisterial environment. After all, the circus was their lifeblood, the big top was their temple, and the audience was part of their soul.

Although the equestrian family members had not performed together as an act for many years, each performed in some capacity throughout the main show. Daviso presented his stunning dressage act; his entrance was singly captivating. Corky, looking ravishing enchanted onlookers with her ballerina-on-horseback routine amid a flurry of paparazzi flashes. Ortans achieved a matchless hand-balancing routine on the Rolla-Rolla, supported by spouse Freddy Cannestrelli, while my parents primarily concentrated on the Cristiani elephants. An act known as "the leaps," which featured Lucio, Freddy, Belmonte, and Mogador, took place atop a superlong ramp that angled downward toward the center ring. Each artist would run toward the springboard and then bounce off, somersaulting over an increasing number of elephants, before landing feet first on an overstuffed foam mat. Amusingly, Lucio revved the action with his wild buffoonery and innate timing. His acrobatic skills were still superb well past his prime, and his spontaneity of wit made the act hugely entertaining.

Pete and Norma waded knee-deep in a sea of merchandise inside the concession trailer while Shaky Paul stayed by the door, allocating supplies for the grease joint and novelty stands. Needing help in the worst possible way, Pete sent for Fisheyes, his devoted stool pigeon and errand boy—burdened with a rather peculiarly shaped bald head, a mouthful of rotten teeth, and thick Coke-bottle bifocals.

"Move, you four-eyed bastard," Pete barked, sneering and chortling under his breath, "or I'll fry your lazy ass on the grill!" In no time flat, poky Fisheyes came shuffling in his direction, smiling the same dumb smile, but he couldn't move fast enough for Pete. My impatient uncle sprang out and goosed him on the sly, quickening his steps.

In between regular jaunts to remind the ushers about the lost art of seating an audience, Mogador wined and dined the local press while Daviso prepared for spec and busied himself combing a perfect chess-square design on the hind end of his gorgeous dressage stallion, Kashmir.

Lucio, decked out in top fashion, trekked straight to the bandstand—only to solicit an opinion from our hip clarinet player. "How do I look, E-Flat?"

"Super, Mr. Bossman, super," he answered with a thumbs-up sign. "I do dig your silk threads. Remember me at Christmastime!"

"That's just what I wanted to hear," Lucio replied, smiling and ignoring the footnote. "If I'm calling it right, we have a full house of beautiful women."

"Better believe it, Mr. Bossman. Here, take my binoculars ... I've got a bird's-eye view, and I can name a few!"

"Ha!" Lucio laughed. "Keep an eye out for me. I have some important business that can't wait ... if you know what I mean." Then he conveyed an arrogant look as he swaggered off to the grandstand to schmooze with a pool of responsive movie stars.

After tending other obligations, Daddy focused on the five Cristiani elephants. My parents were a class act, performing with their beloved pets Christy, Carrie, Babe, Emma, and Shirley. They pampered each one according to individual needs, making sure the elephants felt secure as the stars of the act. Still, my father's classic style and my mother's effortless grace made it work.

I mustn't forget to disclose that Daddy would go to great lengths in order to avoid embarrassment in the ring. Before the act went onstage, he spoke the same familiar words that prompted the bulls to empty themselves of all the ground fertilizer they could muster. As expected, they'd lift their tails and assume that familiar posture while forcibly expelling blocks of runny dung and lakes of pee *on cue*—summarily releasing a ghastly rankness that carried in the wind a note of warning to the breathing-impaired. When satisfied by their cooperative display, Daddy happily tweaked his black-satin bow tie, brushed his tuxedo clean, and then fanned the air in a laughable effort to clear it. As soon as his clever stars gave Daddy the usual signal, he gave them high praise for having such outstanding discipline. Normally, my father's grateful voice summoned forth even more oozing blocks, just for good measure. Christy (lost to pneumonia aboard a ship returning from Rio de Janeiro, Brazil, after a joint venture with Ringling in 1961) was a most contented beast, and the smoothest-riding elephant I'd ever known. This uncommonly gentle-hearted soul just lumbered on with the flow and, even in the worst possible circumstances, followed orders without a rumble of discontent.

Carrie was the trusted keeper of the herd. She had a broad head and fat trunk, which made her a forceful worker for setup and tear-down. Way back when, Daddy beat the pulp out of elephant handler Steve Fanning when he caught the handler tearing at poor Carrie's ear with a sharp bull hook during setup. Afterward, Steve crawled under the elephant truck to dry up; the incident jolted him into permanent sobriety. Before the end of the season, he hired on with a prominent Florida carnival and managed to hold the job to his dying days.

Persevering Babe was strangely in love with Shirley. If ignored for long, Babe would behave in a manner unbecoming of her otherwise good nature. Carrie, of course, refereed fair and square. Shirley was Burmese, so her features were altogether different from those of her Indian sisters. Her butterball frame and short legs actually resembled a cartoon sketch of *Dumbo*. In an elephant beauty contest, she would've won the crown, hands down. On the other hand, beautiful, Shirley could be rather ornery—not unlike gals of the same image.

Lastly, there was Emma, our pet elephant who was precious beyond words. She happened to be the Phyllis Diller of the herd: an adorable, totally unaware clown. Furthermore, her skin was shades lighter than the rest; she had darting albino eyes, long legs, and a slender, steadily swinging trunk.

But alas, after dimple-faced Shirley became Emma's self-appointed guardian, Babe took any opportunity to land swipes. During one risky jump in mountainous Tennessee, Emma got the short end of the stick when Babe attacked from behind and impulsively bit off half of her tail. The racket forced the driver off the road right on the edge of a dangerous ravine; it's frightening to think of what could've happened. Luckily, Emma followed last in line; regardless, neither man nor beast would've dared approach her wounded backside, for she was destined to be tail-sensitive for the rest of her days. We were amazed how quickly she learned to elevate her bandaged boo-boo whenever a bag of fruity treats came her way. Emma (named after my Nona) was the youngest, but she grew to be the tallest—after which she didn't know what to do with her size. Like Daddy, she was forever the worrywart, and with good reason, considering the pitiable state of her knobby stub. Small wonder why he was partial to her; Emma was his muse.

The Cristiani elephant herd was distinctive in every way, acclimatized to any situation, and known in the industry to be the best-natured herd in the business. Their exemplary behavior could've been in part attributed to the fact that they were handled in a rarified gentle fashion with maximal care. Daddy and those mammals enjoyed a priceless bond: the elephants empowered him to understand them in a way no other human could boast. Most people are familiar with Disney's classic animated feature film *Dumbo*. When recalling the memorable scenes where the elephants aired their differences in moralizing gossip sessions, keep in mind that, just like the Cristiani herd, they spoke as though members of an elite club of sages—and who's to say they were not? Perhaps it was mere conjecture on my part but, like Daddy, I was able to slip into their skin and decipher all that was said between them while they dined on clumps of choice timothy hay or rich-tasting alfalfa (used sparingly—too much gave them the runs). Obviously, we never heard the words, but when compared to Dumbo's winning cartoon stars, the Cristiani elephants' mannerisms, gestures, and expressions were undeniably similar.

The Cristiani Bros. Circus had advertised fourteen bulls for the past few seasons: Norma and Pete's well-trained herd, Mary, Maude, Bessie, Tonta, and Norma (traveling on the show between spot-date layoffs); the remarkably-disciplined family of five Cristiani elephants and four unruly Africans belonging to businessman Tony Diano.

Pete and Norma's herd remained under the expert supervision of Rex and Barbara Williams until the dynamic duo became disenchanted with the demands of their contract and left the act months before the LA date—at which point I stepped in to learn the routine. The breakup was a great loss for both parties; up until then, the act had been a moneymaking machine and would never again be presented in the same way, because Barbara Williams was *the* most sensational elephant performer in all of circusdom. Sultry Barbara, known for her gravity-defying body, utilized her great timing and agility while flawlessly performing alongside ruggedly attractive Rex. Circus aficionados will agree that the partners had a certain seductive chemistry that played to the audience. Barbara, though not a beauty in the truest sense, had fiery-red hair that fell below her back, Mae West curves, and abundant sex appeal—a compelling combination as she worked through the complex routine with light-footed ease.

Tony Diano, a fat and squatty Sicilian from Canton, Ohio, had an ego twice the size of Texas—gained from earning megabucks in the dull but lucrative concrete business. Since the machismo challenge of big-game hunting brought needed melodrama into his life, he wore in-your-face safari garb and a superior smile. During his excursions to the savage plains of Africa, Mr. Diano captured a mix of exotic animals—then leased them to circuses and carnivals for profit. Hunting down poor, disadvantaged animals not only earned him kudos among his peers but served as the perfect tax shelter for his main hobby. Our show manager, Uncle Lucio, leased four of Mr. Diano's young Africans together with the infamous Asian bull, Big Tommy. (In future years, he was cleverly elevated to near-mystical stardom when featured as Ringling's modern-day Jumbo). No two ways about it: Lucio's megalomaniac, fair-weather friend knew how to speculate, intimidate, and manipulate. "If you want Big Tommy," Mr. Diano had said in a deceivingly genial manner, "the runaways go with 'em—or it's no deal."

Tommy's impassive behavior was unprecedented. Unlike any other nearly mature bull, he never turned mean or even mildly aggressive. The handsome beast had massive tusks that crossed at the base. Naturally, he guaranteed a front-page headline the instant he was photographed leading our much-anticipated circus parade down Main Street, USA. Anyway, hear me out: for better or worse, Tommy was my mount in spec. Instead of riding on his head, I balanced myself on the crisscross of his mighty tusks in standing position, holding his studded halter with one hand and waving with the other. I'll say most of the time, it was no joyride, because our tusked superstar had this really nasty habit of dropping (and playfully slinging) his scary-looking male organ the whole time. And, because all eyes were aimed on it, I stayed motionless as a mannequin until I disappeared out the back door—pondering the question, "What makes him do that?"

Interestingly, the original owner of Tommy, Ben Davenport, bet the farm that his quiet spirit wouldn't last, and everyone else would have wagered the same. Seeing as Ben had known that the proud-stomached magnate salivated to own the striking bull, he plotted to offer him prestige of ownership. The passed-down tales vary, but the story goes something like this—believe it or not! With sprayed-on sweat that worked much to his benefit, Ben acted out his spiel, talking through his teeth in a low hum. "Tony, I confess I've had the black ass lately, but I'm in a shit pile and need the money. Well, hell, Tommy is yours for a fast, under-the-table cash deal."

"OK, you cunning son of a bitch," groaned Mr. Diano. "Sign him over."

Wheedling Ben reveled in his manipulative exchange. He danced in his stolen alligator boots like vain Geronimo, confident that he'd soon see the day when his green-eyed adversary would be stuck with an unmanageable killer elephant in musth, unable to give the violent beast away—even to a zoo. (Musth is a sexually aggressive condition that occurs annually in male elephants fifteen to twenty years of age. Bulls in musth are primed to mate so they are extremely dangerous to humans and other male elephants.)

As far as I know, Big Tommy never did go into musth! His unflappable behavior stymied everyone in the business, especially the rejected cows who lusted after this magnificent male specimen in aroused beastly fashion. Occasionally, they'd bribe him with seductive rear swings, grinding out an open proposition to "come on up and see me sometime." But Tommy, though well endowed, couldn't have cared less. In my mind, he was just a really strange old boy who paraded with a special swing of his own.

Mr. Diano went on to make a small fortune, openly hissing and preening as the proud owner of the only asexual (or whatever) performing bull in the business. For years on end, the very mention of that particular barter gone wrong made Ben quake with rage.

*   *   *   *

By now, Antoinette and I (being at the vain age when looks count for everything) decided to scrape up what seemed like a small fortune for a bargain-rate hotel room an easy walk from the midway. Considering how broke we were, springing for a modest hotel room was a shocking indulgence. All avarice aside, rewarding ourselves with an infinite channel of sparkling, hot bathwater was the most excellent justification for emptying our piggybanks. But our financial problems were nothing compared to everything else going on: equipment stuck on the road, water-truck problems, last-minute program changes—with the addition of Con Colleano, the great tight-wire star who, despite ill health, still put on one heck of a performance.

Pandemonium erupted inside the wardrobe bus as everyone tried to fish through piles of crushed costumes, leotards, tights, makeup kits, and countless personal items deemed indispensable. My mother was in a sweat trying to recover the sewing machine when Aunt Corky hurried inside.

"Marion," Corky griped, "what happened? Where's my production costume?"

"Corky, the racks broke," Mom divulged. "Didn't you hear the wardrobe bus had a blowout? It just pulled on the lot last night. Oscar said it rolled over an embankment. Then the mechanics had to double back for the cannon truck—engine trouble again."

Wanda, one flaky showgirl who fooled no one into believing her Mae West "once I was Snow White, but I drifted" line, rushed up the steps, expressing concern for our bus-driving clowns Billy McCabe and his (conjoined at the hip) partner, Tweetybird.

"Billy is about to crack," cried Wanda. "He's still shaking glass from his hair."

"I heard all that," Corky hissed with an unctuous smile, "but I'm supposed to be at the front door right now! Somebody's got to lend a hand here."

Just then, my normally relaxed aunt Ortans tapped on the spiderweb-cracked window, clutching her upturned bucket. She could be funny in her delivery, often unintentionally—like just then, when she was boiling mad. "Where's Jane?" she asked. "The kids said Jane borrowed my water. *Borrowed?* What's her problem? Could she be having her period, again? Our water tank's 'taking a leak.' It's piss-full of holes, and Lardo's truck has a flat. *I need aqua!*"

Everyone laughed, except Corky, who was getting more irritable by the minute. She wasn't a bit interested in her sister's ongoing water war. There was much talk about MGM's plan to make a circus musical, to be filmed largely on the Hollywood studio lot. Corky heard rumors that people associated with the film were discouraged because they had not been able to find the ideal bareback rider to double gorgeous Doris Day in the dazzling ballerina on horseback sequence—so, naturally, looking her best was very important. Corky was struggling mightily to solicit help. "My makeup kit and black tights are buried somewhere under all this cockamamy mess," she yelled. You could cut the stress with a knife!

Seconds later, Mogador took one giant leap inside the wardrobe bus—nostrils flared, neck veins popping to a dangerous level. "Corky, what's going on?" he demanded, with unblinking, bloodshot eyes. "Papa's having fits at the front door. He needs help!" Corky pressed her palms flat on her brother's chest and ordered him to freeze.

"Wait! I just dropped my best eyelashes," she cautioned. "Watch ... your ... step!"

Mommy felt it was her responsibility to bottle the sizzling tension—before this potentially explosive situation got out of control. "You'd better go. I'll find everything," she said meaningfully, patting Corky's shoulder. "Go help Papa. Go ... go!"

The Pan Pacific (home of a thousand dramas daily) was a beehive of activity. Who could stand idle while nature's clock raced ahead with no thought of our mere mortal apprehensions—or even the slightest offer of sympathy for whatever God's law did not permit us to see? Family members separated in various directions—outwardly immunized against the very idea of negativity while endeavoring to catch every fly in the ointment. We had a packed big top—packed to the rafters—and the heavenly California sun was shining through. Besides, there was always something about the City of Angels that stirred the circus heart and gave us all courage and extended hope.

It was hard *not* to believe in miracles—and I believed.

*   *   *   *

My theatrical face was powdered before the bugle call sounded. How I loved that look! It did something to the hair of my flesh. I had a different stance; I held my head up, looking for compliments. With spare time to nose around, I slipped into my slop shoes and robe and headed for the bandstand to survey the straw house. (In olden days, workingmen were ordered to spread bales of hay around the hippodrome track to accommodate the overflow of late arrivers. So, most appropriately, in circus terms, "straw house" simply means capacity crowd.)

Stylish Gilbert Roland was seated in the front row reserved section—shading the assertive, squinting eyes that had become part of his mystique behind dark tortoiseshell sunglasses. The desirable actor was impeccably dressed; it seemed he would never appear in public in violation of his own standards. Mr. Roland, whose fine image was hardly inconspicuous, nodded politely while riveted to the operational spark of it all. I wasn't an autograph hound, but … wham! I was absolutely starstruck.

The pulsating mood inside the big top caught the attention of our throaty voiced ringmaster, Jerry Eagle. But just as he zigzagged past the cat cages to check things out, he bumped into cat trainer Eddie Kuhn—a sweetheart of a guy and a rare exception to his breed.

"Jerry, tell me I'm not dreamin'. We've got a straw house. Man alive, I could smell it coming," said Eddie, blotting his forehead. "Are we on time?"

"Yes, sir, Mr. Kuhn. We're goin' after 'em full bore, and we're definitely on time."

Jerry, about to turn away, saw Uncle Daviso walking briskly toward him from the opposite direction, tagged by Spaniard Gene Mendez. Although handsome Gene was the humblest of humble fellows, the Seitz-Mendez high-wire presentation proved to be one of the classiest acts of its type to ever to grace the circus stage. He and his partner were famous for performing a unique sequence of spine-tingling drop-off stunts with the slickness of a pair of black panthers.

Gene started to speak out, but Jerry, sensing his concern, interrupted him midsentence.

"Stop," said Jerry with a crooked smile. "I know the question, and the answer is …" Daviso's killer look straightened his smirk in a hurry. Red-faced Jerry duly cleared his throat. "Sir, absent of unforeseen delays, we're precisely on schedule!"

Guest entertainers paced in and out of various house trailers that surrounded the backyard in a semicircle. Their noticeable angst added new elements of romance and mystery to the high-voltage atmosphere. As it turned out, my older sister, Bonnie; her quiet, unassuming husband, Reggie Armor; and her kids, Reginine (Sa Sa) and Jay were resting up in LA until their next spot date with the sensational "Flying Armors" flying act. Forgetting all bias, Reggie, who not only accomplished the wrist-to-wrist triple, but also the *unprecedented* triple and a half to the legs was superbly graceful as a flying trapeze artist. An absolute vision in the air, he was—that rare individual other performers loved to watch. By chance, the Flying Armors had some time off after their successful performing tour throughout Scandinavia and the Netherlands, so Reggie was able to fill in for injured flyer Billy Woods in the Flying Ray Dels flying act.

On my nosy beat, I caught sight of a black-and-white horse trailer with a shiny palomino tied alongside. His strikingly beautiful head burrowed in a bucket of nutty oats. As I approached, he lifted his locked jaw and challenged me with his velvety, smooth distended nostrils. Next, the tricky gelding put his ears back and simultaneously drew up his hind leg—cautioning me to stay clear. A little voice told me he meant business and was in no mood to be stroked by another blond. Who knows—maybe, in some strange way, he sensed my purpose: I was only interested in his young master. (Never fib to a horse!)

After investigating every nook and cranny of the surrounding area, I found exactly what I was looking for: a white trick-riding saddle propped against the trailer ramp. Still, it didn't behoove me to stick around like some dimwit, so, before I could make a spectacle of myself, I split.

*   *   *   *

Pete and Norma's elephants—Mary, Bessie, Maude, Tonta, and Norma—were an intimidating 1950 wedding gift from Ben Davenport. The spirited herd performed an amazing center-ring act, renowned for swiftness and stunning progression of elephant-girl mounts. Aunt Norma had worked the act herself until it interfered with her already taxing schedule: concessions, caring for her small kids, and keeping a close eye on sly Pete. (About that time Barbara and her husband, Rex, came into the picture.) Naturally, I was honored to follow in Barbara's footsteps, but that was easier said than done. Daddy didn't approve. Although style and showmanship were in my genes, I fell way short in the strength and agility departments … nothing new there! However vulnerable I may have been, I managed to maneuver fairly well and was proud of my achievements. But beyond the veneer of outward pride, I never hit a comfortable plateau. Cognizant of my shortcomings, somewhat obstinate, and devoid of mature reason, I forged ahead in defiance of serious misgivings. God was with me as I practiced high-speed twirls while suspended from a wrist loop (attached to the elephant's harness) plus swift-lifting front-leg and freestanding head mounts. In truth, I never came close to mastering the act Barbara had performed with spiderlike grip and a remarkable sense of balance.

Although I was braver than I had ever been thus far, I cringed every time I performed the lay-down (the trick that put me at Mary's mercy while she crawled over my body). Though I tried to discount the danger, I lived with the real possibility that even an overcautious elephant could lose balance and unintentionally scrape or crush a vital body part. One time, while still rehearsing under the trainer's scrutiny, Mary barely pressed on my knee with her elbow. Fortunately, I only suffered a bruised kneecap that immediately swelled the size of a honeydew melon. My confidence shrank to nothing as I limped to the dressing room, hollering for help. *That's it—I quit!* I said to myself. *Why am I here doing this insane thing? Daddy's right!*

To make matters worse, in the early rounds of on-the-job training, I had to deal with an altogether different crisis. Humorous as it is in retrospect, I didn't view it as such at the time. Both of my costume straps popped at the same time during the matinee performance in a small brewery town up in the east. As a result, I suffered the vulgar disgrace of flashing my then-perky boobs to a bought-out house of rowdy, half-tanked factory workers while Maude, an elephant in the herd, whirled me around in a spread-eagle pose (left hand in a wrist loop and left leg gripped in her trunk). Flustered by embarrassment, I made a clumsy early exit to the racket of hubba-hubba catcalls keening at my back. Later, I became a sitting duck for a rash of jokes that didn't amuse me—or my protective dad.

New chain-halter headpieces for the herd were introduced months later, shortly before the LA date. Granted, they were glitzy enough, but they made grabbing a secure hold terribly awkward without the necessary leather hand grips, which were nowhere to be found. But in hindsight, maybe nothing would have prevented my fate. What-ifs are pointless. Obviously, I was already in the habit of courting disaster twice a day. Most, if not all of me, ached as I toddled around—feigning cool confidence prior to showtime. The five mature bulls worked with such speed that it'd be next to impossible to recover from even a minor fall and stay clear of the descending tonnage—except at nineteen, green in life and used to getting my way, I didn't care.

*   *   *   *

Distracted by a teenager's fancy, I ignored the ticking clock even as I watched the backyard swelling ceremoniously in preparation for spec. Performers fell silent as they contemplated the magnitude of their debut in this glamorous West Coast mecca. Everybody appeared distant—a little glazed over and slightly duck-footed, in need of personal space. The clowns, however, chatted nonstop as they sashayed about in a flower-power huddle—articulating in normal helium-squeak jargon.

As a matter of fact, I was dealing with my own naked self-interest that had me by the kazoo: I longed to steal the attention of (macho-to-the-grave) Gilbert Roland while keeping visions of James Garner alive. Yet, I preferred oiling around incognito, daydreaming from afar. Despite that girlish desire, nothing could keep me from searching for yet another object of my affections: the elusive trick rider who, incidentally, would've made a perfect stunt double for the *Maverick* star.

Months earlier, back at the Sarasota winter quarters, I'd noticed his photo résumé, strategically placed on Uncle Lucio's desk. He definitely got my stamp of approval, so I was greatly disappointed when my uncle's offer for a full-time summer job went flat. His name was Benny Rossi, a hunk trick rider and rope spinner from Oklahoma, christened with a dreamy cleft chin and wary boyish face that packed a wallop. By chance, I caught his flirty, naughty eye for a split second while he was in the midst of calming his rearing, back-stepping golden warrior. I took that as a positive sign; my legs went to Jell-O. Wanting to make my presence known, I sauntered up close and introduced myself to this shy but self-assured Italian.

Nearly twenty-year-old Benny was lean and nicely muscled with a full head of curly, dark hair that was sweetly intoxicating. At present, I felt both intimidated and frustrated by his "I've been around" look—a sure indicator that I was hamburger. Just when my teenage pheromones were starting to surge, Benny introduced his horse, Navajo. Again, the grumpy horse pointed his head toward me— only this time, he exposed his mammoth piano-key choppers. He lunged— I jumped—he missed! Then, as if his moves had been choreographed in advance, Navajo spun around, cut the cheese in my face ... and nearly dumped on my foot. My winded response was, "We've already met!"

There was an uncomfortable silence while Benny showed a mortified grin. "Navajo's very high-strung," he cautioned, grappling for words. "It's his breeding. He's the perfect mix, you know—half Arabian and half quarter horse." I nodded, but I was not impressed ... with his cranky, ill-mannered horse, that is. At that time, aspirations of reeling Benny in with conversation didn't pan out. We did have a conversation, but it was chit-chat—polite and short. Navajo wouldn't stand still, and frankly, my timing was off. Nonetheless, I got the distinct feeling that I might've sparked a small flame or at least piqued *some* inter-est—but the uncertainty made me less than confident, and I was miffed. With due precautions, I moved back a ways to check myself out, thankful the horse hadn't drawn blood. It makes me laugh now to think that I was truly bucking a mighty impulse to fall flat and lay prostrate before this splendidly clad Don Diego. Fortunately, I snapped to before I melted like whipping cream on hot fudge. By some stroke of genius, I decided to play it cool and vetoed my idiotic whim in the nick of time.

While doing my homework the former year, I had learned that Benny's mother, Mary, was married to Obert Miller—who, along with his sons, Dory and Kelly, owned the longstanding Al G. Kelly & Miller Bros. Circus (a large animal show out of Oklahoma). Actually, Benny and I had lived our lives in eerie parallel—at least when it came to the large proportion of time we spent in boarding schools. Benny had graduated high school with honors in 1957 from the top-ranked Missouri Military Academy, located in Mexico, Missouri. After his three-week contract for the Los Angeles date ended, he planned to return to the University of Oklahoma for the fall semester—accompanied by Navajo, of course, set to board three miles away.

Right then, Benny was in a transitional quandary. Having been nominated by Carl Albert, then Speaker of the House, he was facing the one-shot opportunity to enlist in the United States Air Force Academy. Yet, the satisfying joys of liberty caused him to reconsider an extended military career.

Mary had divorced Joe Rossi after twenty-five shaky years of marriage—when Benny was only three. Benny's support-fleeing father, Joe Rossi—by then a respected circus bandleader—never lost his Italian colloquialism; oddly, he punctuated his broken English by sidestepping into a peculiar repertoire of smiles. Mary's five children were a product of that marriage: one daughter, named Evelina, and four outstandingly handsome studs—Rex, Mark, Jimmy, and Benny. Sadly, Mark, known to have a shy personality much like Benny, had been killed in World War II—days after he shipped off to Burma. Mark, a true war hero, received the Purple Heart and Silver Star for valor at the hopeful age of twenty-three.

Benny's oldest brother, Rex, who was twenty-years his senior, was a champion trick rider and trick roper. Rex was the sort of likable character whose company was enjoyed, but only in limited doses—or more bluntly, until one tired of his windiness. Mary had Rex when she was a mere child of barely fifteen; plus, her childbearing life with Joe Rossi was terribly impoverished—and, in Mary's words, tough as hell. Consequently, her firstborn little cowboy grew up tough—and unable to eradicate the prickly vestiges of his deprived youth. Besides wearing that chip, the independent Rex took no bull, having left home himself at age fifteen to join the Tom Mix Wild West Circus to study his craft under the bossman's wing. Clutching an open invitation to stay at his buddy Hoot Gibson's place, Rex was Hollywood bound. In record time (with the help of Mr. Gibson's strong studio links), he became a sought-after stuntman and worked nonstop for a long period. Thus far, this now-urban cowboy had worked in a legion of films that covered a broad range of Hollywood themes, but in the rodeo circuit, he was mostly renowned for his "under the belly" stunt and other daring revolutions atop his favorite golden steed, Apache.

In his day, Rex regularly doubled Bob Steel, Duncan Renaldo, Gene Autry, Roy Rogers, and an imposing list of other celebrities in a series of ever-popular swashbuckler films. All of these actors, I suspect, enjoyed his company ... for a while. The Cristianis were genuinely fond of Rex—even amused by his harmless bogus bluster—and therefore resigned to his fabled promises to stick out a single season. They knew Rex as good as anybody. He worked for them before the rodeo season started when it suited him ... and when it didn't, after the rodeo season got under way, he was gone. He simply blew the show without a moment's notice. When broke and still spending, superhyper Rex, supported by an arsenal of Rolaids, managed to hock everything of value except his teeth— maybe yours, but never his.

For love of the game, Benny aspired to emulate his oldest brother's horsemanship and, as everyone was about to witness, met the challenge with stud style. Frankly, the Cristianis had been the first to exploit this action-packed roughrider sequence that climaxed with a spirited Roman-riding team leaping through a giant ring of fire as an energizing precursor for the main event. Repeating the fast-paced trick-riding sequence as an opening act was a smart move on my family's part because—using history as a guide—the ever-popular display would surely match the expectations of the hip California crowd.

Good grief, I'd lost track of the hour. Spec was under way. How on earth could I have been so reckless? What was I thinking? Next thing, I scrambled toward the dressing tent to worm into my brand-new black and bronze costume with leopard trimming—but not before I shot a hot, flirtatious beam at Benny, the groovy looking cowboy—who, to my chagrin, happened to be looking the other way. Just shoot me. I was late! Everyone else was out there in full wardrobe, leading the way. Lucky for me the elephants trailed the parade ...

After spec, I aimed for the bandstand with my cousin Antoinette to watch Benny's gelding gallop full speed up and down the track, performing a series of risky maneuvers. For the first time ever, I entered my usual tunnel of anxiety feeling sinfully good. Daddy and his brothers were blown away as Rex Rossi's baby brother performed with cocksure ability and pure guts, barely missing track lights, aluminum poles, and numerous aerial-act wires—astride a horse bred to fly as if winged. My new romantic challenge looked awesome. He was magnificently skilled, sensually aloof, and trousered to a tight Western T. He vaulted bewitching Navajo from every angle, using the trick riding saddle as a tool to execute his daredevil stunts. Antoinette remarked, "Unlike Rex, blowing his own horn is *not* Benny's style."

"Let me put it this way, kiddo." I grinned. "That's only *part* of his appeal!"

When Benny completed his alternating laps, he joined Betty and Nancy Elliot, the talented mother-and-daughter trick-riding and Roman-riding team, on the front hippodrome track and shyly raised his white cowboy hat amid deafening applause. That was pretty impressive, I thought, but when I noticed a band of California cuties abandoning their reserved seats, I smoldered with jealousy. There's something macho about cowboys—they draw women like flies. Just as Navajo flew out the back door, the fans swept into view. It was so obvious where they were headed, darn it. I could smell their ocean scent a stone's throw away.

"They're in cahoots," I bemoaned. "Navajo's the bait. He lures them in."

"I don't doubt that for a minute," said Antoinette as she elbowed me in the ribs.

If whistle calls from my admirers counted for anything, I was in great shape, but next to my supersvelte competition, I felt downright fat. This time, I needed courage and aplomb to fabricate a quick scheme, so I put my mind to work. Instead of concentrating on my act—the sensible thing to do—I butted myself up on a bull tub, acting out moronic improvisations like some silly lovesick schoolgirl. A wasp waist couldn't hurt, I discerned, but short of forcing down a bionic tapeworm I was left in the lurch. While I liked being Kim Novak-blond and noticed every single whistle and wolf-in-heat look that came my way, a circus Lolita I was not! Although never a crusading moralist, I remained a terminally straitlaced virgin, the identifying mark of drummed-in convent coaching. But at the same time, I ached to look vivacious, having long ago decided that sticking to my moral code was my prerogative … and if anybody had difficulty with *that*, the problem was theirs to solve.

In all truth, I was functioning under the influence of a very potent aphrodisiac, with my heaving breasts hurting—in a good way—from the thrust of Cupid's arrow, which made me a prime candidate for heartache. The instant I'd met the man of my dreams, I experienced the heart-stopping phenomenon of love at first sight. You should've seen me; my head was charged with enough sizzling energy to drive me to the moon. After our first brief encounter, I walked away rather sheepishly, like a confused woman-child poised on the precipice of life, her mating pheromones bubbling over the edge. At the combative age of nineteen, I'd become bewilderingly unafraid, guiltless, and determined as a mad-eyed huntress—feeling liberated at last from the repenting tomb of self-denial, which for too long imbued my mind with a fanatic convent mentality. And because this oppression had sapped the blood of life from my youthful energy, I wanted to break away—be free to consider the delightful mystery of my thoughts....

Suddenly I took joy in the erotic emotions that had just knocked me off an utterly boring pedestal. Being Catholic born and bred, I longed for time out, alone, in my own little corner of the world, to try and unravel the knottiest of teenage dilemmas. Only now, little did I know that my girlish fantasy would soon be interrupted by an untimely twist of fate.

*   *   *   *

Seventy minutes or so into the performance, the big top was pulsating with enthusiasm. By all indications, the show was a sensation. Performers returned uplifted, exhaling sighs of relief under the shrill banshee cries of approval that accompanied their exit from the ring. As I awaited my impending entrance, I tried to absorb their high; my efforts turned out to be unnecessary, as their enthusiasm was contagious. It was as if I were having an out-of-body experience. My euphoria invoked all the breathless symptoms of vertigo, which tellingly said this much: the air was sweet!

Only two more acts were scheduled before the cannon finale. The flying act, an audience favorite, was a smashing hit. Reggie Armor's announced triple and a half to the legs and his somersaulting passing leap had been flawlessly executed. This gave the *Ray Del's* catcher, muscled Ray (Slick) Valentine, and his beautiful buxom sister, Rosie, (who did the passing leap with Reggie) reason enough to beam with pride as they exited the ring to repeated shouts of "Bravo! Bravo!" So far, the show was running like clockwork, without even one noticeable misstep.

The clowns entered the arena to occupy the crowd with the popular popcorn gag (where a candy butcher, carrying a full tray of popcorn—purposely trips over an obviously bad tempered stick, sitting in the reserved section). The staged altercation was meant to give workers time to clear the flying-act rigging before the three-ring elephant extravaganza was introduced. The elephants were already lined up behind the back door—nervously trumpeting and squealing and blowing mucus from their snouts, anticipating their ground-shaking race into the center ring. The pressure was on. My empty stomach talked up a storm as I stood by, awaiting my cue.

The people seated in the reserved section bordering the bandstand went wild with excitement. Kids abandoned their seats and hung over the side rails shouting, "Wow! Look, Pop! Look, Mom! Quick!" Regular circusgoers knew that this particular section was the perfect place to view the commotion though a crack in the back curtain. I suppose the opportunity to eyeball the platinum-blond circus girl—dwarfed by a frenzied herd of prehistoric mammals nervously nudging her back—could hardly be ignored.

Without warning, I began hyperventilating—suffering from the same condition that had plagued me since childhood. At this point, I grabbed an adrenaline-dissolving breath and scanned the straw house. Good grief ... I was starstruck by the count of prominent Hollywood celebrities situated throughout the primary front section. My mouth went bone dry as I pondered the thought: very soon all eyes were going to be on me.

CHAPTER 23

▼

THE ELEVENTH
HOUR

Don't part with your illusions.
When they are gone you may still exist,
but you have ceased to live.
—Mark Twain

"Laaadieees and geeentleeemeeen, all eyes on the center ring. The internationally famous Cristiani Bros. Circus proudly presents …"

I crossed myself and prayed out loud, half scared but presenting a sassy picture of confidence—all while attempting to restrain the five jittery pachyderms breathing down my neck.

Please Lord, no mistakes. Not today … not on press day.

My power of concentration was broken the instant I was forced to wiggle around two scrambling photographers as I tore through the back door, in advance of the almost sixty tons of mature bulls who pursued me. Once we were inside the center ring and the trunk-up salute had the audience's attention, the act swung into play. Focused in the alchemy of the spotlight, I confronted the lead elephant, Mary, for my first mount. That part went brilliantly—except, as she lowered her head, she gave me such a look. Her portentous "break a leg" wink caused a sudden rush of emotion. That was one heart-stopping moment I'll never forget. Naturally, one never knows for certain what any animal is thinking, but the look she gave was more eloquent than speech. Had Mary's troubled glare been an admonition? Had she tried, with rumbles too low for man's acoustic range, to alert me of danger? It has since crossed my mind that maybe she had.

The initial mount onto Mary's curled trunk cued a fast-swirling waltz that had to be executed with measured precision. At any misstep, there wasn't much I could do but pray. Alas, on that fateful day, the brush was tighter than normal, and the tight-fitting chain halter pinched my fingers bloody. Despite the pain, my basic survival instincts told me to hang on for dear life, or else. But when streams of blood came trickling down my right arm, I felt faint—"good-bye world" pathetic, like one might feel right before a terrible car crash.

By either fluke or providence, Mary released me from the hold of her trunk. Surprisingly, that judgment was her call, and in itself strange. In a moment's time, I went sailing backward over the ringcurb. Lucky for me, the startling twenty-foot trajectory cleared me from the path of her mighty successors. If Mary hadn't given me the escape I needed, I would've been fatally wounded—trampled to death in an unavoidable tragedy. As it happened, the fixed aluminum ringcurb snagged my left heel in flight, and the force of impact resulted in a grotesquely shattered ankle and multiple fractures in my lower leg. That said, I can recall only one conscious sensation: my body acquired a cosmic chill, in part cut adrift from the awesome reality of the moment. Eyewitnesses later told me it was beyond mere luck that my limp body miraculously quilted in among a slew of intricately placed flying-act stakes, where I was safe and—thank you, God—not impaled. At least I was spared that torturous plight.

Primal screams hammered my head, and my eyelids grew heavy. Before nodding off into blackness, I captured a dreamy carousel of wraithlike forms and psychedelic images, totally drained of color. Simply put, I had been catapulted backward with bone-crunching power and lay bare in a state of limbo. Wherever that place of limbo is, I spent a minuscule amount of time there while the merciful Lord decided what to do with his lovesick circus girl. A defiant woman-child, no less, who had put him on the spot round heaven's clock, demanding answers to perplexing questions without wait—many of which, she complained, stayed forever pinned to his almighty sleeve. I reckon he must have weighed the pitiful dictates of my subconscious plea for life while, cold as ice, I fought to inhale and exhale.

A legitimate consideration for a reasonable God!

The next scene had me sprawled on a blanket, abutting the back door. Shock intensified as I lay shivering within an illusionary bubble, beneath a multiplicity of deformed faces fading in and out of focus. Presently, there was no reality—none whatsoever, as if I were suspended in the hereafter. My hysterical daddy kept moaning "nooooo, nooooo" while he paced around in circles grabbing his head. Daddy's primary concern was finding the best orthopedic surgeon available, so Bonnie marched him straight to the office wagon to speak with sponsors who were already calling around—pulling strings on my behalf. I nodded in agreement when I heard this sentiment: "What a blessing we're not in some isolated two-horse cow town!"

Bodies shifted positions, alternating, trying to edge into an available niche. The absence of speech was maddening—none wanted their emotions to escape before me. Although the ugly word "amputation" was never mentioned, the alarming prospect stuck in my mind—and, for that matter, everyone else's. Then I heard a slur of descriptive voices in the background.

"Gosh, Vickie's leg looks like a run-over plastic pipe."

"Look ... her anklebone's sticking out."

"It looks bad. I hope they won't have to ..."

I wasn't jolly to hear the gory details of my unenviable position; I blocked it out.

Gilbert Roland bent down to his knees, looking dazed. "I'm so sorry," he whispered. I couldn't help but gape into the actor's wonderful, expressive eyes, momentarily, for I saw in him a man who had long been observing life with an understanding of its strange turns—knowledge worth passing on. Genuine concern had motivated him to bounce from his ringside seat after witnessing my accident. On an ordinary day, I'd have leaped at the chance to know this cinema icon I so admired, even accept his heartfelt sympathy, but not today. I was both heartbroken and embarrassed for him to see me in this condition. All the other artists had performed flawlessly and I didn't get even get past the first trick; that was inexcusable. I couldn't get over the guilt that I had shamed my family by ruining their much publicized opening day performance. Besides, I looked anything but dignified, and the atmosphere was too funereal. Right then, I didn't want to think, see, or feel.

My mother didn't look well—she was breathing heavily, in solid rapid gasps. That worried me. If given a choice, I would've blinked everyone else away, like a genie. Openly ashamed of my flop performance, I prayed for my broken body to take on the transparency of fairy wings. Unlike the watching crowd, I couldn't look at my leg, because I feared a disconnection of some kind; still, the blood flow was minimal, and that was a mental comfort. But the way idlers stared across, hawklike, as if looking for the bottom of a mystery, told a story I preferred to ignore, so I blocked it out.

All at once, Kilowatt, a sorry sight in greasy overalls, ordered some gaudily made-up woman with shaved eyebrows, smeared red lipstick, and two-inch-long fingernails—the image of Gloria Swanson in her Oscar-winning role in *Sunset*

Boulevard—to back off. She didn't. Now that, if nothing else, was funny. Welcome to Hollywood!

Settling for a hellish life of compromise was not exactly what I had in mind. How quickly I accumulated answers that weren't answers at all. At this point, every hypothetical angle I put together went up in smoke. In a failed attempt to get past this surreal nightmare, I kept babbling on, relatively lost in a singsong of nonsensical thoughts. Pain, as yet, hadn't filtered through my numb body, and I dealt with the trauma as best I could. But the moment a well-intentioned person made an unwise move, I panicked: *"Omigod no, don't touch my leg!"*

After that unnecessary scare, my chattering teeth bit my tongue and—yuck—my mouth had that awful coppery taste of blood, which didn't help the situation. Even if it never dawned on me to ask why I'd missed seeing Benny's concerned face in the crowd of onlookers, something got my attention. I do recall, for no significant reason, thinking how nice it would be to have a concave tummy for a change, so in my disoriented state, I decided to starve myself, although at that point I wasn't sure why. Using that course of thought, I devised a plan that suited my needs. At least I'd end up rib-showing skinny, as I was seldom seen. I hated hospital food … that was one plus. I was hard-pressed to think of another right then, but I pushed.

My mother and little sister, Carin, wept in grim silence—bent at the waist and traumatized like never before, unable to tolerate the jolting sight of my dislodged limb. My teeth kept chattering, so my mother pulled the blanket up to my chin. Little Carin wouldn't budge. She was a pathetic picture, picking bits of sawdust from my hair.

"Vickie, everything will be all right," she said, sniffing, trying to be brave.

Bonnie, who always wore her feelings on her face, returned alone and repeated Carin's words in a cracking pitch. "Yes, everything will be all right."

Because the elephant display preceded the Zacchini cannon act, the propmen were cued to move forward while the band picked up the pace. The propmen worked diligently, raising the net and tightening ropes around the wooden stakes in record time. As soon as the side ring had been removed and the familiar silver cannon was pulled into the arena, the audience went dead silent. All at once, the great Munoz (Manuel Zacchini's protégé) appeared in the spotlight, wearing the trademark white leather jumpsuit and fighter pilot's headgear that fans have come to know. After a round of applause, Munoz rode the nose of the silver cannon high above the crowd. Young Munoz looked awesome—like an indestructible android on a mission to the stars. He balanced himself with dramatic showmanship until the hydraulic mechanism locked into position. Next, Munoz climbed inside the nose, awaiting Zacchini's final question: "Munoz, are you ready?" Then came the countdown: ten, nine, eight …

I never tired of watching the daredevil jump, especially after a satisfying performance, so I could imagine the drama unfolding with my eyes closed. Immediately after the thunderclap of the Zacchini cannon finale, sirens blared through the backyard. Then, a disembodied voice echoed, as though from another time and place.

"It's coming! Shit, somebody move that clown car!"

There was a brief wave of deathlike stillness, and then the earth shook with a tremor. "Here's the ambulance … she's going to St. Vincent's Hospital. Stand back!"

As the paramedics lowered the stretcher, I turned chalk white. In a spasm of sheer fright, I wrung my hands and prayed out of the depths of distress.

Sweet Mother of God, help me. Everything will be …

On my journey to St. Vincent's, I was flanked by two reassuring paramedics, but after they wheeled me inside the icy-cold emergency room, the trauma worsened. I vaguely recall feeling a trifle shamefaced when a nurse walked up and snipped off my costume and tights. My thoughts were still fragmented, full of ugly flashbacks best forgotten. But my insensibility lifted somewhat when the preliminary exam exposed my breasts to some breathy intern who appeared desensitized with noble intent. I immediately motioned to some woman scribbling notations on her clipboard, but she didn't respond. What if I were sleepwalking through the entire scene, and no one was real—the intern, the nurse, even the unresponsive note taker—no one at all? *Maybe I'm dead,* I thought. *Oops, that's it … I'm really DEAD!*

Grouped antiseptic types ogled over me, all speaking in clinical hieroglyphics— except Mr. Whatshisname (noisily sucking breath mints). Seeing as my brain was stuck in one lumpy chaos, I kept blabbering absurdities in a barely audible voice: "He's so skinny—waaay too skinny—and where did he dig up that skinny tie? Nurse, what's that? I really hate shots! Needles make me faint." I had a powerful gag reflex, so I started retching. Hospital odor is what it is: plain terrible.

"Help me sit up … please! Help, I'm going to throw up! Where's Mommy?" I implored. "Need some water! Cottonmouthed … thirsty! Please, just a sip!" After a gap of silence, I got the same vacuous look and heard the same pompous utterances … but, because I was both alert and scared as can be, I didn't merely gloss over the nurse's words; I dwelled on them.

Her words were fresh and sharp: "Later, Miss Cristiani, later. Later!"

"Why?" I asked, with a prickling sense of injustice.

"Because," she answered without a thought.

"Because why?" I insisted. All at once, the nurse smiled down and looked toward the door.

Panic! The assigned specialist had arrived. X-rays showed my leg had sustained seven breaks. Now I knew exactly how Humpty Dumpty felt after his ill-fated somersault. God, another needle! Forget it, if I'm dead; dead people don't feel a thing.

"Ouch ... darn!" I protested. "Eh, tell me ... what's in that needle?" I had little difficulty reading the nurse's mind: *Take a wild guess, honnnnnn ...*

Now, what do you suppose nurses do to dratted patients like me? Stick 'em!

$$*\qquad*\qquad*\qquad*$$

After recovering from surgery, I was completely absorbed in my appearance and terribly put out because I couldn't bathe or wash my hair. Looking my best was a lost cause, but I held the thought that with a little female voodoo, I might be transformed into a ravenous creature capable of inventing a love potion that really worked. But why waste time on impossibilities, Benny could show any time—albeit with some lame excuse. More realistically, I had to wonder if he'd already dropped in without my knowledge—maybe when I was heavily sedated. Horrors! My groggy efforts failed to free sawdust and other debris from my disheveled hair. No doubt, vanity helped me face my adversity with a combination of energetic daring and innocent na|veté.

Swelling was an issue. While one side of my ankle was stitched together, the lesion on the opposite side was left to drain, which lessened the risk of infection, I was told. At some point, hideous metal clamps were inserted—although I'm not exactly sure when the procedure took place. In any case, my poor leg, pieced together like the Frankenstein monster, would never look the same. And due to the severity of the fractures, three steel screws secured my left ankle, so little hope existed, if any, of walking without a noticeable limp. In a state of denial, I bit into my thumbnail and made a ho-hum face, contemplating the thought of hobbling about stiff-footed for the rest of my life. Why should I reconcile myself to that sort of thing? Forget that baloney—I had other plans.

The language outside my door indicated trouble ahead: "Much depends on therapy and how well she mends." But the gravity of my injury didn't register— at all. Honestly, I had no inkling. Conceivably, God made me tune out the entire episode ... or perhaps it was just the audacity of youth. For the world, all I wanted was makeup, shampoo, a telephone, and some ego-boosting gowns.

Immediately, I scratched out an illegible reminder on my notepad. Without question, I needed my own gowns.

My parents were hollow-eyed with fatigue. They'd regressed back into a fragile state. But that's not to say they weren't grateful that we could exclude even the tiniest speculation of amputation, which was a godsend. Regardless, now I had to cope with some wicked pain. While I wasn't bent on giving in to the physical agony, my left side felt as if it'd been raked over by a giant claw with mean, tearing hooks. At whatever hour those horse-size pain pills did kick in, the burning sensation from my gross-looking clamps and sutures lingered. In one cowardly moment, I faced the music out loud: *Vickie Belle, this may not turn out well!*

Since my fall had been picked up by local news shows, I had an assemblage of concerned visitors, except one: my handsome love interest. The hall traffic was heavy with a constant pipeline of recovering patients, part-time candy stripers and—though forgivable—a few oddball strays eager for voyeuristic thrills. In every instance, I'd smile with polite restraint and do my best *not* to return the stares. Being unable to rest in my usual scrunched-up position wasn't easy; for me, this was the worst part of wearing a full-leg cast. Shortly, my slanty-eyed, nice-as-can-be day nurse apologized in her usual winsome way and closed the door behind her.

"Shot time, Miss Cristiani," she laughed, squinting playfully over her bifocals.

"It's over," I grumbled back. "See, I've become a genuine sideshow oddity … the buxom blond circus girl, thrown from an elephant. I feel like an exhibit in Ripley's museum."

"That's nonsense," the nurse replied, checking my chart. "You just happen to be the glamour queen of this floor. Congratulations, Miss Cristiani; how you've managed to stay looking so beautiful is a mystery to me. What's your secret, circus girl? Enough compliments … roll over, nice and easy."

"Darn … darn!" I winced at the sting and clutched my pillow with a death grip.

King-size needles fit for Kong himself pumped thick penicillin into my rear three times daily. The shots weren't always planted with care, so I had my list of favorite jabbers. Some nurses, sapped of energy, must've been furloughed from hell, for my shameful backside looked like Mars. "The evil brigade," as I called them, managed to tattoo my tail end with blackish lumps, patchy scabs, and a mosaic of bloodstained prints.

After continually fighting off a combination of the most offensive odors, the word "perfume" came to mind. So I folded my hands in prayerful style and begged my mother to bring my perfume, and she promised she would. At once,

the world was a brighter place … but not for long. After all, I was carrying an op-
pressive burden: knowing my accident had nixed my budding romance before it
had a chance to bloom into a meaningful relationship. To think otherwise would
be silly; not even Antoinette could change my opinion.

The next morning, I brooded over the particulars of past days. Finally, I
achieved total recall as to why I wanted to reduce my flesh to the bone. Even if
Benny was interested in dating one or all of those anorexic dolls, he should've
called … sent flowers … something. My former scheme to make him fall for me
didn't have a chance. Strangely, my bedridden state sharpened my senses like a
wolf basking in the light of a full moon. Every annoying moan, groan, and griev-
ance was amplified—as if the ebb and flow of the floor were being hotwired into
my nervous system faster than greased lighting. So when the nurse's aide placed
the breakfast tray at my throat, I made an angry fist and wagged my tongue with
all the gumption I could muster. "I'm sorry to be a pest … but please dump that
smelly tray?"

When all the madness subsided, Antoinette reported that Benny had suffered
a terrible spill himself—only two days after my accident. Given my own predicament, the news had been hidden from me. Difficult as it was to hear, I needed to
know exactly what had happened. During his third trick lap around the hippodrome bend, a lone guy wire caught him by the leg and face—peeling him off his
mount while the rest of the horror-struck team rode on, cringing in their saddles.
Frightened Navajo ran wild, flying like Pegasus, sensing the mishap. Taken unawares, the spectators drooped their heads briefly, sickened by the ugly sight of
Benny's slashed face. Swelling distorted his face even before the crew could assist
him offstage. By then, blood had soaked clear through his black-and-white riding
suit. Many vacant, watching faces opted to turn away from the image of Benny's
disfiguring lacerations. Lucio, infuriated that the grips had failed to clear every
hazardous cable on the track, shouted brazen orders over the lively music. "Son of
a bitch … where's that idiot Jake? Find that *stupido*! He's the one …"

Belmonte had panicked. "Tweety, run up front and wait to spot the ambulance."

Ronnie, our juggling clown, pressed an ice pack to Benny's mouth. "Can't
stop the bleeding!" he moaned. "For crying out loud, what in hell's holding the
paramedics?"

The ambulance delay obviously caused excessive anxiety. Benny, now wincing
with pain, was in dire need of attention. Surprisingly, after sensing the obvious
urgency, the very kind-hearted David Nelson insisted on giving him a momentous ride to the hospital in his polished Porsche. David indicated that if he and
Benny left immediately, they could beat the ambulance to the hospital. Without

wanting to seem unappreciative, Benny hesitated only because he feared the gore might spill over and damage the young actor's leather upholstery.

But David, being as charitable in real life as he was on his long-running TV show, persisted, showing little concern for his swanky sports car. These aren't his exact words, but they're close enough: "It's just a car. Don't worry about it!" David stayed with Benny until he was situated comfortably, with the emergency ward's sterile crew tending to his bleeding wounds. Astoundingly, the x-rays showed that Benny had suffered no broken bones. Regrettable as the mishap was, Benny got a lucky break in defiance of the odds: that hanging guy wire could've lopped off his head in one fell swoop. Everybody expected his injuries to be far worse than later revealed. Even including the monitored abrasion on his skull, the unpredictable repair of tender lip tissue, and thirty-five stitches inside and outside of his mouth, the prognosis was relatively good. Of course, the recent double whammy had everybody on edge. Shall we say that the superstitious notion of accidents happening in threes, especially feared by entertainers the world over, was showing its uncanny veracity.

The Nelson brothers, partners in their own flying act (David the catcher and Ricky the flyer) hardly missed a performance. Conceivably, in their minds, the chaotic circus lot was much more stimulating than the *Ozzie and Harriet* TV set. The pair studied every aspect of my brother-in-law Reggie's stomach-tightening maneuvers and recorded each transfer—no doubt mindful of the superstitious worry that kept everybody on their toes. Prior to Benny's tumble, David had arranged a party at his bachelor pad, so they were already acquainted with one another. It was punishing to know that, if invited, I could've been a guest at the fun soiree—also attended by then-aspiring actor Mark Goddard, who'd worked with my cousin Antoinette at the prominent Palm Tree Playhouse in Sarasota and later costarred in the long-running TV series *Lost in Space*.

As luck would have it, when both David and Ricky opted to escort my flirtatious cousin on one of her many visits, I was in seventh heaven. The fact that David and Ricky Nelson—the idols of every teenager in America—actually came to see me at St. Vincent's lifted my spirits to no end.

"Hi, I'm David, and this is my little kid brother, Ricky," said David, knuckling Ricky's cheekbone. That line had us all laughing! My silent thought: *How unreal is this?* Who in their right mind wouldn't be tickled pink? They looked gorgeous as ever, and their demeanor was true to their shy persona—exactly as I had imagined, as if they'd stepped right out of a movie magazine. Really, in my day, did anyone not watch *Ozzie and Harriet*? Incidentally, the Nelsons' surprise appearance upped my stock with the nurses overnight. Ricky showed a second time with Antoinette—carrying a large, spicy, hot pizza. My cousin had joked that I looked so skinny, an updraft could send me floating to the ceiling. No question, I'd pushed away every tray of yucky hospital food the staff had thrown at me. Tea-soaked cotton balls would've been tastier (gross, I know). Well, no wonder I craved all the bad stuff—anything oozing with artery-clogging cholesterol. At least it explains why I actually wolfed down an entire pepperoni in front of Ricky Nelson!

True to form, a freakish third accident occurred just one week later, during the leaps. Goose, the propman who was dumb as an oyster—and who, I should add, had to adjust his right shoe in order to accommodate six and a half toes— happened to be the chosen one to brace the springboard from underneath the ramp—for Belmonte's swan dive over five elephants. Drumroll, please ... whoops! Because Goose neglected to duck on cue, the impact scored a knockout blow that rendered him unconscious. At first, Goose looked dead as a smashed barfly until he managed to snap alert, slowly morphing into America's first conehead as sympathizers applauded his startling recovery.

Even though he had just experienced what might've qualified as the most painful crown in circus history, the witty slouch recovered without a hint of what had gone wrong. He growled back into position the day after and smarted off, as usual, while sitting on the edge of a bull tub, legs a-dangling: "Shhhit, I'm tough as any bastard ken be. Got fo', maybe five chillun' I know of ... soos, Lawd willin', I isn't done workin'. I jes needs three fat babes and a barrel of Ooo-zark moonshine." He crowed this last bit, spitting streams of tobacco juice against the wind. "Whaddaya want me ta do ... ferget showbiz? No-sir-ree! Ain't noooooo way in hell!"

The weather stayed beautiful for the duration of the straw-house engagement. Thankfully, no additional freakish accidents befell the crew. Aunt Norma, being the pro she was, took my place without missing a beat. Celebrities of varied stature visited daily, mingling with performers and crew. Apparently, they really loved hanging around, but I missed all that.

Benny's brother, Jimmy (a dead ringer for actor Cesar Romero at his best) was fresh out of the military. Although he had been an ace pilot for years prior, his duty didn't involve flying military aircraft. Actually, Jimmy was always somewhat of a wizard when it came to airplanes, having learned to fly—and even assemble—twin-engine private planes in his early teens. But now, just like Benny, Jimmy was in a transitional period, not knowing where to turn next. Big brother Rex, who probably set a record for slugging wisecracking "shit-kickers" or anybody else who gave him lip around the rodeo circuit, revealed that his two punk brothers were punch-happy wops, just like the Cristianis—and had a bad reputation for whipping any dude who looked at them cross-eyed. While Jimmy, four years older than Benny, had a mania for stunt flying and a desire to become a professional pilot to pay the bills, he couldn't shake the showbiz bug. (Down the road, Jimmy Rossi's bill-paying job evolved into a spotless thirty-two-year career with American Airlines.)

Surprisingly, upon witnessing Benny's tumble from the sidelines, Jimmy, an able trick rider himself, was so overcome by his impromptu desire to uphold the old adage "the show must go on" that he miraculously managed to rein in his brother's rearing—and frothing—horse and then, like some phantom rider, completed the remaining laps without losing life or limb. In the meantime, nobody could blame the propmen for storming the track, thinking Jimmy was some jobless actor seizing the moment to get his mug on TV. The chase itself was hilariously funny—Abbot-and-Costello funny, I was told!

"Grab that horse! Grab 'em!" (Fat chance!)

"Hey, stop! It's part of the show!"

"Noooo it ain't! That guy's crazy as a coot!"

Jimmy's sudden call to active circus duty while Benny was drowning in blood was next to insane, considering Navajo's seemingly unbreakable bad habit of hugging the slanting quarter polls around the bend. Casting that disparaging episode aside, Jimmy performed for the rest of the engagement without a hitch. He even inherited Benny's fickle harem of female fans, which enabled him to saddle up Navajo with a strongbox of preening confidence.

Coincidentally, Benny ended up at St. Vincent's just one floor down from me. I'm still clueless as to who sent the first note, but I can remember the lightheadedness, and my desperately tenacious grip on this well-deserved serendipity—while reaching over to anoint my neck with Chanel. Somebody sensed the chemistry. We had become soap-opera stars overnight, so our slick note-passing act gave the nurses something to talk about besides the bellyaching gripes of bedpan duty. On a deeper level, insecurity took the wind right out of my sails, especially once I mulled over the conundrums that rejection phobia imparts to the brain. When I heard that Benny and Jimmy had indeed visited my room the night of my surgery, I turned pomegranate red. Even though the news was encouraging—and, at last, exactly what I wanted to know—I scarcely made a sound. Swell! I must've looked great: drugged, hair mussed, and drooling.

With nothing better to do, I daydreamed through a labyrinth of plots that stopped short of a happy ending. The first night Benny felt healed enough to take the elevator up to my room, I questioned him, nonchalantly, about the flock of sun-kissed babes—with a fair piece of acting, I might add. Predictably, he responded with a grin so broad he almost pulled a stitch. But seeing as his nonanswer made me wonder more than I cared to, I smirked up at the ceiling to let him know I didn't need a hanky. What's more, later in the day, when I meanly stared him down, I saw in Benny's face neither apology nor regret. At wit's end, wobbly with lust and ready for the kill, I shooed away his sizzling-hot, hormonal advances, thinking, *This guy should suffer some necessary pain.*

Mommy and Carin didn't fly home until after they got assurance from my doctor that I would be all right in their absence. Carin had already missed a week of school, so they needed to leave when they did. Interestingly, bright, on-the-ball Penny Singleton, who had starred in the original *Blondie and Dag-wood* TV series, was the current president of the AGVA (American Guild of Varity Artists), which provided our medical coverage. She was an angel in disguise and dealt with all matters having to do with my hospital stay. Initially, there was a problem of some sort, but that's all I know to this day. Our AGVA dues may have been in arrears; whatever the problem was, Penny worked it out.

My sister Bonnie, a shrewd businesswoman with a darling petite figure and perfect set of Barbie doll legs, stayed wholly informed of my ever-improving condition and helped our father make the right decisions in regard to my well-being. No one messed with Bonnie. She got things done—her way or no way. Understand, because of the almost ten year gap in our age, Bonnie and I hadn't spent all that much time together since childhood. We did see each other on occasion, but her performing schedule made it difficult to connect in a sisterly way. Even though we loved each other dearly, her inflexibility never changed; our relationship alternated between hot and cold. Bonnie had a way of distancing herself so you couldn't get too close. She had reasons—many founded, and many unfounded, though all were quite real in her mind. Daddy and Bonnie had a communication problem that, sadly, was never resolved. No doubt, there was an iron wall between them, and it bothered me terribly that they had such a problem clearing the air and starting anew.

My fiercely independent older sister was foolproof smart, multilingual, and further gifted in that she had a true photographic memory. Mindful of Bonnie's ability, Daddy, being a saver, had put enough money aside to send her to college in order to pursue a career as a foreign correspondent. Instead, Bonnie ran off and married the day after graduating from the costly Nazareth Academy in Arizona and was divorced within a year. Daddy, being only human after all, was hurt beyond belief—although he blamed himself for not seeing it coming. I once read, "A parent's wish cannot be ordered." And so, as the adoring daughter, I suppose *I* was the one who got the attention, the locket, and the roses.

*   *   *   *

On his second visit to my bedside, Benny came purposely to patch things up—asking, in a he-man sort of way, if he could try once again to win my heart. Incidentally, he could and did—only now that I didn't want to just talk, he did. The first time he called me sweetheart and ran his callused hand over my bare shoulders, I had what must've been an epiphany. Candidly, I was over being too shy to accept the very desires that gave my conscience something to chew on. Privately, I pleaded with myself to stay cool, but I had not an ounce of will or strength to pull away. Thoughts of sensual pleasures controlled my mind and body and could no longer be silenced at will. I'd never before known that certain weightless sensation, unwinding inside me like a rope, until now. Had I actually witnessed Moses parting the Red Sea, I couldn't have been more baffled. Stuck somewhere on the side of the road, I dueled with the dilemma of whether to quell my dizzying emotions or bathe happy, lathering in the nature of my passion. Yet, I was lucid enough to know that I'd been swept away by the wild romantic passes of one's first love—that Benny and I were howlingly moonstruck and feverishly courting one another in the frenzied fashion of youth. Our situation was a bit awkward, I suppose (we weren't exactly jitterbugging). But hey, hallelujah—from my outpost, things were definitely looking up.

EPILOGUE

▼

The wise man must remember that while he is a descendant of the past,
he is a parent of the future;
and that his thoughts are as children born to him,
which he may not carelessly let die.
—Herbert Spencer

After LA's tremendous success, business took a nosedive for the balance of the California tour. Advance sales were negligible; the show continued to hemorrhage money. Frankly, it was like watching the collapse of a house of cards. Despite the publicity boost of *Roll Out the Sky*, the 1959 season came to a disastrous end. The cargo of corporate and personal debt was astronomical; it was impossible for the Cristiani Bros. Circus to regain its financial footing.

Honestly, I don't believe anyone was prepared for the awesome shopping-center boom of the 1960s. Groundbreaking malls shot up like mushrooms from coast to coast.

Almost overnight, thriving cities became dismal ghost towns—and, in turn, a string of tented circuses went belly-up. For decades, advance men slept and worked out of panel trucks while tacking box loads of lithographs on every available storefront and roadside structure on seasonal routes. In conjunction with local media promotions, this advertising blitz had been the marketing backbone of every traveling show in the country—and it worked. But a new age of suburban sprawl obliterated the success of that affordable campaign. Circus owners soon found out that the outmoded lithograph blitz failed to generate business. Sophisticated circusgoers weren't about to drive miles out of town only to sit for ninety minutes inside a hot tent. Dollars earmarked for major city advertising had to be tripled in order to steal an apathetic populace from their bona fide leisure option: the supercool malls. After the rapid fall in attendance, overall rise in costs, and new safety laws, nothing remained. Bear in mind P. T. Barnum's famous quote: "A funny thing happens without publicity: nothing."

From then on, air-conditioning had America hooked. "Sweat" was a dirty word. Summer temperatures inside the malls were so frigid that thin-skinned shoppers needed parkas to prevent frostbite. Yea to comfort, boo to heat! Credit-card spending became the opiate of the masses. Throngs of happy campers from every stratum of society stampeded to blockbuster sales in savage fury, as if embarking on an impulsive excursion to the World's Fair. In addition, other variables affected the Cristianis' battle to withstand the unstoppable changes of the modern age—changes that threaten traditional customs to this day.

All things considered, my family waged an honorable fight, even if it was like trying to sandbag the Mississippi. Independent of that thought, I believe that obsession, in any form, directs one on an orderless course. Everything has a price tag, as the saying goes … except most people are deaf to that wisdom amid the thunder of stress. Consider, too, that failure has no ally in this ageless passage: humans share one common condition that makes us all cocreators of our own fortunes—or misfortunes. I've always viewed the world perceptively, and I've always been a close reader of character. I watched my family's annihilation. Boom! I participated. Any dagger at my father clawed at my heart. Feelings were ugly; false accusations were flung with no thought of the lasting repercussions. There were terrible arguments over what each would take from what was left; the Cristiani elephants were included in the debates and they were anything but friendly. Survival was the issue, but not survival for one and all—not anymore. Sadly, this is what it had come down to.

Resentment grew. Everyone hurt inside, feeling increasingly ill from the pain of failure. It was as if family members had developed a tumor—a malignant tumor that grew into a maniacal eight-hundred-pound-gorilla with blood on his hands. Our faces were askew, armed with counterfeit smiles and soulless eyes that bulged in the sulfured air of contempt. I swear it was like watching the cursed transformation of Dorian Gray in a world gone to hell. Everybody had that blank "What now?" look—the panicked look of a deer caught in the glare of an oncoming headlight. In desperation, wrong decisions were made—with predictable results. The spiraling downfall was particularly hurtful for my grandparents, who witnessed the sickening cesspool of kindred rage. Naturally, the interplay of pride and incivility made it wholly impossible to close the widening breach that blew loyalty to smithereens. I cannot judge—or canonize—any family member, because the wounds were penetrative on all sides. This ugly chapter was not the end—only the eleventh-hour prelude to the kiss of death!

*   *   *   *

My God, the next few years were hard—spent in denial, with haunting attempts to survive the end of an era ... one golden to many in the circus world, but never more golden than to the Cristiani family. Notwithstanding obvious blunders, I conclude that the collapse of the Cristiani Bros. Circus was hastened by the evolution of our modern-thinking society. Yet, I'm bound to say that an addiction to false hope precluded any sensible inclination my family might have had to morph with the times by daring to reach out beyond the orbits of their own existence. In this failure to adapt, the Cristianis were at end defeated by loyalty to the canvas sky. This final blow took away their prance; it left them wallowing like wounded sparrows, wingless and whipped. The next couple of years generated some futile projects that went nowhere, which created even more headaches and prolonged the inevitable split.

Everyone was fighting to pay bills back home in order to save personal possessions: homes, automobiles, and other investments. Lucio discussed selling the elephants. Daddy said, "Not on your life!" They went at it head to head, with fire in their eyes. During one layoff in South Carolina money was so scarce Daddy went door to door asking local farmers if the elephants could graze on their farmland. Their generosity was astounding. The farmers came together willingly and contributed barrels of wheat and bales of hay so the elephants could get their daily fill.

At some point, Tony Diano, offered to care for the Cristiani elephants at his animal compound in Canton, Ohio. "Just temporarily," he declared, "at least they'll be fed and cared for. You can pick them up whenever you want." Although the gesture was uncharacteristic, the elephants' welfare came first. For this reason alone, the five Cristiani elephants were dropped off at the Diano compound along with the herd's diesel-tractor and custom-made semitrailer. In no time, my suspicious uncle Pete advised Daddy to collect the elephants as soon as possible. He told Daddy that the Cristiani elephants were needed for a string of winter dates up north and went on to say that the Texas dates were open as well, which was wonderful news. But when Daddy arrived in Canton to retrieve the elephants, Diano said ... not so fast.

Apparently, there had been a whole lot of manipulating going on over the past year. Frankly, the right hand didn't always know with the left hand was doing. Under the circumstances, obtaining financial backing by conventional means was out of the question. Unbeknownst to Daddy and to my knowledge everyone else, Lucio (acting as show manager) had obtained a substantial business loan from Tony Diano—guaranteed by a shocking list of mortgage-free collateral

... and Diano had the papers to prove it. According to Tony Diano, the elephants definitely belonged to him. Demoralized and at the point of exhaustion, Daddy checked into a small Canton hotel room and, with Pete's help, managed to hire a fine lawyer who was not a Tony Diano fan, and waited it out. Pete flew in for the trial. I'm not sure of all the particulars, but the court ruled in Daddy's favor. Understand the Cristiani elephants had been in my mother's maiden name, Marion Bendixen, all along and therefore were never legally part of show assets. It was said that upon hearing the verdict handed down by the fair-minded judge, Diano unleashed his anger by hollering the worst foul words imaginable at Daddy and Daddy's lawyer in front of the judge, which almost landed him jail for contempt of court. Fortunately, the elephants only missed the first engagement by a day.

As expected, the family had to face a litany of consequences for the "done deal" that turned brother against brother. Shortly after Diano returned to Sarasota to collect his debt everybody went off in different directions, doing whatever they could to make a living in the business. Daddy struggled to meet expenses for a while but he eventually went on to make a comfortable living booking the (in-demand) Cristiani elephant act as an independent contractor. In later years, my sister, Carin, and her capable son, Brian, took over the responsibility.

Those who may be interested should know that the Cristiani elephants were never sold. There were many offers, but Daddy made it clear that selling his beloved pets to another circus or zoo would never be an option. He cared too much for their well-being to ever do such a thing. At the appropriate time, the bulls retired to a lovely free-roaming compound in Georgia to live out their natural lives.

*   *   *   *

During the process of writing *Spangles*, various mind-altering sentiments eased my conscience. Finally, I saw my family as they were unable to see themselves: not so good, but also not so bad. Contentious theories and misconceptions will never be absent, I know, but the extent to which they are dwelled upon is not in my hands. Personally, I'm satisfied that our situation was not unique; friction thrives in any family facing ruin. And in artistic circles such as ours, it thrives luxuriantly. Tempers explode like kegs of dynamite, capable of annihilating the mighty players along with the weak. Up until the writing of this book, I had an itching need to find a salutary outlet for my pent-up animosity; I was absolutely convinced that any type of reunion was hopeless to the grave. But on the day of reckoning, all the poison left my body. Something bad died inside of me, seemingly overnight, as though I'd succeeded in squashing the head of a hideous serpent.

After reexamining the dysfunctional aspects through the prism of humor (as time so graciously affords), I made a supreme effort to lay down the blade. But what matters most, now and forever, is this: I've reassessed that friction and have since determined it was far outweighed by love. Dignity precedes the Cristiani name and, as we move through the threshold to the twenty-first century, not one circus family has come close to matching their accomplishments and charismatic appeal. Within the sawdust furrows of the center ring, this amazing equestrian troupe secured an indelible mark and, as a matter of course, wrote a most remarkable chapter in the America circus story.

As Papa Cristiani now knows, his vision cannot be erased, for it is etched in the annals of circus history—even if embellished now and again by a spoonful of folklore and wonder. My spirited grandfather might also consider what I believe to be true—that is to say, essentially, that his sons' personal flaws only worked to fuel their exalted ambitions. While I do not wish to secure an epitaph predisposed solely to my emotions, the circus of yesteryear remains a monument on the landscape of America.

I confess that I still pine for our gigantic big top, groomed for doors; the titillating sideshow, amid sixteen-foot-high banners suitably stylized and painted with exaggerated strokes of shockingly irreverent naughtiness; and the exotic menagerie—rumbling with the ballyhoo of animal talk intoned at showtime. Those colossal tent cities were the final relics of a bygone day one should not wish to forget. It was a friendlier era back then, a wholesome and grand time to be coming of age—and, in my own mind, a time best represented by the American circus. Really, I ought to thank my lucky stars that I was able to record my compiled dower of memories while I still had it this side of heaven. At its very worst, circus life shifted wildly between chaotic and sublime. At best, pure and simply, it was magic.

As we moved out of the sixties, sleazy entertainment was in, and wholesomeness was passé—eschewed like some weird condition contracted back in the dark ages. I mustn't get carried away, but now that we're confronting the new millennium and the outbreak of uncertainties after the terrorizing 9/11 attack, moral values should be more sacred than ever. It saddens me that my grandchildren will never enjoy the playground of my youth. All evidence suggests that the circus as I knew it, animals included, is nowhere to be found—except in the minds of old-timers and poetry of books. Regrettably, I can foresee that, on one frightful day in the not-too-distant future, a child with a mirthless smile will look up at some unsuspecting soul only to ask, in a tone of sniffling wonder, "Where are the clowns?"

*   *   *   *

When young, one lacks the wisdom of the old. When old, one lacks the fearlessness of the young. In the scheme of things, life, as many have reasoned, is indeed nothing more than a series of tradeoffs. At nineteen, I had little wisdom ... but I also had little fear. With more wisdom, I would've feared that I might never walk without a cane. With time I got wiser, and with time, I walked without a cane. In hindsight, fearlessness was the governing power that got me back on my feet. Today, I walk normally in high heels; flatfooted, I tend to limp. Although I have the mobility to get by, I can't run ... but I'm in no hurry now.

Benny fully recovered, with only one insignificant scar on his mouth—an apt reminder of his daredevil past. We had a no-frills Catholic wedding on January 27, 1961, followed by a simple reception at the Sarasota Hotel. The ceremony took place during the height of my family's troubling split. My parents did the best they could with what they had to spend, and everyone came together to celebrate the occasion in top form. Within days, we flew to Los Angeles, then on to Honolulu, Hawaii, for a three-week working honeymoon.

Surprisingly, our marriage has withstood the "for better or for worse" test more times than I care to mention. Given the unsuppressed candor of our hotheaded Italian heritage, who would've guessed? (I'll admit I did *not* inherit my mother's Norwegian cool.) However trivial or intense, our occasional blowups matter little and, thank goodness, have never uprooted the love valued most in our lives—for we've been blessed with two caring, sensible sons, born almost thirteen years apart. Thankfully, both young men reside in Orlando, Florida, and are proud Gator alumnae. Ben Jr., a graduate from the University of Florida as well as UF Law School, has been a practicing attorney for many years. My youngest son, Ryan, graduated from the University of Florida with a business degree and has a challenging job as a financial analyst. Our sons may have amusingly opposite personalities, but they share one thing in common: they remain our proudest achievement.

All four of my grandparents have passed on. My maternal grandfather's lovely Viking oil painting, set in the fjords of Norway, was my favorite wedding gift. It hangs over our fireplace as a reminder of my other half. He inscribed the back side: "Dear granddaughter Vickie, don't ever forget your Norwegian heritage!"

My beloved parents, who loved each other until the last hour of their life, are gone also. Daddy died on December 15, 1987, from complications of Parkinson's disease and a lung tumor—solely caused from smoking, we were told. The news was difficult to accept, because Daddy hadn't touched even one cigarette for over thirty-two years. Only days before, a young Italian priest from St. Martha's Church who spoke perfect Italian, had administered the last rites. The pious Jesuit, visibly taken by Daddy's heartfelt confession (given in Italian), indicated that heaven surely awaited him. I became a different person after Daddy's death; it marked the end of life as I knew it. We had been bonded as one. The moment Daddy died, I felt hollow—bodily separated, as though the merciful Lord had permitted my soul to travel with him, at least part of the way. I loved him so. The sky fell that day in Sarasota. It poured; it thundered; it was black. I took it as a sign.

Shortly thereafter, my mother's health failed. Aside from being stricken with Guillain-Barré syndrome (a rare neurological disorder), she was suffering from congestive heart failure and all the problems related to that condition. Mommy was in and out of the hospital for the next four years. I couldn't grasp why her first valve surgery (which took place at the famous Bailey Clinic in Philadelphia, Pennsylvania, when I was seventeen) had given her nearly three decades of surprisingly good health … yet the pigskin replacement valve she received at Tampa General gave her a mere fraction of time in comparison—despite the advance technology.

I remember that the initial surgery, which saved Mommy's life, was still in the experimental stage. But because Mommy was a nonsmoker, and specific test results were promising, she was declared a candidate and remained on the waiting list for the revolutionary procedure, which involved precisely slitting her severely damaged valve—pioneered by the genius surgeon, Dr. Bailey.

School was an issue for me during that first scare with Mommy. For some reason or other, I didn't return to Holy Names after tenth grade, so Uncle Dave enrolled me at Sarasota High for my junior year, which I completed. Although I eventually got my degree, registering for twelfth grade was a subject of contention with Daddy. I begged him to understand that graduating was not my first priority, and that my grades would suffer under the turmoil of Mommy's life-threatening situation. Even if all went well, Mommy would be at risk for months. Her much younger roommate, a smoker, suffered from infection and never recovered.

Evoking that sharp slice of the past brought me into the stark reality of the present. Once again, I found myself in the same state—falling apart piece by piece, barely subsisting and unable to pretend for one blessed minute that

Mommy was going to get better. My mother's only functioning eardrum had somehow perforated on a return flight after visiting my sister Carin, who was busy performing the Cristiani elephant act in Puerto Rico. "A hiss of air and a pop was the last thing I heard," she said. But thankfully, instead of agonizing over the bad news she counted her blessings for living past the age of eight—recalling the clairvoyant nun who had appeared at her bedside (when she was stricken with diphtheria and scarlet fever) and told her she would live to marry and have two beautiful daughters.

Little by little, our communication deteriorated. Although Mommy never lost her memory or rationality, deafness took its toll. There were moments when she seemed beyond the reach of consciousness. I missed our window-shopping excursions at St. Armand's Circle. I missed lunching on a delicious pressed Cuban sandwich and really, really special 1905 Salad, served at Daddy's favorite dining place—the Columbia Restaurant. Moreover, I'll never forget our special twilight walks on Siesta Key while devouring a pound-packing waffle cone at Big Oloff.

Slowly and unknowingly, my gravely ill mother became lost in the pictorial inventiveness of her library world. Our situation nagged at my spirit and tore at my heart until I had nothing more to give. It hurts me to say that I labored through her daily-care routine feeling beaten and powerless—loathing the very act of watching her drift into the jaws of death. But Mommy, baptized and raised in the Protestant faith, showed the same calm she'd shown all her life, trusting destiny to the fatherly providence of God.

In contrast, I turned into a premenopausal she-devil with horns, on the verge of imploding in a sorry heap and trying my darndest to interpret God's invincible design. Like the prophet Jeremiah, I found my faith was stretched to the break-ing point. "Why," I angrily challenged my Maker, "did you permit my beautiful Mommy to be reduced to a bony shadow of her former self? Why, God," I per-sisted, "are you putting me through such torture at this lost period, when I have the blasted sweats and need regular sabbaticals in the cuckoo nest?"

It bothered me that a satisfactory solution didn't pop up like toast. For a long while, I couldn't pray, confess, or even attend Sunday mass. God himself seemed dead. I felt miserable, abandoned by my very best friend. If he wasn't listening—or, far worse, didn't care—why should I? The instant I showed irritable swings, Mommy dispensed forgiveness without question or pause. Caring for her and watching her die was my test, my ongoing lesson in true selflessness. However true this was, I wasn't in the mood for bargaining. It took the fullness of time for me to see God's side.

My angel mom passed on February 4, 1991.

About thirty seconds before she died, brokenhearted Carin tried to communicate with her, but my mother's eyelids were matted shut. Out of the blue, some troubled nurse, foolish enough to barge through the door unannounced, proclaimed, louder than necessary, "Ms. Cristiani is totally deaf. She can't hear a thing!" I was livid, but said nothing. However, my inward voice screamed, *How dare anyone steal away the sanctity of our privacy!* In defiance, I leaned down and spoke. Most fittingly, Mommy's right hand rested on her favorite Christmas gift—a beautifully illustrated copy of *The Secret Garden*, by Frances Hodgson Burnett. Just then, in what seemed the briefest, purest moment, she answered, clear as a bell: "I love you, too."

Though life goes on, it's hardly the same; yet, in recent years, I've come to know that the death of a loved one, if allowed to do so, can open a secret spring for the living—a reservoir of inspiration, if you will. It's there for the asking. And so, whenever I look up—especially in a pitch-dark night gemmed by stars—I'm startled to receive, by some means, a rush of fond messages that make me smile.

My loving godmother, Ortans, who suffered from emphysema, died one month before Daddy. Uncle Lucio expired two years later, at the uncanny hour of Aunt Chita's funeral mass. That was an awfully cruel hit. Everybody put up a united front, but the embrace was iceberg cold. Although the extraordinary circumstances of that week left the remaining siblings in a state of paralyzed depression, the infernal spell was not broken. What could be done, if anything? Mortality had displayed its wrath before a broken family, all poised to take a fetal position on the therapist's couch. Even the inexorable power of grief couldn't provoke a change in this accusatory climate. Figuratively speaking, the Cristianis were born with inbred tunnel vision, aiming for the pinnacle of the circus amphitheater.

Through adulthood, the brothers had little sufferance for gentle fraternal intimacy. Granted, this sort of unspoken anguish exists pretty much in every family circle, but it is even stronger in a highly stressful atmosphere where competition rules. For heaven's sake, at this stage in the game, everybody needed professional counsel—and, in an emotional capacity, each other. But a member of the Cristiani family biting his or her tongue? Never! Consequently, that pesky little membrane that separates rational behavior from insanity had us all evading one another like the Black Death. Over decades of arduous and rather barbaric athletic training, each rebel became more unknowable to the other. They were frozen in a mindset of damming conviction, acknowledging no goodness or rightness except their own. Their hearts having hardened like cooled lava, they could no longer face the truth.

As dedicated as the brothers were as a bunch, as individuals, each had an unseen side crammed with stowed animosity that stemmed from the raw bruises of childhood. Together, they had survived the best and the worst of times, but now that Nona and Nono were out of the picture, no amount of buffing could hide their bitter jealousy and interpersonal power struggles. But just as life always seems to find a way, so does deep-seated love. Almost a decade later, at the twilight of Christmas 1995, tender words resulting from a single phone call to my uncle Pete became music to my soul. Our brief conversation struck the deepest chords of feeling. This had a redemptive power as soothingly effectual as a refreshing bubble bath. Yet, I wondered then, as I wonder now: with such misgivings, what exactly prompted my call?

From that day forward, the corrupting, evil spell that had kept us from speaking a civil word since 1962 evanesced—expunged by some supernal entity, I suspect. I'm not apt to forget I did more than hold my breath. Telling no one, I headed for McDonald's and celebrated the occasion by ordering the works: Big Mac, large fries, Coke, and hot fudge sundae with nuts.

As for the rest of the gang, the little green monster was still in the woods—though I was confident that, eventually, with Pete's will and persuasion, the cobalt blue sky of peace would be restored, and it was … and not through some fortuitous circumstances, either! Quite the reverse, in fact: our phenomenal thirst for togetherness was a sure indication that the Lord, in all his mercy, had performed a true miracle of reconciliation, saving us all from the fatal undertow of pride. How fortunate we were to have had the opportunity to retrieve our souls—the one priceless possession no mortal can afford to lose.

Poor lost Aunt Jane died much too young from acute alcoholism. My kind and sensitive godfather, Mogador, who went through life with nothing but the best intentions, passed away in 1999 at his home in Las Vegas—one year before his good friend Bob Lax. Surprisingly, Mogador had called Aunt Corky a couple weeks before his death, saying that he was homesick and wished to return to Sarasota—however, he never disclosed his advanced illness or the extent of his gambling woes. My uncle knew all along that I was struggling to complete my book. On his last visit to Sarasota he asked if he could help me out in any way, but I told him that my manuscript simply wasn't fit for review. "Let me know when you're ready," he answered with a hug. And I thanked him with all my heart!

My strongman uncle Daviso, born nine months after Daddy, succumbed at 91. He was amazing in that he never lost his humor or fight. Even though we had discussed the emotional content of my memoir many times, on one particular day filled with heartfelt emotion, he made a very important distinction after I expressed this sentiment: the Cristianis really had a lot of bad luck.

"Yes, that's true, Vickie," he replied philosophically, "but we had a lot of good luck too." And so, I can say for sure that my uncle Daviso was at peace with himself, his God, and the Cristiani legacy.

Another miracle occurred in early 2001. Something came over me while attending Aunt Delia's funeral mass at St. Martha's Church in Sarasota, Florida—wherein I was baptized by its charismatic founder and lifelong pastor, Father Elslander. Notwithstanding the fact that Delia had been twenty-five years younger than Belmonte, her totally unexpected death was a heartbreaker. By happenstance, my sister Bonnie, who in recent years had evolved into a genuinely devout Eucharistic minister, was praying in the side pew next to the altar. At that instant, I had not the slightest doubt that I not only loved her still, but needed absolution from the changed person I saw before me. Bonnie stood up with open arms as I walked toward her, and we embraced. Little said, then and there, we made amends after I'd selfishly shut her out of my life over ten years ago. I believed then, as I believe now, that God intervened by saying, "Enough!" Perhaps he pressed his lips to our ears, thereby ordering us to behold—not through the lenses of judgmental eyes, but through the healing properties that looped our hearts. Who knows—maybe Aunt Delia put in a word, given her embattled relationship with her own sister, Flora. Whatever transpired, his message sounded loud and clear:

> Life has to be played out with time; only then can we foresee its meaning and purpose. If we stop and listen, the answers will fall in order prospectively. Gradually, a reckoning of sorts will occur—a reckoning that sets your spirit free.

So now I know what my mother meant when she said there is beauty in time, for it has only been with time that I have realized the true beauty of my past. There's no better catharsis for your soul than forgiveness, because, in the process, God forgives us. Therefore, we must begin by forgiving ourselves. Forgiveness is the one key element that can arouse our moral nature and free the demons within. In my early years, I was much too busy trying to survive my youth, just like many of my peers. How wonderful it is, later on in life, to look back with unrestricted vision. Again, timing is important, so here the mystery deepens: looking back at the wrong time, when views are polarized, can constrict one's ability to reach the right conclusions. If all this sounds promising, take it from me: it is.

On the surface, I have matured, and my mirrored image shows the wears of time. The good news is that, in many ways, I still cling to the naive child inside, from whom I draw my faith, strength, and hope. If I happen to hear the symphonic pulsation of "Entry of the Gladiators," I can easily regress back into the cocoon of my childhood. The lively melody still churns my innards and conjures up a carousel of candy-sprinkled brilliance—with me safely ensconced inside the cozy cavity of my favorite fairy-tale shoe on the Cole Bros. Circus.

Suspending disbelief, it's easy to picture the long-squabbling Cristianis deliciously young, proud, and ever so cocky, reveling in concert somewhere out there, in their newly minted big top—populated with adoring circus fans. Well, now, that may or may not be a stretch … but who can say with certainty that it isn't true? When I think back even further, way back to my first year at Cardome Academy, I wonder if my (look-at-me) violets are still swaying in the breeze—or if my cluster of trees has been replaced by towering buildings reaching far to the sky. No matter what, my sweet Kentucky violets will always be there, if only in my mind, tossing their little heads as if playing instruments in the symphony of my life.

"Now in telling the story
of the Cristianis …
we tell of creation and glory,
of rising,
and fall:
and again of the rising
where we are all risen;
for each man redeemed
is risen again."

—Bob Lax (*Circus of the Sun*, 1959)

About the Author

Victoria B. Cristiani Rossi grew up in a circus as a daughter of the famous Cristiani circus family, onetime stars of the Ringling Bros. and Barnum & Bailey Circus. She lives in Orlando, Florida, with her husband, Ben Rossi, and their beloved Yorkshire terrier, Precha.

Made in the USA
Lexington, KY
15 December 2009